IF BY CHANCE

Major-General John Strawson served with the 4th Hussars – Winston Churchill's regiment – during the Second World War in the Middle East and Italy. Following amalgamation of the 4th Hussars and the 8th Hussars as The Queen's Royal Hussars, he commanded the regiment in Malaysia and Germany. Later he commanded an infantry brigade and was Chief of Staff, United Kingdom Land Forces.

He was Colonel of his regiment from 1975 to 1985, Chairman of the Cavalry and Guards Club from 1984 to 1987, and Master of the Staff College Draghounds from 1959 to 1961, recording his experiences in a book, *Drag-Hunting*. He is married to Baroness Wilfried von Schellershiem and they have two daughters.

He has written a number of other books including *Hitler as Military Commander*, *The Italian Campaign*, *Gentlemen in Khaki*, *the Duke and the Emperor* and *Churchill and Hitler: In Victory and Defeat*. *If by Chance* is his twelfth work of military history.

JOHN STRAWSON

IF BY CHANCE

PAN BOOKS

First published 2003 by Macmillan

This edition published 2004 by Pan Books
an imprint of Pan Macmillan Ltd
Pan Macmillan, 20 New Wharf Road, London N1 9RR
Basingstoke and Oxford
Associated companies throughout the world
www.panmacmillan.com

ISBN 0 330 49245 4

1 3 5 7 9 8 6 4 2

A CIP catalogue record for this book is available from
the British Library.

Typeset by SX Composing DTP, Rayleigh, Essex
Printed and Bound in Great Britain by
Mackays of Chatham plc, Chatham, Kent

*He who never leaves anything to chance will
do few things ill, but he will do few things.*

MARQUIS OF HALIFAX

*No human activity is so continuously
or universally bound up with chance.*

KARL VON CLAUSEWITZ, *On War*

Contents

Acknowledgements

I would like to thank William Armstrong for his patience and perseverance during our discussions which led to this book. After some false starts we hit upon a variation of Macmillan's successful *What If?* volumes, one which would bring in the element of chance, its effect on the outcome of battles and how this outcome might have changed had chance taken a different turn.

The idea therefore was for me to choose a number of campaigns and battles, explain the strategic circumstances, together with the principal statesmen and commanders involved, and then see what effect chance had in determining the results of various battles. The next stage was to move from what did happen to what might have happened had things fallen out differently, and so to see what longer-term consequences there might have been.

In setting the scene for some of these battles, I have made use of passages from previous works of mine when the events described coincide with those in this book. For permission to do so I am grateful to B.T. Batsford (Chrysalis Books), J.M. Dent & Sons, Hutchinson Books Ltd (The Random House Group), Constable & Co. Ltd, Secker & Warburg Ltd.

I would like to thank Jeremy Trevathan, Stuart Evers and their staffs at Pan Macmillan for all their admirable advice and assistance. My thanks go to the photocopiers of Coates & Parker, Warminster for their cheerful and courteous help. Finally I wish to thank my wife for her invaluable assistance in the production of this book.

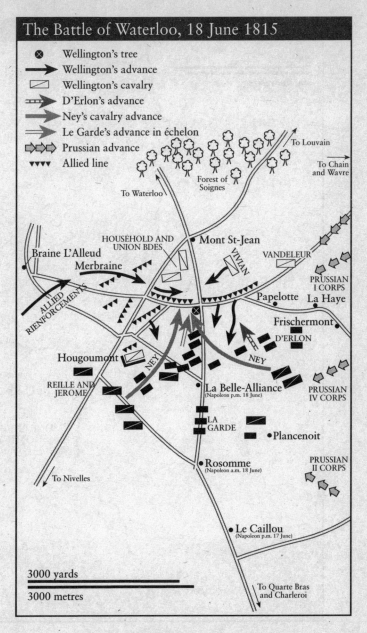

The Battle of Waterloo, 18 June 1815

⊗ Wellington's tree
➤ Wellington's advance
▱ Wellington's cavalry
⇢ D'Erlon's advance
➤ Ney's cavalry advance
⇨ Le Garde's advance in échelon
⬭ Prussian advance
▾▾▾▾ Allied line

To Louvain

To Chain
and Wavre

Forest of
Soignes

To Waterloo

HOUSEHOLD AND
UNION BDES

Mont St-Jean

VIVIAN

VANDELEUR

Braine L'Alleud

Merbraine

ALLIED
RIENFORCEMENTS

PRUSSIAN
I CORPS

Papelotte   La Haye

Frischermont

D'ERLON

Hougoumont

NEY

NEY

REILLE AND
JEROME

La Belle-Alliance
(Napoleon p.m. 18 June)

PRUSSIAN
IV CORPS

LA
GARDE

Plancenoit

Rosomme
(Napoleon a.m. 18 June)

PRUSSIAN
II CORPS

Le Caillou
(Napoleon p.m. 17 June)

3000 yards

3000 metres

To Nivelles

To Quarte Bras
and Charleroi

1. Had Napoleon seized Hougoumont,
it would have given him the world

The First Afghan War:

200 miles

300 kilometres

•Herat

AFGHANIS

PERSIA

Kandal

Helmand

BALUCHI

(UNDER AFGH
DOMINION

ARABIAN SEA

2. The Great Game could have been won there and then

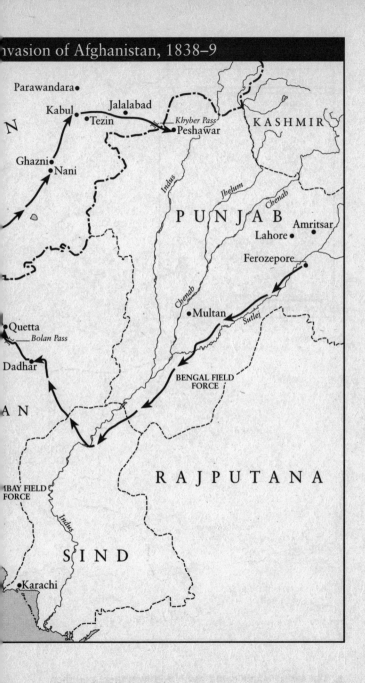

Parawandara

Kabul • Tezin Jalalabad

...N

Ghazni • Nani

Khyber Pass Peshawar

KASHMIR

Indus

Jhelum

Chenab

P U N J A B

Lahore • Amritsar •

Ferozepore •

Chenab

Quetta

Bolan Pass

Dadhar

• Multan

Sutlej

BENGAL FIELD
FORCE

...AN

R A J P U T A N A

...MBAY FIELD
FORCE

Indus

S I N D

• Karachi

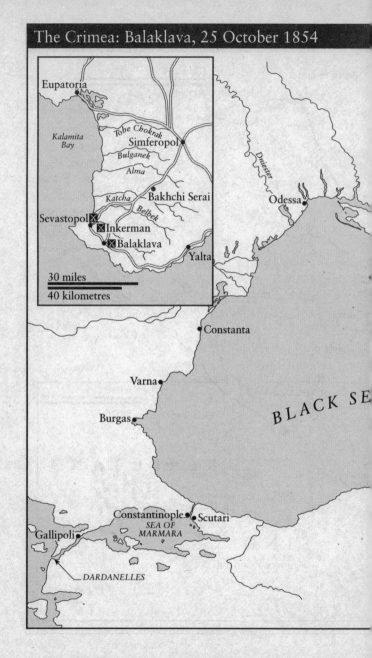

The Crimea: Balaklava, 25 October 1854

Eupatoria

Kalamita Bay

Tobe Chokrak

Simferopol

Bulganek

Alma

Katcha

Bakhchi Serai

Sevastopol

Inkerman

Belbek

Balaklava

Yalta

Dniester

Odessa

30 miles

40 kilometres

Constanta

Varna

Burgas

BLACK SEA

Constantinople

Scutari

SEA OF MARMARA

Gallipoli

DARDANELLES

3. But suppose 'Someone had *not* blunder'd'!

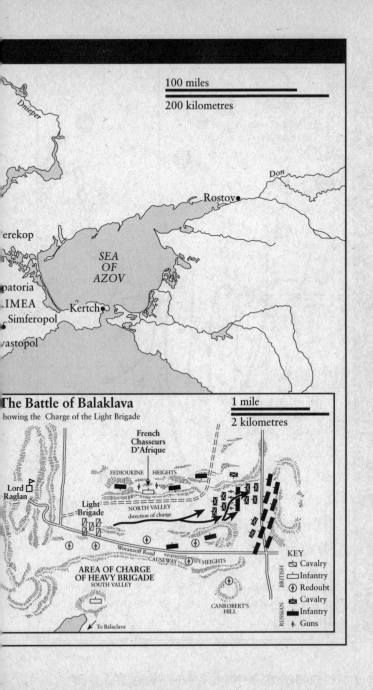

100 miles

200 kilometres

Dnieper

Rostov

Don

SEA
OF
AZOV

erekop

patoria

IMEA

Simferopol

Kertch

vastopol

The Battle of Balaklava
howing the Charge of the Light Brigade

1 mile

2 kilometres

French
Chasseurs
D'Afrique

FEDIOUKINE   HEIGHTS

Lord
Raglan

Light
Brigade

NORTH VALLEY
direction of charge

Woronzoff Road

CAUSEWAY   HEIGHTS

AREA OF CHARGE
OF HEAVY BRIGADE
SOUTH VALLEY

CANROBERT'S
HILL

To Balaclava

RUSSIAN | BRITISH

KEY

⚐ Cavalry
⌂ Infantry
✙ Redoubt
✖ Cavalry
▬ Infantry
⚔ Guns

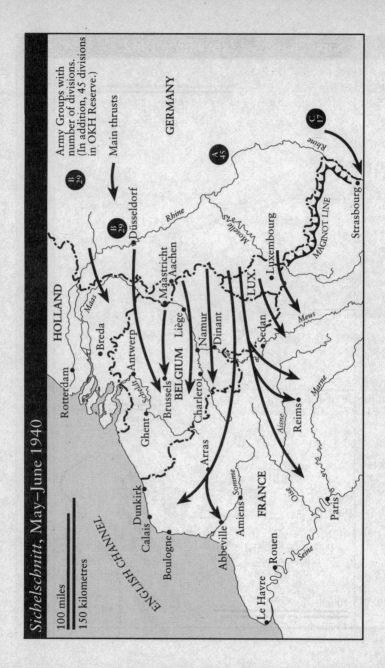

Sichelschnitt, May–June 1940

Army Groups with number of divisions. (In addition, 45 divisions in OKH Reserve.)

Main thrusts

GERMANY

HOLLAND

Rotterdam

Breda

Antwerp

Ghent

Brussels

BELGIUM

Düsseldorf

Maastricht

Aachen

Liège

Namur

Dinant

Charleroi

Arras

Dunkirk

Calais

Boulogne

Abbeville

Amiens

Somme

FRANCE

Le Havre

Rouen

Seine

ENGLISH CHANNEL

Rhine

Maas

Scheldt

LUX.

Luxembourg

Sedan

Meuse

Moselle

MAGINOT LINE

Strasbourg

Rhine

Aisne

Reims

Marne

Oise

Paris

100 miles

150 kilometres

B
29

B
29

A
45

C
17

4. Dunkirk might not have been a miracle after all

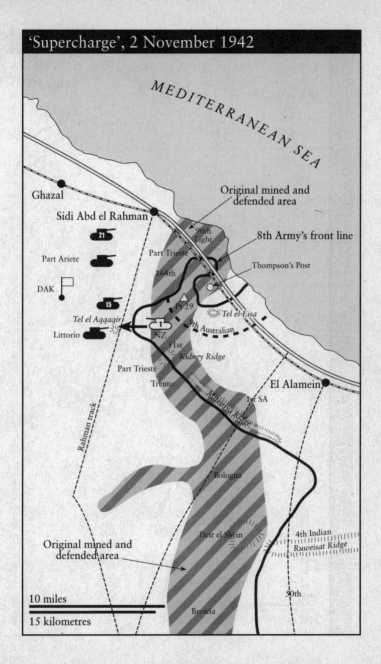

'Supercharge', 2 November 1942

MEDITERRANEAN SEA

Ghazal

Sidi Abd el Rahman

21

Part Ariete

DAK

15

Part Trieste

90th Light

Original mined and defended area

8th Army's front line

164th

Thompson's Post

Tel el Aqqaqir

Littorio

Pt 29

1
NZ

Tel el Eisa

9th Australian

51st

Kidney Ridge

Part Trieste

Trento

Miteiriya Ridge

El Alamein

1st SA

Bologna

Deir el Shein

4th Indian

Ruweisat Ridge

Rahman track

Original mined and defended area

10 miles

15 kilometres

Brescia

50th

5. But what if Monty had rejected McCreery's advice?

The Mediterranean Campaign, 1943–5

SWITZ. AUSTRIA HU

FRANCE

BRENNER PASS

LJUBLJANA GAP

YUC

Toulon

ITALY

SPAIN

CORSICA

•Rome

SARDINIA

ANZIO 22 JAN 1944

SALERNO 9 SEPT 1943

REGGIO DI CALABRIA 3 SEPT 1943

Algiers•

Tunis•

SICILY

10 JULY 1943

•Kasserine

MALTA 10 JULY 1943

M E D I T E R

MARETH LINE

ALGERIA

Medenine

Tripoli•

TUNISIA

200 miles

200 kilometres

LIBYA

6. A lesson in how to forgo not just one advantage, but many

ROMANIA

Bucharest●

BLACK SEA

'IA

'ANIA
urazzo

BULGARIA

GREECE

TURKEY

RHODES

CYPRUS

CRETE

ANEAN SEA

●Benghazi

Tobruk

Alexandria

El Alamein

EGYPT

Berlin: the Rejected Prize, April 1945

BALTIC SEA

Flensburg

BRITISH ZONE

Lübeck

Hamburg

RUSSIAN ZONE

Elbe

Oder

POLISH ADMINISTRATION

FRONT LINE

Hanover

Brunswick

BERLIN

50 miles

Frankfurt

POLAND

Posen

Magdeburg

Dessau

Oder

FRONT LINE

Mulde

Torgau

FRONT LINE

Leipzig

Breslau

Neisse

Breslau

Elbe

Karlsbad

Prague

AMERICAN ZONE

FRONT LINE

Pilsen

CZECHOSLOVAKIA

Nurnburg

Brünn

Danube

Munich

Linz

Vienna

Danube

AUSTRIA

100 miles

200 kilometres

7. If only Eisenhower had taken Berlin
when it was within his grasp

IF BY CHANCE

PROLOGUE

Chaos and Chance

Chaos umpire sits,
And by decision more embroils the fray
By which he reigns: next him high arbiter
Chance governs all.

JOHN MILTON

Those of us who have been privileged to take part in a full-scale battle will probably agree with Milton. During the battle's conduct we will have been conscious that chaos reigned and that chance played a goodly part in the game. All the clear, precise orders which we have received from our immediately superior commanders and which we have passed on in appropriately modified form to our immediate subordinates will have gone for nothing. We have discovered all too soon what von Moltke[1] meant when he declared that no plan survives contact with the enemy. The point was admirably made by Michael Carver[2] in his account of El Alamein when he recalled that to the soldiers taking part, whether infantrymen, tank crews, sappers clearing mines, or gunners, the whole affair 'seemed a chaotic and ghastly muddle'.[3] Nobody seemed to know what others were doing or even where they were. There was always someone firing at something or being fired at, but who and what and why were mysteries. Trying to find out got you nowhere, so that 'in the end one . . . went one's own sweet way, hardening one's heart to the inconvenience, annoyance or anger it might cause to somebody else'.[4] Fred Majdalany[5] who, like Carver, knew all about war at the sharp end, is equally at home in showing how different are the expectations and realities of battle when he records his reactions to reports of the bitter fight for Cassino.

I

He maintains that an official despatch would be almost unrecognizable to the soldier who had taken part in an operation as an accurate description of what had happened to him. He discovers that the day when his company spent hours hanging about in reserve without any idea of what was happening, he was being poured in as a reinforcement. Similarly, the tank crewman finds that on that unhappy morning when all but two tanks of his squadron were knocked out, he was part of a great armoured breakthrough.

The El Alamein battle lasted for twelve days, Cassino for more than four months. Both have been described as decisive. What did they decide?

The battle of El Alamein brought about the retirement of Rommel's Panzerarmee. It enabled Churchill to ring the church bells for what was essentially a British victory. It confirmed Montgomery's mastery of a battle of attrition. It gave new hope and spirit to the British people and their soldiers. Together with the Allied landings in North-west Africa which followed hard upon it, it made possible the defeat of all Axis forces in North Africa and the establishment of Allied control of the Mediterranean. It was a stepping-stone to ultimate victory, the first of a series of battles which slowly but surely brought the war to the gates, and then to the heart of Germany. Compared in purely numerical terms with what was happening at Stalingrad, El Alamein was puny. But for the British it was all-important. It was the turning-point of their fortunes, the redemption of all that Churchill had been striving for, and from that time forth, as the Prime Minister subsequently recorded, victory was to be the order of the day. We will take a longer look at El Alamein in Chapter 8, and see in particular how chance played its part in the battle, but for now we may record what Nigel Hamilton in his new biography of Montgomery had to say about it:

Alamein was crucial to the morale of the free world. No one who lived in Britain, the Commonwealth or even the occupied countries of Europe would ever forget the moment when the news of Rommel's defeat came through. From civilians in factories to resistance workers in Occupied Europe, the sense of a change in the fortunes of democracy was palpable. Alamein thus became a symbol for the free world, and the enslaved world, as much as a military achievement in its own right: a symbol of Allied determination and combined effort in defeating the Nazis.[6]

In this respect El Alamein has been properly described as a decisive battle. Can this also be said of Cassino? Not in the same sense, for the taking of Cassino did not lead to any instant strategic success. Even the subsequent fall of Rome was overshadowed by the invasion of Normandy two days later, and indeed the Italian campaign dragged on for almost another year. Yet, like Alamein, as a symbol Cassino *was* decisive. 'So costly in human life and suffering,' wrote Majdalany, 'it was in the end little more than a victory of the human spirit: an elegy for the common soldier: a memorial to the definitive horror of war and the curiously perverse paradoxical nobility of battle.'[7] We will take a further look at Cassino, too, when we consider the battle for Rome, which showed how General Mark Clark's eye on the main chance frustrated Alexander's opportunity to destroy the German 10th Army after the breakout from Anzio.

What determines the outcome of a battle? The influences are almost too numerous to catalogue. The cause, political stakes, time, terrain, numerical odds, weapons, weather, intelligence, courage and calibre of soldier, skill, resolution, health, even whim of commander, clarity of direction, opportunities seized or forgone, tactics, administrative resources and their use, morale – all these play their part. But there is also *chance*. And chance is a thing of many parts. 'We have ninety chances in our favour and not ten against,' the Emperor Napoleon confidently declared at 8 a.m. on 18 June 1815 while breakfasting with Soult and others of his staff at Le Caillou. But he was about to throw away many of the chances in his favour. Some years before Napoleon had said, 'Give me lucky generals,' yet his choice of generals for his last battle was about as unlucky as it could have been. Later in Chapter 3, we will see how this came about.

Thus one aspect of chance is that of opportunity, a tide in the affairs of men, which, taken at the flood, leads on to fortune. Neglect it, and everything goes wrong. At Salamanca in July 1812 Wellington was quick to see when Marmont had over-extended his army, seized his opportunity and triumphed. Lord Cardigan, on the other hand, when presented with the chance of a lifetime to exploit the Heavy Brigade's success at Balaklava, sat on his horse and did nothing. Had he acted, as he was being urged to do by his subordinates, not only would he have brought off a great *coup*, but the ill-fated charge of his Light Brigade would not have taken place, thus robbing us of a glorious page in military history and a memorable poem by Alfred, Lord Tennyson. Closely allied to opportunity is the business of taking a chance, a risk, as James Wolfe did in scaling the Heights of Abraham and shattering Montcalm's army; or Napoleon in his bold, brilliant style at Austerlitz, risking all by storming the Austro-Russian centre and gaining a crushing victory.

Then there is a third sort of chance. The hand of fate or fortune may be thought of as divorced from human design or endeavour.[8] 'If chance will have me king, why chance may crown me, Without my stir,' mused Macbeth. We may detect chance of this sort in the random arrow which struck King Harold at the battle of Hastings or in the violent thunderstorms on the night of 17/18 June 1815 which so fatally delayed Napoleon's attack at Waterloo. All these interpretations of chance are relevant to our theme, and if chance could play such a leading part in a relatively minor engagement like Salamanca, how much more significant would its influence be when the stakes were really high, when the battle was truly decisive?

This brings us back to the question: what do we really mean by a decisive battle? We have seen that El Alamein was decisive, not because it brought the campaign to an end, still less finished off the German army, but rather because it brought cheer to the 8th Army, signalled a stop to the depressing round of setbacks suffered by British arms, gave a great boost to the nation's morale and seemed to vindicate the strategy which Churchill and his advisers had been pursuing for so long. But it is clear that there are degrees of decisiveness, for the effects of El Alamein, momentous though they were, could not be compared with those of, say, Waterloo, which concluded a war, put paid once and for all to the adventures and ambitions of Napoleon Bonaparte, and ushered in a new era of peace and, for some, prosperity. In considering therefore how chance and other circumstances played their part in determining the outcome of battles, we must include not only those which brought campaigns to a conclusion, but those too which contributed to ultimate victory – or defeat. Otherwise we would exclude such crucial encounters as Plassey, Saratoga, Quebec, Trafalgar, Dunkirk, Moscow and Normandy.

Any account of battles such as these is likely to contain some reference to decisive moments or events when the balance between victory and defeat shifted or even when the outcome of the engagement was actually determined. Sometimes such moments amounted to a single shortlived action performed in the heat of battle. When asked, for example, to pin-point the crucial moment of the Waterloo affair, Wellington, always one for the laconic comment, replied that it was the closing of the gates at Hougoumont. Such over-simplification and taste for terseness tend to obscure the truth that most decisive battles have several decisive moments, and that some of these have little to do with design or calculation, but are the result of chance. At other times decision springs not from a single blow or manoeuvre of short duration, but rather from careful deliberation and discussion. We may see an instance of this in the choice of thrust-line for the breakout at Alamein, which provoked much dissent and delay. The axis of attack eventually chosen was not that originally favoured by Montgomery, but was recommended by General McCreery, Alexander's Chief of Staff, strongly supported by Brigadier Williams, head of Intelligence. Even Montgomery, never lavish with praise for others, remarked that the change of thrust-line proved most fortunate.

Decision may be thought of by some as the prerogative of commanders in the field, but all too often history will show us that it has been *indecision* that has played a major role in settling the issue between two opposing forces. We need think only of Grouchy's indecisiveness on 18 June 1815 when the main action was at its height and when his proper course – forcibly pointed out to him by those under his command – would have been to march to the sound of the guns. Had he done so, his intervention could have turned the scales in Napoleon's favour. Another example is the ludicrous inactivity and dithering of Elphinstone when commanding the British forces at Kabul in 1841/2, leading to the disastrous retreat during which he succeeded in arranging for the destruction of his entire army, with the exception of one man. A glance at Lord Raglan, commanding the British army in the Crimea in 1854, shows us that indecision at the battle of Alma, when an immediate pursuit of the defeated Russians would have resulted in the capture of Sebastopol and arguably the end of the Crimean War, led instead to a prolonged and bloody campaign, whose principal benefit was to compel reform of the hopelessly outdated and inefficient military system. And when, to bring us up to wars within our own lifetime and memory, we recall Hitler not deciding to order his Panzer Divisions to press on against the British Expeditionary Force on 24 May 1940, thus allowing 337,000 British and French soldiers to escape via the beaches of Dunkirk, we can only wonder. For although Churchill made it clear that wars were not won by evacuations, he also pointed out that these evacuated soldiers were 'the nucleus and structure upon which alone Britain could build her armies of the future'.[9]

When we contemplate how chance or mischance, luck or ill-luck, decision or indecision, seizure of opportunity or its neglect determine the course of history, we may perhaps be forgiven if we wonder too how battles might have been lost or won had the dice fallen somewhat differently, had another man been chosen to command, had the orders been more precisely worded, had the terrain been more carefully reconnoitred, and what then might have been the effect of such a change in fortune. The 'Ifs' of history may be what has been called 'an idle parlour game', but they are, like many other entertainments, of gratifying interest. Before examining in some detail how chance and luck profoundly influenced a few crucial engagements during our struggles again Napoleon and Hitler, let us glance at some other affairs which shaped this country's history and in which fortune took a hand.

If ever a man were favoured by chance, that man was William, Duke of Normandy. It was chance that delivered Harold, Earl of Wessex, to the Norman Court in 1064, for had it not been for perverse winds Harold would not have been driven on to the French coast. It was guile, rather than chance, however, which enabled William to persuade Harold to renounce his designs on the crown of England. William, convinced of his own right to the succession,[10] was well aware of Harold's powerful position under the English sovereign, Edward the Confessor, and realized too how easily this position might be converted into sovereignty. With Harold in his power and dependent on his goodwill for return to England, William was therefore well placed to make a pact, reinforced by solemn oath, whereby he would become King of England, while Harold would have to rest content with the assurance of continuing to enjoy the splendid Earldom of Wessex. We may imagine the fury which consumed William when at the beginning of that fateful year, 1066, he was greeted with the news that Edward had on his deathbed recommended Harold as his successor. Hence William's decision to take by force what had been denied him by broken pledge. The business of descending on England was always going to be chancy, but he set about minimizing the risks in a business-like manner.

Halifax[11] made a good point when he suggested that a man must take some chances if he is to achieve anything,[12] and William of Normandy was well aware of it. The mere idea of invading England across the Channel was in itself a major strategic gamble. William therefore took every step he could to reduce the odds against him, both diplomatically and militarily. He was fully alive to the value of propaganda and sought to advertise the fairness of his claim to the English throne throughout the courts and ecclesiastical authorities of Christendom. Even more to the purpose, his martial preparations were thorough, both in the mustering and construction of shipping and the gathering of an army of mercenary soldiers together with the scions of Norman chivalry. A band of well-trained adventurers eager for plunder, which would moreover be attuned to the demands of a lengthy campaign, would be more fitting for his bold enterprise than those subject to feudal levy with a limited period of service.

How large was the expeditionary force that William put together at the Dives estuary in the summer of 1066? Numbers would have been restricted by shipping space, and according to the historian J. A. Williamson, the ports in Norman waters were not dissimilar to our own Cinque Ports, 'able to produce 57 ships between them for the King's service'.[13] Given this restriction, Williamson is inclined to believe that the Norman army was some 4,000 to 12,000 strong, and he suggests that the lower figure is the more likely one. William then had another stroke of luck, for while he was preparing his own expedition, Harold's brother, Tostig, an adventurer and a rival, with the aid of Norway's king, Harold Hardraada, invaded England at the end of August, landing in the Humber.

It is never a sound or sensible strategy to fight a war on two fronts, but this is precisely what Harold of England was required to do. He was fortunate in not having to face two invasions at the same moment, and indeed there was much to be said for the inherent strength of his defending forces. An invading army was bound to be limited in size because of the sheer difficulty of transporting it across the sea, and even though the defending army might itself be limited by the administrative problems of supplying large numbers of soldiers concentrated in one place, the home team could be reinforced, whereas for the invaders, losing the first encounter would mean losing the entire venture. It was in this manner that Tostig and Hardraada failed, for although they won their first battle against the northern Earls near York, Harold roundly defeated them at Stamford Bridge, killing the two leaders and their most valued followers. It was the speed with which Harold acted that had overwhelmed the Norse invasion before the initial landing could be reinforced. But Harold's good fortune was to be shortlived, for no sooner had he repelled the Norsemen, while he was still in Yorkshire, than he heard the news that at the end of September William of Normandy had landed on the shore of Pevensey Bay in Sussex.

Harold did not hesitate. Riding with all haste to London, accompanied only by his personal guard and having ordered the rest of his army to follow, he gathered together what forces he could and posted south to take up a position on what has long been known as Battle Hill. His army numbered perhaps four or five thousand, although there is no reliable record of it. It is enough to suppose that Harold was able to muster a total not dissimilar to the Normans. William in his turn had drawn up his men on Telham Hill opposite his enemy; aware that whereas Harold might expect to be reinforced while he himself could not, he determined to attack, and did so on the morning of 14 October. The battle was not an orderly affair of controlled manoeuvre and fire-power. It consisted rather of a series of Norman assaults on the Saxon position, assaults which were readily repulsed. It was towards evening that the Norman effort seemed to be weakening and many of Harold's men, believing that the day was theirs, rushed forward in pursuit. This was their undoing, for while Harold's army used horses for getting about, they did not fight mounted; William's force included armed horsemen, who rapidly disposed of the advancing Saxons. Yet the battle was still undecided until dusk, when William was presented with the most fortunate chance of all. A falling arrow struck Harold through the eye. It had not been aimed at him, but the result was decisive. Not only Harold was killed, but his two brothers with him. No one remained to rally what other Saxon forces might have been raised. The following day William found that he was King of England.

But for this chance how different might England's history have been. 'Had some nameless bowman's arrow flown three inches wide,' wrote Williamson, 'Harold's statue might stand by Alfred's as that of another hero-king who saved the nation from disaster.'[14] The idea that we would have had no Plantagenets, no Hundred Years War or Wars of the Roses – what would Shakespeare have used for historical material? – no Virgin Queen and thus no Stuarts, no Civil War leading to the Glorious Revolution and the establishment of a governmental system which has more or less survived to this day, hardly bears thinking of. Mention of the Stuarts and the Civil War, however, brings us face to face with another great If of battle.

No two kings of England, indeed no two men, could have been more dissimilar in their purposes, abilities, inclinations or characteristics than James II and William III. James wanted absolute authority in his kingdom, not only for its own sake but in order to promote the cause of Catholicism; William wanted to employ England's economic and military resources to pursue his struggle against the power and ambitions of Louis XIV. James had shown himself to be a competent manager of navies; William had proved himself to be a perseverant deployer of armies. James relished the embraces of women; William preferred the company of men. For James religion was everything; William could take it or leave it. James was thoroughly English;

William was first and foremost an Orangeman. The two men faced each other but once on the battlefield, and the outcome of the contest was to have a profound effect on the future of both England and Ireland.

No controversy concerning the profession of arms raged more furiously in English counsels at the time of the Stuarts than that of whether or not there should be a standing army. Our good fortune in being an island made it possible to ignore the existence of great standing armies elsewhere in Europe, for while the English navy remained in being, these armies posed no threat to England. And since the power of the purse remained in the hands of Parliament, it would not be possible without Parliament's sanction for the sovereign to raise great standing armies at home, which would assuredly pose a threat to England. Only taxation would provide the king with a regular army and only Parliament could provide taxation. The Tudors had been wise enough to recognize this restriction in their power. The Stuarts' refusal to do so led to their undoing. The great irony of this country's military development was that when the time came to acknowledge that the practice of war was a distinct and separate calling, with all the social and political consequences which this entailed, it was not for the confusion of a foreign foe, but for the punishment of an English king.

Other kings had been content, or at least constrained, to rely on the militia. The militia, however, was not enough for Charles I, nor for his faithful minister, Thomas Wentworth, Earl of Strafford. To make Charles as absolute a monarch as possible, Strafford devised his scheme known as Thorough. It depended on realizing what had eluded so many former monarchs: there was one thing, and one thing only, which would enable Charles to rule as he wanted to do – a standing army. All Strafford's attempts to raise one failed, however, and Charles failed too. It was left to Parliament to form and raise the New Model Army, which in Cromwell's hands arranged for the submission first of the Cavaliers and then of Parliament itself. In the end the army overreached itself, and despite its success in putting down all the opposing forces in Europe, once the English had felt the hand of military tyranny, they expressed their disapproval by a series of insurrections, easily suppressed by the iron hand of Cromwell. Yet paradoxically, having rid England of one Stuart king, Parliament now allowed the son of that same king to be restored to the throne without the disturbance of another Civil War. And it was Charles II, feeling perhaps with justification that the Beefeaters and trained bands might not be sufficient to guarantee the security of his household, who contrived to put aside sufficient funds to support a body of guards, thereby no doubt making a serious sacrifice of his own pleasures and dissipations. It was a modest enough body. Three regiments of cavalry, the Life Guards, Blues and Royal Dragoons;[15] a few more of infantry, two regiments of Foot Guards, four of the line, plus the Admiral's Regiment, forerunner of the Royal Marines, totalling some 1,700 horse and 7,000 foot. Such an establishment was hardly likely to threaten 5 million Englishmen with enslavement.

Such a thought was no doubt present in the mind of Charles's brother, James, when he succeeded, narrow, bigoted and dull though he was. But again chance took a hand and presented James with the perfect opportunity to begin his cherished project of building up a standing army. Monmouth, bastard son of Charles II, was unwise enough to venture forth from the comforting embraces of Lady Henrietta Wentworth and land at Lyme in June 1685, mustering a force of some 1,500 men. In spite of some initial success, support for Monmouth remained local and limited, and the great men of the realm – however much some of them might dislike the rule of James, whom they had after all sought to exclude from the succession – were not disposed to risk another Civil War, with an inevitably uncertain outcome, for the sake of Monmouth. So the far more numerous forces that James was able to put together prevailed at Sedgemoor, where the presence of the King's Household troops and regular battalions of Foot brought about Monmouth's defeat.

This was not the only benefit which James gained. Under the guise of assuring the realm's security during the Monmouth rebellion, he had greatly increased the strength of regular forces at his disposal by raising six regiments of cavalry and nine of infantry. He trebled the size of his army to 20,000 troops, more than any former monarch had had in times of peace. If the chance offered to him by Monmouth's ill-fated expedition had not presented itself, James would have been hard put to raise these extra regiments. Yet he was still not satisfied. Happily for England, raising an even larger standing army depended on the ability to pay for more soldiers. And the power of the purse still rested with the House of Commons.

So little did James understand the character of the people he ruled that when opposition to his intention to destroy the Established Church by using his ecclesiastical authority reached the point of London's trained bands refusing to disperse hostile crowds – refusing, in short, 'to fight for Popery' – he formed a great camp of his standing army at Hounslow Heath. Fourteen battalions of infantry and over thirty squadrons of cavalry were assembled together with artillery pieces and ammunition, all with a view to overawing and subduing the citizens of London. But James, who usually got his priorities wrong, had completely misjudged both these citizens and the soldiers, for instead of the soldiers deterring and forcing obedience on the citizens, the ideas of the citizens took a grip on the imagination of the soldiers. Apart from this, the Londoners, once their first apprehensions were overcome, took to the spectacle and active delights of the camp rather as they would to a gigantic fair or circus. 'Mingled with the musketeers and dragoons,' wrote Macaulay,

a multitude of fine gentlemen and ladies from Soho Square, sharpers and painted women from Whitefriars, invalids in sedans, monks in hoods and gowns, laqueys in rich liveries, pedlars, orange girls, mischievous apprentices and gaping clowns, was constantly passing and repassing through the long lanes of tents. From some pavilions were heard the noises of drunken revelry, from others the curse of gamblers.[16]

So much for the effect of James's standing army. Two years later, when all was put to the test, it availed him nothing. For when William of Orange, at the invitation of leading Whigs and Tories, landed at Torbay in the summer of 1688 with an army inferior in numbers to that which James, had he been able to command its loyalty, should have opposed him, this same standing army, so prudently and menacingly collected together by the king, deserted *en masse*. Thus in the contest for England William triumphed over James without a struggle.

A struggle was still to come, however, for in 1689 the Catholic provinces of Ireland declared for James, while the Protestants of Ulster stood for William, hence their nomenclature as Orangemen ever since. James was supported by Louis XIV with troops and money and made his way to Ireland, held a Parliament and attempted to confiscate Protestant lands. The siege of Londonderry followed, relieved at length from the sea.

It was not until 1690 that William was able to leave his commitments in England to confront James. William III was not the first or the last English king to command troops in the field, but he was certainly one whose perseverance and experience progressively enhanced his military reputation. James was no stranger to soldiering either; he had served with credit in the field and had cherished his beloved Royal Navy. But however able or experienced a battle commander may be, much will depend on the material to hand and the state of mind of the commanders themselves. By the time William and James met and opposed each other in the field, the intrepid character of the one had been heightened and hardened by campaigning and heavy responsibilities, while the inherent sluggishness and ignoble nature of the other had been indulged and stimulated by a gradually deepening inflexibility of mind and a wanton misuse of power. Small wonder that the result was what it was. Both kings commanded heterogeneous armies, in itself a disadvantage, for if part of an army turns out to be totally unreliable, disaster may follow.

Let us first take a look at James's army. It probably amounted to some 30,000 men of which about one-third – the French infantry and the Irish cavalry – was of high quality. Not so the remaining two-thirds. Both the Irish dragoons[17] and the Irish infantry were inferior. The best they could do in an encounter with the enemy was to fire off their weapons once and then take to their heels bawling for mercy. That such behaviour should be imputed to plain lack of courage has been shown to be false by a thousand instances of Irish bravery in contests all over the world. More to the point was not so much the idea that such soldiers had been badly trained, but that they had been trained in a totally deficient manner. Above all, no sense of discipline or steadiness had been instilled into them. What, therefore, was more likely to encourage ill-discipline than an incitement to bolster their wholly inadequate remuneration by marauding? It was hardly to be expected that such a mob would be capable of standing up to the steadfast, well-drilled actions of well-led and well-trained opponents.

William's army was very different from James's. It was a little larger – some 36,000 in all – and was even more variously composed. There were Englishmen, Dutchmen, Germans, Danes and Finns. But Macaulay has reminded us that among this mixed assembly 'were two bodies of men animated by a spirit peculiarly fierce and implacable, the Huguenots of France, thirsting for the blood of the French, and the Englishry of Ireland impatient to trample down the Irish'.[18] William therefore had a slight numerical advantage, whereas James had adopted a strong defensive position on ground of his own choosing. But the real advantage lay with William by virtue of the quality of his soldiers and his own determined leadership. This leadership was admirably displayed by his courageous conduct. The excitement of battle seemed to dissolve all his cold reserve and acted upon him like an intoxicant. On 11 July 1690 William was always to be seen where the danger was greatest. Twice he came near to paying the price for his insistence on exposing himself to enemy fire. One ball struck his pistol, another the heel of his boot, but he paid no heed to the pleas of his lieutenants to retire to some more secure position from which he could issue orders. No wonder the troops under his command, inspired by his example, gained ground.

James did little to emulate his rival. He watched the battle from a safe distance. When we consider what was at stake, we may wonder at such behaviour. There he was, with the eyes of all upon him, the eyes of those who were ardently supporting his cause and of those who were bitterly opposed to it. He was after all the legitimate King of England, Scotland and Ireland, and had come to fight for his rights and for the rights of his heir. And yet when all was to be won or lost, when he observed his rival, William, despite his wounds, leading a charge through the mud, rallying the Enniskilleners, and inspiring his troops to gain further ground at a moment when determined leadership and a counter-blow might have been decisive – at this crucial point, when the future of the House of Stuart was in the balance, what did James do? Observing that the day appeared to be going against Ireland and fearful that his escape from the field might be intercepted, James quit the scene of battle and galloped towards Dublin.

Put the case, however, that William's strength had failed, that one of the balls which struck his accoutrements had instead struck him. Put the case that the French auxiliaries and the Irish cavalry, more daringly led and controlled, had swept down on William's troops when they were engaged in the tactically vulnerable business of crossing the Boyne. Put the case, in short, that James II 'wrested victory out of heretic Fortune's hands' and that William, rather than himself, was obliged to flee the field. What then? We may perhaps conjecture that James might have remained King of Ireland for a time, but there would have been fierce resistance at Enniskillen and Londonderry. Louis XIV might have been tempted to ship reinforcements to James, and then much would have depended on the activities of the Royal Navy, James's own special protégé. The fickleness of loyalties is usually determined in the end by the power of the purse. And this power still remained with the English Parliament, whose leading members would have seen to it that James was never allowed to return to England. England had had its fill of the Stuarts, as subsequent events in 1715 and 1745 were to show. Pretenders to the throne never got further than being pretenders. And we must remember that the very standing army which James had created, and which men like Marlborough had ensured would not fight for a cause which embraced absolute monarchy and Catholicism, would have stood firm in upholding the rights and freedoms so triumphantly acquired by the Glorious Revolution. Sooner or later, no doubt, England would have tried to re-establish her ascendancy over Ireland.

Yet the idea of an independent Emerald Isle as early at 1690 is intriguing. How would the country have aligned itself during England's interminable wars with France? Would fox-hunting have reached its heights without the enthusiastic support of English landowners? Would there have been such mass emigration to the United States or Australia by disenchanted Irish families? Perhaps an independent Irish administration would have ruled its own people in such an enlightened way that the shadows of famine, eviction, murder and sullen hostility would never have stalked the valleys and hills of that beautiful country. But whether there could have been a reconciliation with the Protestants of Ulster must remain in question. The defiance of Londonderry, so marked and so triumphant in 1689, would have been unlikely to change in subsequent years. Could some accommodation have been reached between the rival factions whereby a degree of religious toleration and civil liberty for the Protestant North was observed? What an infinite sum of misery, bloodshed, recrimination and wrangling would then have been saved. We may predict more confidently that the Irish would still have bred magnificent horses and would have continued to provide splendid soldiers for the ranks of the British army and a generous flood of brilliant general officers. Yet we might have looked in vain for the Somerville and Ross stories of an Irish R.M. or the early novels of Anthony Trollope. What would we have done without Wellington's Irish regiments and all those men who served the British Empire in every part of the world? Kipling would have been robbed of some of his Barrack Room Ballads and his history of the Irish Guards.[19] Think of Alanbrooke, Alexander, Montgomery, Templer, whose contribution to our survival against the power of the Third Reich was so incalculable.

Let us move to an even more colourful seat of war – India. It cannot be said that many of Britain's great captains distinguished themselves when they were young. Unlike Alexander, who conquered the world before he was thirty, or Napoleon, who at twenty-seven shocked Europe with his Italian campaign, Marlborough was fifty-four at Blenheim, Wellington forty-six at Waterloo, Montgomery fifty-five at Alamein. Yet there were notable exceptions. Robert Clive was only twenty-five at Arcot, James Wolfe but thirty-two when he triumphed at Quebec. These two men showed what a handful of redcoats commanded by soldiers of genius could do, overcoming daunting odds with almost insolent ease, and winning for the Crown great tracts of Empire. Their exploits were ripe for the intervention of chance. Let us accompany Clive to his splendid victories and Wolfe to his rendezvous with the last enemy and look at the coin's other side.

There are two great ironies about the career of the man who

became known as Clive of India. In the first place, although in his youth he acquired the reputation of being so fierce and imperious that he was charged with being addicted to fighting, his schoolmasters rated him a dunce. Nothing good was to be expected from one who combined inadequate intellect with unmanageable temper. His family was therefore content to accept for him the post of writer in the East India Company, and in 1743 he was posted to Madras. Once there, neither his duties nor the climate suited him and he found no outlet for his audacious spirit. He recorded later that he had not enjoyed a single happy day since leaving England. Indeed, so discontented was Clive, and so displeased with him were his official masters, that he attempted suicide. Twice he tried to discharge a pistol at his head; twice it failed to go off. At this point, having assured himself that the pistol was properly loaded, Clive became convinced that he was destined to do something great. His opportunity came in 1751.

The second irony lies in the consideration that a Frenchman's vision of founding a great European empire on the crumbling remains of an Indian monarchy should have led in the end to this same empire falling into the hands of the British. There was nothing unusual about the British and the French being at war, nor was it uncommon for initial French successes to be gradually reversed by the British. So it was in the Carnatic in the middle of the eighteenth century. Had it not been for Dupleix, Governor of Pondicherry, Clive might never have been heard of, for it was Dupleix's imperial ambition which made him seize Madras, threaten Trichinopoly and, in alliance with Indian pretenders to the throne, set himself in the way of becoming master of the Carnatic. Yet it was Clive, now a captain and commissary to the troops, who saw that unless some bold, dramatic blow was struck, the French would become absolute masters of the southern part of India. He therefore proposed an attack on Arcot, capital of the Carnatic.

Not many soldiers of twenty-five possess the foresight, the thorough-ness, the political sagacity, the determination and the inspiring leadership which Clive was now to show. Having persuaded his masters in the East India Company that what he proposed was necessary and that he himself was the man to achieve it, Clive set off with a mere 500 soldiers, less than half of whom were British, 300 being sepoys trained by the East India Company. Only two of his fellow officers had seen action before.

After a march from Trichinopoly in appalling weather, Clive arrived with his puny force at the gates of Arcot, whose garrison, panic-stricken, instantly rushed out of the fort, allowing Clive and his men to occupy it without a fight. Up until now the enterprise had been little more than a raid, but now Clive set about putting on it the seal of a decisive victory. Knowing that an attempt to regain the fort would shortly be mounted, he took two steps, one precautionary, the other bold. He prepared for a siege and made a night sortie to disperse the enemy reinforcements that were gathering to attack him.

Before long the siege began in earnest. Rajah Sahib, who conducted it, mustered some 10,000 troops against Clive's small band, which had now dwindled to about 300 troops, only one-third of them European. For the day of the assault Rajah Sahib chose the Mohammedan festival of Husein, which augured well for the Moslem cause. All those who fell in battle against the infidel during this festival instantly atoned for whatever sins they might have committed during their lives and found themselves translated to that paradise represented by the garden of the Houris. Yet Rajah Sahib did not rely solely on this alluring prospect. Drugs reinforced the fanaticism of religion so that the besiegers, 'drunk with enthusiasm, drunk with bhang',[20] rushed furiously to the attack. They were led by armoured elephants whose sheer weight and momentum were expected to batter down the gates and demolish the defences. But a spirited reception awaited the attacking hordes, and the first to feel the accuracy and discomfort of musket-balls delivered by disciplined redcoats were the elephants themselves. So dismayed were these huge beasts that they turned about and fled from the fusillade that had greeted them, thereby scattering or trampling underfoot those unfortunate enough to follow in their wake. This initial repulse did not dampen the ardour of Rajah Sahib's men, however. They attempted to raft their way across the defensive moat and attacked over the dry parts of it with great courage and dash, but Clive's direction of his artillerymen, together with the disciplined accuracy and volume of the British infantry, took such heavy toll of the fanatical hordes that assault after assault was defeated. Hundreds of the assailants had been killed while Clive had lost but a handful of men. The following morning Rajah Sahib's army had gone. What had begun as a venture to strike a daring blow had become the beginning of the end for the French in India.

If, by chance, Clive's first attempts at suicide had succeeded,[21] there would have been no triumph at Arcot. Or if the elephants had ignored their punishment at the hands of the British redcoats and had surged on to trample down the defences and make a passage for the attacking hordes, Clive would surely have perished. And then, without Clive, what would have happened in India during the Seven Years War? At the battle of Plassey in 1757 Clive commanded a mere 3,000 men and pitted them against Surajah Dowlah's host of nearly 60,000, including more than 40,000 infantry, 15,000 cavalry and fifty huge guns which required great teams of oxen to pull them and elephants to push. It was these two armies which met at Plassey. One was incomparably superior in numbers; the other was astonishingly superior in discipline and valour. By his victory there Clive determined India's future. Without him there might have been no British India, jewel in the crown of the Empire. It might all have been French instead. Yet Clive did it, and what he had done on one side of the world, Wolfe was to accomplish on the other.

When we think of the Seven Years War, we think too of the Year of Victories, 1759, and its architect, William Pitt, later Earl of Chatham. Isaiah Berlin once described Winston Churchill as 'one of the two greatest men of action his nation has produced'.[22] He did not reveal who he thought was the other one, but it must have been Pitt that he had in mind. The resounding success of the Royal Navy and the British army under Pitt was not only the result of his command of large resources and the strategic skill with which he deployed them. Pitt also achieved success because, like Churchill almost 200 years later, he inspired the nation. 'The ardour of his soul,' wrote Macaulay,

had set the whole kingdom on fire. It inflamed every soldier who dragged the cannon up the heights of Quebec, and every sailor who boarded the French ships among the rocks of Brittany. The Minister, before he had been long in office, had imparted to the commanders whom he employed his own impetuous, adventurous and defying character.[23]

One of those commanders was James Wolfe, and if Wolfe had bitten some of his fellow generals, as George II had suggested when he had been told that Wolfe was mad, the Seven Years War might not have lasted so long. As it was, in a single encounter on 13 September 1759 outside the walls of Quebec, Wolfe conquered an entire province of Canada, which together with Amherst's subsequent occupation of Montreal, established British supremacy in Canada. Wolfe has sometimes been likened to Nelson, and indeed the two had much in common – frail in constitution, fearless in action, indomitable in spirit.

It was in the preliminaries to his triumph on the Heights of Abraham that Wolfe displayed such daring. All depended on the use of a little-known footpath at L'Anse au Foulon (Fuller's Cove), a steep track which led up the bluff from the St Lawrence river to the Plains of Abraham, some two miles west of Quebec. All depended, too, on the calmness of the night, which enabled Wolfe's men to embark with the skilful and dauntless support of the Royal Navy, then scale the cliffs by the narrow, precipitous path and confront Montcalm's 16,000 men and strong artillery with little more than half that number. It was by the discipline, accuracy and sheer volume of Wolfe's infantry fire power as directed by him that the issue was decided. As the two armies confronted each other, Wolfe

ordered the line to lay down till the enemy came close, when they were to rise up and give their fire . . . the enemy huzza'd, advancing with a short trott (which was effectually shortened to a number of them) they began their fire on the left, the whole of them reclining that way, but received and sustained such a check, that the smell of gun-powder became nauseous; they broke their line, to all parts of the compass.[24]

During the exchange of volleys, Wolfe received his mortal wound, yet his immortality was assured, for 'no event has ever been more celebrated on canvas than Wolfe's capture of Quebec. Wolfe died in every style from the classical to the naturalistic to suit all tastes and rouse one general emotion.'[25]

Wolfe, like many another soldier, had a deep love of literature, and after completing his reconnaissance on the evening before the battle, diverted his fellow commanders by reciting for them from memory almost the whole of Gray's *Elegy*. He would rather, he concluded, be the author of those lines than enjoy the glory of defeating the French on the morrow. How prophetic was his repetition of one line of the *Elegy*, for in his case the path of glory did lead but to the grave. Yet if by chance Wolfe had not learned of that obscure footpath from one Captain Robert Stobo, if the recent storm had persisted, putting paid to any amphibious operation, if delay had forced the Royal Navy's ships to withdraw for resupply, if Wolfe's health, always precarious, had further deteriorated, there would have been no further glory for him, no victory for Pitt, no Canada for the British. The Ifs of history might have seen to it that there was not only a French India, but a French North America too.

The Year of Victories was not confined to Canada, however. In West Africa, in the Caribbean, in India, in Europe, British arms were triumphant. Pitt's strategy of destroying French sea power and relieving France of her possessions overseas had succeeded. At the battle of Minden the British infantry had won plaudits even from their enemies, the French general, the Duc de Contades, commenting that to see a line of infantry break through three lines of cavalry and tumble them into ruin was to witness something he had thought to be impossible. Yet even though the Peace of Paris in 1763 confirmed British conquests in Canada, North America, India and the West Indies, Pitt, now out of power, foresaw that it would not be long before France took up arms again to seek retribution and restoration of her losses. When this time came, it was because Britain found herself at odds with her own people, the Colonists of North America.

Although an over-simplification, it would not be inaccurate to say that the loss of the American Colonies was brought about by the inflexibility and stubbornness of the one man who most ardently desired their retention – George III. In this achievement he was ably assisted by Lord North. Neither of them could see what Edmund Burke so clearly perceived and so eloquently tried to impress upon others: that magnanimity was very often the wisest policy and that 'a great empire and little minds go ill together'.[26] Alas, both North and his sovereign did have little minds, and set about trying to coerce the uncoercible. Even though Pitt pointed out that America could not be conquered, and General Howe, who succeeded to the command in America in October 1775, advised that the country could not be held, the king still persisted. As a result he was obliged to stomach Burgoyne's surrender at Saratoga.

Let us accompany Gentleman Johnny as he proceeds to lose an army. The strategy, if it may be called that, was devised by the then Secretary of State for American affairs, Lord George Sackville, who had distinguished himself at the battle of Minden by his disobedience and cowardice. The plan was to detach New England from the rest of the Colonies by two internal thrusts. Burgoyne with his 7,000 men was to move from Canada through the Hudson Gap towards Albany, while Howe would join Burgoyne by driving northwards towards New York. But timing was difficult, and Howe, realizing that he would have to remain inactive for too long, thus allowing Washington to act against him, decided instead to provoke Washington into battle by seizing Philadelphia. He did both, but it meant that he could not now join Burgoyne in the Hudson area. Thus Burgoyne was left with no choice but to retire or attempt to force his way through to Albany unsupported. But he found himself surrounded by enemy troops and unable to break through. As Burgoyne and his army fell back on Saratoga, depleted in numbers, short of provisions, harassed by incessant rain, impeded by mud so thick that the exhausted, starved horses and oxen could not drag guns and ammunition-wagons out of bogs, the soldiers themselves exhausted, wet through and hungry, the American forces under General Gates hemmed them in. Gentleman Johnny's own conduct was an example to all. Sergeant Lamb reported that 'in the heat, fury and danger of the fight he maintained the true characteristics of the soldier – serenity, fortitude and undaunted intrepidity'.[27] It was not enough, however, and on 14 October Burgoyne asked for terms. Three days later the formal instrument of surrender was signed. Gates was triumphant, Burgoyne unrepentant, maintaining that if his entire command had been British – some of it was German – he would have fought his way through.

If he had done so, or if Howe had been able to reinforce, if in short there had been no surrender at Saratoga, the consequences would have been profoundly different, for Burgoyne's capitulation changed the whole nature of the war. From that time forward, thanks partly to the persuasion of Benjamin Franklin, the US ambassador to France, the French decided to give their open and whole-hearted support to the Americans. Thus the balance of power was significantly changed, and Britain was no longer able to rely on the key to success in the American War – command of the sea. And it was want of this supremacy at sea which brought about the further disaster of Yorktown and thus the emergence of American independence. Without the active intervention of France, Saratoga might have been retrieved, and British authority in the American Colonies re-established. If George III and his footling ministers could then have been persuaded to understand Burke's plea for magnanimity and to have inaugurated a system of representation before taxation, there might have been another great British Dominion, stretching from the Atlantic to the Pacific. What an Empire we would have had then!

As we observed earlier, the Ifs of history may be illusory, but they provide harmless entertainment, and may indeed be of value in learning further how to tackle or not tackle dilemmas still to confront us. English history is littered with such Ifs. Many of them concern our struggles with France. The most striking of our opponents there was Napoleon. It was he who noted that wherever he turned, if there were water enough to float a battle-ship, he would be confronted, and thwarted, by the Royal Navy. And the darling of the Royal Navy and England's greatest hero was Nelson.

ONE

St Vincent: 14 February 1797

It shall be my watchword – Touch and take.

NELSON

In recent times there has been an attempt to disparage the character of Lord Nelson.[1] He has been called 'a natural born predator' whose private life was reprehensible, who was mentally unstable, who allowed prisoners of war to be unjustly executed, who manipulated his own image to the point of outrageous idealization, who circulated stories of his own valour in such a way as to overshadow the exploits of others. This curious vogue for debunking and demeaning our past heroes strikes a sour note to those who, like Nelson, but in a minuscule way by comparison, have spent most of their lives in some sort of military service. Happily, when we contemplate Nelson's character in the round, it is not difficult to show that these detractors – whose motives must puzzle the most objective of us – are profoundly mistaken, however conscientious they may have been in their search for detail.

Of course Nelson had his faults. He was vain, restless, intense, egotistic. Yet he was also lion-hearted, kindly, paternal, his name to this day the touchstone of naval excellence. He seemed to possess an unrivalled instinct for sensing the feelings of the lower deck. No wonder sailors longed for Nelson to command them. No wonder his captains were a band of brothers. Nelson was said to hold the four aces of leadership: imagination; the ability to inspire; confiding in subordinates and acknowledging their contribution to success; and above all the offensive spirit, the overriding determination to bring the enemy's fleet to battle and then annihilate it. This last was the kernel of the Nelson touch. When he explained to his captains his intended tactics at what became the battle of Trafalgar, they were overcome with emotion.

Trafalgar was a victory which a few years later would facilitate the deployment of a British army on the south-western extremes of Napoleon's empire, and keep it there, properly supplied and reinforced, until the Emperor's own armies had been driven back to France by Wellington. When Nelson sighted the combined French and Spanish fleet off Cape Trafalgar on 21 October 1805, he and his captains knew exactly what they were about. Nelson had repeatedly outlined to his subordinates how they would 'surprise and confound the enemy', bring about what he always sought – 'a pell-mell battle' – and so accomplish the absolute destruction of the enemy's fleet. When he expounded his plan to sail direct for the enemy centre, then split and divide them, so that each half could be destroyed in detail – the plan which he lightly defined as 'the Nelson touch' – his captains were electrified by the sheer beauty of it. 'It was new, it was singular, it was simple . . . it must succeed.'[2]

Never were Nelson's four aces of leadership played to more advantage than at Trafalgar. His imagination enabled him to picture the circumstances of a forthcoming battle with such clarity, such boldness and such unrivalled determination to bend the enemy to his will that his spirit permeated the whole fleet. There was no need for further signalling. They all knew what to do, although his last signal, the renowned 'England expects . . .' had such an effect on Napoleon, when he heard of it, that he ordered a comparable call to duty – *La France confide que chacun fasse son devoir!* – to be inscribed in every French man-of-war. Nelson's second ace, the ability to inspire, was so strong that it animated the whole of his command. His confidence, his enthusiasm, his dedication to duty, and the sheer professional heights of seamanship and gunnery that had been achieved, meant that every captain who served with him aspired to be another Nelson. The third ace, consulting and confiding in subordinates, listening to their views and giving credit to their actions, produced a unique atmosphere of mutual confidence, trust and reliance. The last ace, the offensive spirit, embodied Nelson's greatness as a fleet commander. It was an absolutely overriding resolution to engage the enemy at the closest possible quarters and utterly destroy him.

Yet it would be absurd to ignore Nelson's shortcomings. On the one occasion that he and Wellington met – it was on 12 September 1805 in Castlereagh's ante-room – he at first appalled the victor of Assaye by speaking of himself in trivial and self-indulgent language – 'almost all on his side, and all about himself, and really, in a style so vain and silly as to surprise me'. Once Nelson had discovered to whom he was talking, however, it was a different matter, and Wellington later commented:

All that I thought a charlatan style had vanished, and he talked with good sense, and a knowledge of subjects both at home and abroad, that surprised me equally and more agreeably than the first part of our interview had done; in fact, he talked like an officer and a statesman . . . I don't know that I ever had a conversation that interested me more.[3]

Admiral Sir John Jervis, later Earl St Vincent, was not blind to Nelson's faults, however much he admired his brilliance in command at sea. 'Poor man,' he observed, 'he is devoured with vanity, weakness and folly.'[4] It was certainly true that Nelson made a fool of himself over his obsession with Emma Hamilton.[5] But the explanation for it was clear enough. When the two became lovers, it was for Nelson the very ecstasy of love, and Emma was no longer obliged to simulate pleasure for he yielded to her as much as she yielded to him. They both embarked on the adventure of pleasure with the same slight anxiety about their ability to please or be pleased, and the same ease, the same trust. They were equals in pleasure because equals in love. Was not this love indeed? None but the brave deserve the fair, they say. If ever a man of heroic stature deserved the kind of love he longed for and Emma gave him, that man was Nelson. When the detractors already referred to hint that Nelson's so-called mental instability led to his 'suicide-in-all-but-name' at Trafalgar, it is plain that they have not studied the letters Nelson wrote to Lady Hamilton before the battle or have understood the ardent longing he felt to return to the arms of Emma and their daughter, Horatia.

The truth of the matter was that from the very beginning Nelson had something of the poet and the mystic in him. 'Nelson was the poet in action,' wrote Aubrey de Selincourt, 'in his grandest moments he ceased to belong to this world and entered a realm as visionary as Shelley's.' It is this which helps us to understand the emotional reaction of his captains when they listened to his exposition of the Nelson touch. It was honour which predominated in Nelson's mind. He coveted honour in the way that both Hotspur and Prince Hal did. He even misquoted from the Crispin speech in *Henry V*, substituting the word 'glory' for 'honour'. But the acquisition of honour and glory was not the sole key to Nelson's character. He desired recognition as well. 'I am the child of opinion,' he wrote. And his first real taste of recognition came with the battle of St Vincent.

1797 was a bad year for England, sometimes described until the beginning of the Great War in 1914 as 'the darkest hour in English history'. Europe was dominated by France, the whole Rhine delta was in the hands of the French, and their armies poised for invasion. Ireland was on the point of rebellion. Discontent was seething at home. The fleets of both Holland and Spain were at France's disposal. The Royal Navy was abandoning the Mediterranean, and Sir John Jervis, commanding a fleet, fifteen sail of the line, had declared on 13 February 1797 that a victory was essential to England at this time, for everything was going wrong elsewhere. Clearly some striking success for Britain was needed. Admiral Jervis and Commodore Nelson were just the men to deliver such a success.

The engagement off Cape St Vincent, the south-west corner of Portugal, was remarkable for two things: first, Jervis's admirable indifference to the daunting size of his enemy's fleet. When the captain of his flagship, *Victory*, reported twenty Spanish sail of the line, Jervis replied: 'Very well, sir.' Then, on the next report's being of twenty-seven ships, nearly double their own strength, Jervis retorted: 'Enough, sir, no more of that. The die is cast and if there are fifty sail of the line, I will go through them.' This splendid spirit so impressed a huge Canadian, Captain Hallowell, who was standing near the Admiral, that he slapped Jervis on the back, enthusiastically endorsing this defiance by saying, 'That's right, Sir John, and a damned good licking we'll give them.' That they did so was due in large measure to the tactical brilliance and remarkable action of Nelson.

Second, when Nelson in *Captain*, third from the rear of the British line, saw that his Admiral's orders to the fleet might allow the two Spanish divisions to join up and bring greatly superior fire-power to bear on the British, he acted with what Arthur Bryant called the 'instinct of genius' and contrary to orders; indeed, contravening a cardinal rule of naval warfare, he bore out of the line of battle and headed straight for the main Spanish division. By bringing them to action, he sought to prevent their reunion with the other Spanish vessels. It was an act of the utmost daring to take on five enemy ships of the line. But the tactic succeeded. Nelson was supported by Collingwood in *Excellent* and he in turn was followed by Troubridge's *Culloden* and Frederick's *Blenheim*. What transpired was what Nelson always aimed at – a pell-mell battle in which British seamanship and gunnery would triumph. Nelson even went so far as personally to board a Spanish first-rate, the 112-gun *San Josef*, via the eighty-gun *San Nicolas*, which Nelson, as always eager for closer action, had rammed with his own ship, *Captain*.

This further act of cool courage appealed to the British fleet, and the use of the *San Nicolas* became famous as Nelson's Patent Bridge for Boarding First Rates. The outcome of the battle was eminently satisfactory. Four Spanish battleships were captured; the rest of the enemy fleet, still outnumbering the British, limped back to Cadiz; the junction of the Spanish and French fleets had been prevented; the threat of England being invaded was removed. Nelson himself, longing for recognition and fame, was made a Knight of the Bath and a Rear-Admiral. 'His sudden exploit', wrote Arthur Bryant, 'caught England's imagination . . . For all men knew him now for what he was. That knowledge was the measure of his opportunity. The years of testing and obscurity were over, the sunrise gates of fulfilment opening before him.'[6] Nelson's next great task would be against the endeavours and ambitions of Napoleon himself.

Yet if by chance Nelson's *Captain* had not been where she was near the rear of the British line, if, say, she had been nearer the van, the opportunity to act as he did would not have presented itself. The battle might then have developed very differently. There would have been no doubt about Jervis's intention to 'go through them', but the decisive action of Nelson's cutting off one division of the Spanish fleet and pulverizing it would have been unlikely to occur. No doubt British seamanship and gunnery would have given the Spaniards something to think about, but in the end numerical superiority alone might have enabled them to avoid such a significant defeat. And then the threat of invasion might have persisted in a more menacing way than it did. After all, Napoleon, following his triumphant victories with the Army of Italy, had been appointed to the Army of England. Not that he thought much of the idea of an invasion when the British navy still enjoyed command of the seas. 'Too chancy,' was his comment. 'I don't intend to risk *la belle France* on the throw of a dice.' Instead, he turned his thoughts once more to Egypt, with the ultimate view of striking a blow at India itself, where an ally, Tippoo Sultan, would be ready to cooperate with him in ejecting the British from India once and for all. So in March 1798 General Bonaparte was appointed Commander-in-Chief, Army of the East, and two months later he set sail from Toulon, himself sailing in the huge 120-gun flagship, *L'Orient*, taking with him his army of soldiers, scientists, artists and philosophers. With him too went nearly 200 ships, 1,000 guns, plentiful ammunition, 700 horses and some 20,000 men – later this force would be reinforced by another fleet sailing from Italian ports. The idea was to make Egypt a French colony as a preliminary move in the ultimate aim to strike at India, and bizarrely enough 'to improve the lot of the natives of Egypt'.

In the same month Rear-Admiral Sir Horatio Nelson had re-entered the Mediterranean with a powerful squadron, bent on the traditional mission of search and destroy. The consequences of these two expeditions were to be dramatic indeed. If the battle of St Vincent had not been so decisive, if Pitt and his fellow ministers had not felt themselves secure enough to despatch a fleet to the Mediterranean, if Nelson had not distinguished himself sufficiently at St Vincent to demonstrate his eminent fitness to command a fleet, or had not recovered from his dreadful wound at Tenerife, which resulted in the loss of his right arm, we would not have found Earl Spencer, First

Lord of the Admiralty, writing to Earl St Vincent on 2 May 1798 with instructions which led to Nelson's shattering victory at Aboukir Bay:

When you are apprised that the appearance of a British squadron in the Mediterranean is a condition on which the fate of Europe may at this moment be said to depend, you will not be surprised that we are disposed to strain every nerve and incur considerable hazard in effecting it.

Should St Vincent decide not to command the squadron in person, the task should be entrusted to Nelson. These were Spencer's instructions. The decisions and actions that Nelson was now to take present us with another great If of history.

On 19 May 1798 General Bonaparte, not yet twenty-nine years old, set sail from Toulon for his great mission in the East and headed with the principal part of his expedition in the direction of Genoa. Nelson, who had sailed from Gibraltar on 8 May with three ships of the line and five frigates, learned from a captured French corvette nine days later that the French were preparing to leave Toulon with fifteen ships of the line and thousands of troops embarked on the transports. It was at this point that the power of nature intervened: a violent storm battered Nelson's flagship, *Vanguard*, off the Sardinian coast, and it was only the daring action of Captain Ball in *Alexander*, who took *Vanguard* in tow and brought her to safety, that prevented the flagship's being wrecked. The same storm, however, carried the French fleet out of Toulon and over the horizon before Nelson received both his orders from St Vincent and the reinforcements with which to carry out these orders – to pursue the Toulon fleet and destroy it. At this time Nelson had no information as to the likely destination of Bonaparte's expedition. The instructions he had received made no mention of Egypt. Yet Nelson's strategic instinct told him that it must be there that Bonaparte was bound for. His appreciation was strengthened when he further learned that the French had captured Malta and had sailed east on 16 June. He had already written to Spencer saying that he believed the French were aiming to possess Alexandria with a view to invading India, and this latest intelligence – false as far as the date of Bonaparte's sailing east from Malta was concerned – made up his mind. It was unfortunate that Nelson's acute lack of frigates precluded his seeking more accurate information. But in his overwhelming desire to destroy the French fleet and transports and acting on the intelligence he had, Nelson set course for Alexandria. Meanwhile Bonaparte had actually left Malta, not on 16 June, but three days later.

The result was that instead of chasing the French fleet to Alexandria, Nelson's squadron was ahead of it. Yet the two fleets nearly converged. When on 22 June Nelson's lookouts caught sight of French frigates on the horizon, he concluded that they could not be part of Bonaparte's main force which, according to his intelligence, had left Malta six days earlier. He therefore sailed on. The night was hazy and during it Nelson's line of battle sailed across a line on which the French fleet was converging. At dawn the following day neither fleet was visible to the other. It was, Arthur Bryant wrote, 'one of the decisive moments of history'.[7] There the two men were, England's greatest sailor, France's greatest soldier, within an ace of clashing, and had it come to that, the result could not have been in doubt: an early end to one of history's most eminent stars, either drowned or made prisoner; some of the later Grande Armée's most brilliant generals out of the running; Nelson's annihilation of a French battle fleet anticipated by more than a month; no battle of the Nile or cosseting of its victor by Emma Hamilton.

And the cause of it all? Lack of frigates which, said Bryant,

robbed Nelson of a victory that should have been Trafalgar and Waterloo in one. Again and again St Vincent had pleaded with the Admiralty for more frigates: pleaded in vain. He had had to send his brilliant subordinate into the Mediterranean with too few, and these had failed him. Treasury parsimony, the unpreparedness of a peace-loving people . . . had contributed to this fatal flaw. It was to cost Britain and the civilized world seventeen more years of war, waste and destruction.[8]

Yet we must remember that Nelson did catch up with the French fleet in the end and more or less annihilated it. He became the hero of the Nile. Those who relish attacking Nelson's vanity should recognize his own cognizance of it. His comment on the storm which had nearly wrecked *Vanguard* was to the effect that he believed 'it was the

Almighty's goodness to check my consummate vanity', while a few years later, before Trafalgar, the West India merchants whose possessions had been saved by his vigilance voted him their thanks, and the *Naval Chronicle* went so far as to suggest that the praise heaped on Nelson was such that he was in danger of being made a demi-god – but for his modesty!

We may perhaps pursue this point by referring again to those who seek to tarnish Nelson's reputation. That he longed for glory, honour and recognition is not to be denied. Indeed, in quoting Henry V's admission to coveting honour as applying to himself, he acknowledged as much. 'I ever saw a radiant orb suspended which beckoned me onwards to renown,' he confided to Captain Hardy. But it was not just for himself that he sought renown. It was for England too. The most cherished praise that a military commander can receive comes not from his superior officers, but from those serving under his command. And it was from these very men that Nelson received unstinted devotion and admiration. 'He was a man who led by love and example,' observed Bryant. 'There was nothing he would not do for those who served under him. There was nothing they would not dare for Nelson.'[9] So that when we read that Colin White, director of Trafalgar 200 (the bicentenary of the battle of Trafalgar and Nelson's death), talks of Nelson's claiming all the glory for himself after the battle of St Vincent instead of sharing it with his fellow officers, we may readily dismiss such insidious calumny. On the very morning after the battle we find Nelson writing to his friend Collingwood, who had supported him with *Excellent*:

'A friend in need is a friend indeed' was never more truly verified than by your most noble and gallant conduct yesterday in sparing the *Captain* from further loss; and I beg, both as a public Officer and a friend, you will accept my most sincere thanks. I have not failed, by letter to the Admiral, to represent the eminent services of the *Excellent*.

It may, however, be noted that whereas Jervis made no special mention of individuals in his dispatch – for fear of offending by exclusion or inclusion – in his private letter to Lord Spencer he drew attention to the exploits of Nelson, Troubridge, Collingwood,

Saumarez, Hallowell and Admiral Parker. Nelson's own account of the battle, which was signed by two of his fellow officers, Captain Berry and Captain Miller, did understandably outline his own contribution to victory. It was sent to another old friend, Captain Locker, who was given permission to pass it on to the newspapers. His account did not satisfy everyone and indeed it was unlikely to do so, for just as Wellington once observed that it was impossible for a participant to recall every detail of a battle, so Collingwood commented on the difficulty for one who is engaged in it to relate all its circumstances. Jervis, with his customary sense of fairness and justice, wrote to all captains to 'convey the high sense I entertain of the exemplary conduct of flag-officers, captains, officers, seamen, marines and soldiers, embarked on board every ship of the squadron'. He asked his captains to give his thanks and approbation to their crews.

Thus it was clear that whereas Nelson's tactical brilliance and personal gallantry had greatly contributed to the victory, the whole fleet had shown its skill and mettle. This spirit of the British navy as a whole was what men like Jervis and Nelson had always striven for. Yet it was Nelson's part in it all that fired the country's imagination. Jervis had emphasized beforehand how essential a victory was to England. Now they had one, and in Nelson they also had a hero. In 1775, sailing in *Dolphin* from Simon's Town to the Isle of Wight, Nelson, depressed and despairing over the bleak prospects of ever rising in his profession, suddenly experienced a surge of joy and confidence.

After a long and gloomy reverie, in which I almost wished myself overboard, a sudden glow of patriotism[10] was kindled within me and presented my King and Country as my patron. Well, then, I will be a hero, and, confiding in Providence, I will brave every danger.[11]

By 1797 he had braved dangers enough and had indeed become a hero. It was this self-surrender, as Bryant put it, that was the real core of the man. Before setting off for Trafalgar he wrote to his friend Davison that in spite of having much to lose and little to gain, he went because it was right to do so and he would serve his country faithfully. The esteem in which Pitt, the Prime Minister, held Nelson was manifested in his honouring him by accompanying him to his carriage after their last meeting. And as Nelson's barge left Southsea to row him to his flagship, *Victory*, hundreds of people were there to give him three cheers. 'I had their huzzas before,' he told his flag-captain, Thomas Hardy, 'I have their hearts now.'

Nelson was anxiously awaited by the fleet. 'For charity's sake,' wrote Captain Codrington, commanding *Orion*, 'send us Lord Nelson, ye men of power!' They wanted him not just for his professional mastery, but also for his personal qualities. One of the captains, who made up the Band of Brothers and who had fought with him at the Nile, Alexander Ball, summed up the feelings they had for him:

Lord Nelson was an admiral, every inch of him. He looked at everything, not merely in its possible relation to the naval service in general but in its immediate bearings on his own squadron; to his officers, his men, to the particular ships themselves, his affections were as steady and ardent as those of a lover. Hence, though his temper was constitutionally irritable and uneven, yet never was a commander so enthusiastically loved by men of all ranks from the captain of the fleet to the youngest ship-boy.[12]

Even Nelson, despite his absolute confidence in his own tactical plans and in his ships, captains and crews, was obliged to concede that nothing was certain in a sea-fight. 'Something must be left to chance,' he observed. Yet before closing with the French fleet at Aboukir Bay, when Captain Berry asked him what the world would say 'if we succeed', Nelson replied: 'There is no *if* in the case.' He was certain of success. Who would live to tell the story was a very different question. His success was absolute, and yet the question may be put: if by chance he had not destroyed the French fleet, what would Bonaparte have done after defeating the Egyptian and Turkish armies? Hauled his fleet across the desert to Suez and descended on India? Followed Alexander's footsteps through Persia to the north-west frontier? As Napoleon himself put it: 'Had it not been for the English Navy, I should have been Emperor of the East.' He would not have been deterred by the hazards of any such venture. As it was, however, he was thwarted at Acre, where the Turks, aided by another sailor,

Sidney Smith, put a stop to his plans, and it was by the courtesy of this same sailor in sending Bonaparte the latest news-sheet from Europe, the *Gazette Française de Francfort*, that Bonaparte learned of the French Republic's perilous condition. She was at war with England, Turkey, Russia, Austria and Naples. Corfu had been lost, Zurich taken by Austro-Russian forces, northern Italy had been invaded, there was fighting in Holland. France itself was in economic turmoil. There was but one course of action for him – to return to France. Leaving the Egyptian command to Kléber, he embarked in a frigate, *Muiron*, on the night of 22 August 1799 and with three other vessels sailed for France, taking with him Berthier, Murat, Marmont, Bessières and Lannes. He was never to return to Egypt. Indeed, the whole Egyptian campaign had been futile.

Yet if he had not gone there, Nelson would not have had the opportunity to triumph at the battle of the Nile, and so bring about the circumstances in which Bonaparte was constrained to hasten back to France and begin the political and military intrigues which led to his becoming First Consul. It was not long after his assuming this position of power that Austria was once more in arms against France. This challenge to both the French Republic and his own position at its head led to a battle in which Bonaparte faltered and was saved by the timely action – and as chance would have it brilliant coordination – of three of his subordinates: the battle of Marengo.

TWO

Marengo: 14 June 1800

Give me lucky generals.

NAPOLEON

During his voyage back to France on board *Muiron*, Bonaparte frequently referred to the importance of luck. No matter how strong his belief in determinism, 'all great events hang by a hair and I believe in luck'. On the other hand, nothing should be neglected which could promote a man's destiny. His main concern when he contemplated the situation in France was that he might be too late to take advantage of it, that 'the fruit might be overripe'. He was going to need all the luck going. As things turned out, not only did he neglect nothing which might bolster his cause, but he had the devil's own luck as well.

There was serious work to be done, for while Bonaparte had been in Egypt, the Directory, a government of lawyers, had fallen from favour, and every sort of intrigue was under way to bring about change. This was not to be wondered at for everything was going wrong. Bonaparte's glorious conquests in Italy had been forfeited, the Treasury was empty, widespread disorder reflected widespread discontent. The armies, except for Masséna's on the Frontiers of Switzerland and Brune's in Flanders, had been defeated. The Allied campaign in the Netherlands may be summed up by saying simply that their armies had advanced in drenching rain from Den Helder to the line of the Zype Canal, where they stuck fast in the mud, while the Dutch people did not so much as lift a finger to support their supposed liberators. After much dithering and recrimination, the Allied armies withdrew and were evacuated. One more British expedition to the Netherlands had ended in failure. No wonder

Macaulay condemned Pitt's military administration as that of a mere driveller.

Despite their losses elsewhere, the French were still defying their enemies further south. The Austrians under Archduke Charles were poised to invade France by crossing the Rhine, while the hideous butcher, Suvorov, whose military doctrine was to go bull-headed at the enemy, and whom Byron called half demon and half dirt, was coming up from Italy towards Nice. Yet if either did invade, Masséna would be able to emerge from his Alpine bastion, pounce on their communications and sever them from their supply columns. There was a third threat to Masséna. Korsakov, reputed lover of Catherine the Great and a celebrated *bon viveur*, was commanding an Austro-Russian army at Zurich. But Masséna, undeterred by the prospect of a simultaneous attack from three sides, concentrated his force outside Zurich at the very time when the Allies did not concentrate against him. Archduke Charles took his army off towards the Netherlands; Suvorov had been slowed down by snow and harassed by French forces under Lecombe; and Korsakov had dangerously extended his position to the west of Zurich, prompting Masséna to attack him with his entire force, driving him out of Switzerland and capturing 8,000 men, guns, money and supplies. Suvorov then abandoned his offensive. Thus Masséna had plucked the flower, safety, from the nettle, danger. His cold, crafty, calculating waiting game, played with great patience and perseverance, harbouring the opportunity to pounce on vulnerability, had saved the Republic from invasion. By the time it was next threatened, Bonaparte would not only be once more in command of the army, he would be the political leader of France.

The process by which this came about was set in train by the Abbé Sieyès, one of the Government's Directors. He hit upon the idea that he himself would be an excellent replacement for the Directory. But others would need to be similarly persuaded, among them that great survivor, Talleyrand, and the Chief of Police, Fouché. There would also have to be a soldier to wield the sword for Sieyès. At first Sieyès thought of Bernadotte, Minister of War, but he was too circumspect. Moreau might do, but he was too timid. It was, however, Moreau who made the crucial suggestion when he heard on 13 October 1799 that Bonaparte had landed at Fréjus. Bonaparte, Moreau told Sieyès, was the man to manage a *coup d'état*. And manage it he did.

There was a lot of preliminary manoeuvring to be done, and between 16 October and the end of that month, Josephine's *salon* – Bonaparte had forgiven her dalliance with Lieutenant Hippolyte Charles and they were now on more comfortable terms – was crowded with politicians and soldiers, while her husband ruminated, gauged the temperature and formulated his plans. After deliberating for two weeks, he threw in his lot with Sieyès and Ducos, another Director, and assured himself that the support of those soldiers essential to him if it came to a fight would be forthcoming. The men who mattered – Berthier, Murat, Lannes, Marmont – had been with him in the Italian and Egyptian campaigns. All would later become Marshals of the Empire. Bonaparte also made sure of Sérurier and Moreau. He still had to get the Military Governor of Paris, Lefèbvre, on his side, but he was manipulable enough. Bluff and naïve, Lefèbvre fell for Josephine's blandishments and Bonaparte's smooth confidences. Bernadotte, on the other hand, continued to sit on the fence. The conspiracy would have to proceed without him. The first step was to get the soldiers into their proper positions. On 9 November Bonaparte's supporters fastened their grip on the key places and deployed their troops in readiness. Marmont, one of Bonaparte's oldest friends and, like him, an artilleryman, was fittingly enough in charge of the guns; Murat, one of history's greatest cavalry leaders, was with his hussars and chasseurs at the Palais Bourbon; Lannes – who while in Egypt, not having seen his wife for more than a year, heard that she had given birth to a bouncing boy – was in command of the Tuileries; Macdonald was at Versailles; Sérurier at St-Cloud. By the end of that day all the Directors were rendered impotent and it only remained for Bonaparte to appear the following day and confront the Council of the Ancients and the Deputies at St-Cloud for the whole *coup d'état* to be complete.

Few things daunted Bonaparte, but one of them was a hostile mob, and this was precisely what he had to face in the Council Chamber at St-Cloud, outside Paris, on 10 November. When he addressed the Council of the Ancients, he struck quite the wrong chord, speaking to them not as the statesman they expected, but as soldier, bragging that the god of Victory and the god of Fortune marched with him. He was greeted with angry shouts. Worse was to come when he entered the Orangery to address the Five Hundred Deputies. At once he was accused of violating the law. Angry Deputies crowded round him, clawing and striking at him, shouting that he was a dictator and should be outlawed. Bonaparte was rescued by four stalwart soldiers and led outside. His brother Lucien, who was President of the Five Hundred, then made an attempt to restore order and sent an urgent note to Bonaparte telling him to act at once. After making an appeal to the soldiers – 'I led you to victory, can I count on you?' – powerfully reinforced by Lucien, who swore that he would run his own brother through should he jeopardize the freedom of Frenchmen, Bonaparte ordered General Leclerc, a comrade-in-arms at Toulon and husband of Bonaparte's sister, Pauline, to clear the Orangery, together with Murat. Murat, who never stood on ceremony, acted with his characteristic blend of eloquent bravado and practical action, inviting his grenadiers to chuck the Deputies – 'these blighters' – out of the Orangery window. This action effectively put a stop to all opposition and early the following morning, 11 November 1799, still at the Orangery, the new Government formally took office.

There were to be three Consuls – Bonaparte, Ducos and Sieyès. They all swore their loyal service to the Republic. The principles of Liberty, Equality and the Representative System would be upheld. But none of this counted for much when about a month later Bonaparte became First Consul and virtual ruler of France. He was thirty years old. He moved to the Tuileries in February 1800, telling the 'little Creole', Josephine, to 'sleep in the bed of your masters'. It would not be long, however, before he found himself at the head of the army, once more confronting the enemies of France. He would have preferred to concentrate on matters of peace, but neither Austria nor Great Britain was prepared to follow suit. That Bonaparte wished for peace was made clear by his declaration to the people on becoming First Consul that he knew they wanted peace and that the Government wanted it even more. He himself wanted to set about the gigantic task of overhauling completely the organization of France and the conduct of its affairs. He went so far as to send a message to King George III proposing a settlement and asking 'why the two most enlightened nations of Europe should go on sacrificing their trade, their prosperity, and their domestic happiness to false ideas of grandeur?' His own ideas of grandeur were to take huge strides in the coming years and he would create for himself a position and fame unparalleled in contemporary history. Yet it must be borne in mind that all the wars fought by him up to 1807, when he sent troops into Spain to conquer Portugal, were defensive wars against a series of coalitions, sponsored by England and joined by Russia, Austria and Prussia. And while waging these wars to preserve the integrity of France, Bonaparte was generally successful. It was only when the wars of aggression began that his game began to go wrong.

Bonaparte's overtures to George III met with a dusty answer. George instructed his Foreign Secretary, Grenville, to write to Talleyrand and reject any idea of negotiating with the First Consul. This rejection could have been couched in firm, diplomatic and inoffensive language, but Grenville chose to employ irrational and tactless pomposity, demanding restoration of the Bourbons and a return to pre-revolutionary frontiers. It was, of course, Pitt who was the arbiter of this dismissal of Bonaparte's peace offer, and when challenged in the House of Commons as to the purpose of continuing the war, against which there was now high feeling in the country, he justified his policy on the grounds of security. He went so far as to speak of the danger which threatened the world as being the greatest that had ever done so, one that had been resisted by the nations of Europe, and with notable success by England. Jacobinism, which had previously been embodied in the persons of Robespierre and Barras, the Terror and the Directory, had not gone away. It had now 'been centred and condensed into one man, who was reared and nursed in its bosom, whose celebrity was gained under its auspices, who was at once child and champion of all its atrocities and horrors'.[1] There was no security for England in making peace with Bonaparte. The prosecution of war, on the other hand, would attain security. Yet for the time being, as far as making war on land was concerned, it would have to be left to the Austrians. The irony of it all was that this brought about another triumphant victory for Bonaparte, and in spite of Nelson's destruction of the Danish fleet at Copenhagen and the recapture of Egypt by Abercromby, England did make peace with France. But by then Pitt had ceased to be Prime Minister and Addington was in his place. How did Bonaparte set about beating the Austrians?

During the early months of 1800 the First Consul was obliged to interrupt his formidable task of organizing France's finances, judicial system, Civil Code, religion, educational structure, its roads, ports, canals and countrywide administration, in order to raise another army to beat off enemies which were gathering again to overthrow the Revolution once and for all. France was being threatened on two fronts – from the Rhine and from Italy. Bonaparte positioned his Army of the Reserve at Dijon from where he could reinforce either front. It was to Italy that he marched for, whilst the Army of the Rhine succeeded in checking the Austrians at Biberach, south of Ulm, the position in Italy was potentially much more dangerous. It all depended on that old fox Masséna, who was defending Genoa, hemmed in by the Austrian army on land and by the British navy at sea. Masséna defied all the odds – starvation, disease, a mutinous army, a rebellious population – hanging on at all costs, for the Austrians dared not advance beyond Genoa leaving French forces, albeit weak, astride their communications. Towards the end of May 1800, Masséna heard at last that the First Consul had crossed the Great St Bernard Pass with the Reserve Army (not as depicted in David's famous painting mounted on a full-blooded grey charger, but on a mule well behind the main body), and was in Lombardy at Marengo, positioned between Vienna and the Austrian army under Melas. Masséna could now march out of Genoa with his bedraggled remains of an army and leave the rest of the business to Bonaparte.

Somewhat later in his career, Napoleon – we may refer to him thus now, as after the peace of Amiens in 1802 he was confirmed for life as First Consul and would from then on be known as Napoleon – made his plea: 'Give me lucky generals.' At Marengo in June 1800, making the mistakes he did, he needed plenty of luck himself – and got it! Having dispersed his forces too widely, astonishing in a general who knew all too well that concentration was a cardinal principle of war, never to be breached, and failing to give the Austrian commander credit for being able to mount a concentrated attack on him, Napoleon was dismayed to find his divisions being pushed back and his entire position in danger of disintegrating. There was but one measure that could save the day – a counter-attack. It was then that three of his subordinate commanders came to the rescue. First, Napoleon sent a desperate plea to Desaix, who with his infantry division of some 5,000 men had earlier been sent off south to cut the road to Genoa: 'For God's sake come back.' At about five o'clock Desaix returned and, according to Correlli Barnett, more or less took charge of the situation, commenting to Napoleon that although one encounter seemed to have gone wrong, there was still time to win the battle. Meanwhile, Marmont, who was in charge of the guns, and who had been fighting all day, supplemented his five pieces of artillery with five from the reserve and eight from Desaix, making up a battery of eighteen guns. Thus Marmont was able to deliver an effective bombardment against the advancing Austrians, enabling Desaix to go forward. On the flank with 400 cavalrymen was young General Kellermann, and their charge just as the Austrians were trying to recover from the combined shocks of Marmont's discharge of cannister and Desaix's assault completed a perfectly combined action of horse, foot and guns, which transformed the fortunes of a battle the Austrians thought they had won.

'The French counter-attack,' wrote A. G. Macdonnell, 'was, *by chance* [author's italics], one of the most perfectly timed tactical operations by combined infantry, artillery and cavalry in the whole history of warfare.'[2] First came Marmont's bombardment with his eighteen guns which lasted for some twenty minutes. Then Desaix went forward with his infantry – he was killed by a bullet in the head while leading his men in the attack – and Marmont, having limbered up four of his guns, was there in support. It was another instance of close cooperation between arms, for in an effort to counter the counter-attack, a battalion of Austrian grenadiers was pressing forward against Desaix's men, and seeing them but fifty yards ahead, Marmont unlimbered his four pieces and let the advancing closely ranked Austrian grenadiers have four rounds of cannister from each gun fired at point-blank range. To cap it all, just as the Austrians were reeling from this fresh blow and Desaix's infantrymen were surging forward, young Kellermann came charging in from the flank with his heavy cavalrymen. The enemy broke and fled. 'A minute earlier,' said Macdonnell, 'or three minutes later, and the thing could not have succeeded, but the timing was perfect, and North Italy was recovered in that moment for the French Republic.'[3]

Napoleon's own part in the battle had been positively undistinguished, yet the victory confirmed his position as First Consul and enabled him to make peace. When Berthier consoled an Austrian officer after the battle, however, by pointing out that his army had been defeated by the greatest general in the world, the reply was that it had been Masséna's iron hand that had won the battle of Marengo by resisting siege in Genoa. To which might be added – Genoa certainly *and* chance!

But what if Desaix had not come back? Correlli Barnett is quite clear about it: 'If Desaix had not returned in time, the resulting defeat would have put an end to his [Napoleon's] career.'[4] Evangeline Bruce is equally definite: 'Bonaparte had gambled his future and almost lost it; had Desaix not arrived in time his career would have ended then.'[5] Very well, let us hypothesize that chance does not favour him after all, the Austrians win at Marengo, Bonaparte is dismissed from his position as First Consul; what might have happened then? We might consider first what would *not* have happened, for whatever else might be said about Napoleon, it cannot be denied that he was totally unique. He was a comet shooting through his own generation and many others to come, a man whose imagination, ambition, capacity and sheer magnitude made him stand up peerless among his contemporaries. He was a modern Caesar and bestrode this narrow world like a Colossus. His capacity for work was prodigious. And it was after Marengo that the business of putting France in order really began. It may be doubted whether anyone else would have embarked on quite so radical and comprehensive a programme as he did, but Napoleon held two winning aces. First, he was immensely popular; indeed, the royalist Mathieu Molé observed that with the exception of

America's first President, George Washington, no chief magistrate of a republic had ever been so universally popular. The second ace was power. When Napoleon and Sieyès had discussed what form the Republic's executive should take, it was Napoleon who got his way. There were to be three Consuls, but only the First Consul would make decisions. Napoleon was therefore able to set about the complete reorganization of France's internal affairs. Most of his measures were instituted in the two years 1800–1802, the so-called 'ardent years of the Consulate'. It was then, wrote Evangeline Bruce, that 'he laid the foundations of all the administrative and fiscal achievements that were to be his real monuments, created the tightly centralized administration that survives in France, much modified, to this day, restructured the judicial and public educational systems, and created the Bank of France'.[6]

His greatest, most enduring achievement was the Civil Code, more renowned as the Code Napoléon. This was essentially a matter of the law. Following the Revolution in 1789 there had been so many decrees, regional codes and rulings by autonomous courts that, as Napoleon himself put it in writing to Talleyrand, France was 'a nation with three hundred books of laws, yet without laws'. Now the whole matter of law and justice was to be put in order. The Code Napoléon was founded on a number of principles: all were to be equal before the law; there would be an end to feudal rights and duties; property would be inviolable; marriage would be a civil act, not a religious one; there would be freedom of conscience and freedom in choice of work. Without Napoleon, we may take it that all this would not have been done, nor would the Concordat, the pact between Napoleon and the Pope recognizing Roman Catholicism as the official religion of most French people, have been brought about. And then Napoleon was utterly dedicated to work. During the early months and years after becoming First Consul, he would work for sixteen, even eighteen, hours a day, seven days a week. Apart from the time he spent in the Council Chamber at the Tuileries where he presided over the Council of State, much of his day was passed in his study, dictating to his secretary. There, as Vincent Cronin put it:

Napoleon answered letters, issued orders, made minutes on Ministers' reports, checked budgets, instructed ambassadors, raised troops, moved armies and carried out the thousand and one other duties which fell to the head of government, always totally immersed in the task in front of him, always completing it before going on to the next.[7]

It was this ability to concentrate which was the key to his powerful intellect. At a time when in his own words *la carrière ouverte aux talents* was there for the taking, Napoleon showed the world how his own quite exceptional talents opened up for him a career of dazzling distinction.

Added to this, of course, was his supreme confidence. In establishing the Code Napoléon, he was sure that it would endure. He was right. It is still the law of France, with some amendments. To make the whole thing work, Napoleon established in each *département* a new type of official, the prefect, a system of administration still in being today. When we add to all this a new criminal code, a reformed educational system, the Legion of Honour and the building of roads, canals and ports, there seems to be no end to his achievements. Yet there is one more we must look at, without which all the rest might have gone for nothing – creating the Grande Armée: 'It was to be a real, full-dress, organized, trained fighting machine,' wrote Macdonnell. 'Its training ground was to be the north-east coast of France, and its objective was England.'[8] This was the army which was to be Napoleon's tool for dominating the affairs of Europe for the next decade, and against which only a small British army under Wellington was able to nibble away in a theatre of war which the by then French Emperor regarded as a side-show. Napoleon's army was certainly on the grand scale. It was a highly efficient fighting force, as regards both numbers and quality. Organized into seven corps, positioned at Hanover, Utrecht, Flushing-Dunkirk, Boulogne, Montreuil and Brest, it consisted of some 200,000 men. The Corps Commanders, all of whom were destined to become Marshals of the Empire, represented about the most glittering array of military talent that could be gathered together.

They consisted of Bernadotte, who, despite his fence-sitting during the 1799 *coup* and his lack of regard for the First Consul, did at least promise cooperation; Marmont, Napoleon's friend and artillery expert, who was very earnest, painstaking, concerned with his men's well-being, and who loved building things; Davout, who was later said to be the only one of the Marshals who really understood what Napoleon's theory and practice of war was all about; Soult, who was another great builder and an excellent trainer of young officers; Lannes, the courageous leader of so many attacks, who had been the First Consul's envoy in Portugal to bully England's oldest ally into neutrality; Ney, the fiery red-headed cavalryman, who worshipped war and battle for their own sake, who studied hard to master infantry tactics, and whose admirable concept of operations was 'fast marching and straight shooting'; Augereau, swaggering, rough-mouthed and full of intrigue, but a bold man in a tight corner; and the cavalry under Napoleon's brother-in-law, Murat (he had married Caroline Bonaparte), the most dashing of cavalry commanders, and whose subordinate generals, Lasalle, Colbert, Sainte-Croix and Montbrun, were all young, illustrious, good-looking and rash. Later, Bessières with the Imperial Guard was added to this star-studded community.

Would some Bonaparte substitute have created such a weapon of war? And who might that substitute have been? There was no lack of intrigue against the First Consul even in the early days, enough indeed to satisfy even those arch manipulators of power, Talleyrand and Fouché. Envy was a great breeder of intrigue, and there were plenty of Napoleon's erstwhile comrades-in-arms who envied him. Some of this envy was cloaked under protestations that the principles of the Republic were not being consolidated. Such men as Sieyès, disgruntled by his own former disappointment, Moreau, Oudinot and St-Cyr, did not understand what it was that Napoleon was striving for: first, the organization of France so that order would replace disorder, proper administration take the place of corrupt practices, and a system of beneficial government would prevail *subject to the will of one man*; second, Napoleon's ardent desire to heal old wounds, to bind together conflicting interests and loyalties, in short a programme of recon-ciliation and stabilization which would fuse the nation into one united

France. It was all very well for Augereau and Lannes to make a fuss about the Concordat, and point to the countless number of lives which had been lost 'to get rid of this nonsense', but the fact was that the people as a whole enthusiastically welcomed the return of Catholicism after twelve years of State-enforced atheism. Among the ranks of other intriguers and malcontents were Jourdan, Brune, Macdonald and Masséna. Yet, as A. G. Macdonnell pointed out: 'In all the intriguing against the Consulate it was the attitude of Bernadotte, as in 1799, that was the key to the situation.' Bernadotte's ambition was boundless – he did become after all King of Sweden later – but his intrigues with Moreau and Sièyes were not conducted with the discretion and secrecy which such dangerous goings-on demanded, and it was Davout, a devotee of Napoleon and at this time Commander of the Military Police, whose successful espionage uncovered the plot for a *coup d'état* against Napoleon. Had it come off, we may speculate that it would have been Bernadotte who headed the new Government.

No Emperor Napoleon, then, no plan to invade England, no Austerlitz, no crushing of Prussia at Jena or Russia at Friedland, no Treaty of Tilsit, or aggression in Spain, no Peninsular campaign by Sir John Moore or Wellesley . . . the catalogue stretches on. Instead we may imagine a consolidation of Republican measures, peace-making with England, Talleyrand as Foreign Minister, Fouché still Chief of Police, the other generals bought off with military commands or political posts, no Grande Armée for conquering Europe, but an Army of the Republic for defending France's frontiers against the hostility of Austria and any allies she could muster. And if by chance it were not Bernadotte who was called upon to rule France, of one thing we may be sure. France would not have reinstated the Bourbons. It took another decade or so of Napoleonic sovereignty to bring about that ill-fated design 'to call back yesterday, bid time return'.

As it was, however, Marengo had confirmed Bonaparte as First Consul. It would not be long – shortly after the Peace of Amiens was concluded in March 1802 – before Napoleon received an over-whelming vote of confidence from the French people, confirming him as Consul for life. From there it would be an easy leap to become

Emperor of the French. As Emperor he was to command the Grande Armée in countless battles. In doing so he would often be mounted on a grey Arab stallion named Marengo.[9] It may seem strange that Napoleon should have called the horse said to be his favourite charger after a battle in which his own part had been so undistinguished. Yet it was the result of the battle, rather than its conduct, which proved to be so significant. On 14 June 1815, when giving the army its Orders of the Day for the morrow, he charged his soldiers to recall the glorious anniversaries of Friedland and Marengo, both fought on that day. There is some controversy as to whether or not Napoleon rode Marengo at the battle of Waterloo. Marengo's skeleton is on display at the National Army Museum, and the accompanying caption states that the Emperor *did* ride him. Other sources contend that Marengo was the horse on which Napoleon escaped from the battlefield. Some claim that it was a white mare called Desirée that carried him. Of course, Napoleon would have had more than one charger at hand. The outcome of the battle was certainly not what he desired. Indeed, whichever horse he rode, it availed him nothing at Waterloo.

THREE

18 June 1815

To be killed at Waterloo would have been a good death.

NAPOLEON AT ST HELENA

The historian Jac Weller is said to have complained that the Ifs of Waterloo made him wince. I fear we must make him wince again. No doubt these Ifs are countless, but for our purposes here, we will choose five chances which contributed to Napoleon's defeat and examine the consequences had chance taken another course. First, Napoleon's chance meeting with Ney as he moved forward on the Charleroi road and his capricious and fatal appointment of Ney as field commander; second, even given this mistake, the interference by Ney in countermanding Napoleon's order to d'Erlon to join him at Ligny when Ney himself was dithering at Quatre Bras; third, the thunderstorm on the night of 17/18 June which delayed Napoleon's attack; fourth, the gates of Hougoumont, the closing of which Wellington somewhat arbitrarily claimed was the decisive element of the battle; and fifth, the Emperor's imprecise orders to Grouchy, together with Grouchy's own incomprehensible error of judgement, which led to his 33,000 men taking no part in the decisive encounter. We will look at what effect on the battle there might have been if any of these five occurrences had been different. Such speculation will lead us to two further questions: what if Napoleon had won? What if he had been killed?

Napoleon's choice of subordinate commanders for his last campaign must strike us as capricious, to say the least. Of course, the field was somewhat limited. There were few of the old hands who supported the Emperor on his triumphant return from Elba. Marmont, St-Cyr, Victor and Macdonald stuck to their new Bourbon loyalties.

Augereau and Berthier had gone to ground. Soult, on the other hand, despite his former allegiance to Louis XVIII, had rejoined the Emperor. So had Mortier and Suchet. Masséna, perhaps wisely, chose to be unwell. Murat, King of Naples – who would never have allowed the cavalry to be handled as Ney did – impetuous as ever, on hearing of his brother-in-law's resumption of power, committed the egregious folly of turning on his Austrian friends and attacking them with Neapolitan soldiers, who of course ran away, leaving Murat to fly ignominiously to Toulon. Napoleon had created one more Marshal – Grouchy – who might have turned the scales at Waterloo had he acted as a Marshal of France should. The Emperor had one other worthy supporter, the iron, uncompromising Davout, who accepted the Ministry of War. If instead he had been with Napoleon in the field, either as Chief of Staff or as the Emperor's immediate lieutenant, what a world of difference he might have made. The Ministry could have been left to Soult, for however devious Talleyrand and Fouché might have been, they would never have risked a *coup* against Napoleon while he was in command of the army. But all in all it must be conceded that the Emperor would not be fielding the first eleven for the battle to come.

Those who have suggested, as Andrew Roberts in his recent book has reminded us,[1] along with that eminent Napoleonic expert, David Chandler, that Napoleon deliberately appointed a second eleven in order to enjoy the greater share of glory himself after a victorious campaign, are surely wide of the mark. Napoleon's whole future, and that of France, was at stake. Not to have taken every step to promote success would have contradicted Napoleon's entire creed. He may have been a gambler, but he was not in the habit of throwing away aces in the middle of a game. This is what makes it all the more extraordinary that he should have chosen Ney to be his field commander before the battle got under way. Ever since the battle of Borodino, when the fiery, red-headed Marshal had launched his tirade against his Commander-in-Chief for not being right up at the front and for refusing to release the Imperial Guard, Ney, despite his heroic rearguard action in the Russian campaign and unfailing courage at Leipzig, had been unbalanced, at times hysterical. Although temporarily in disgrace because of his promise to Louis XVIII to bring the usurper back to Paris in an iron cage, Ney was to be entrusted by Napoleon with absolutely crucial responsibility in the forthcoming battle, a responsibility which Ney was temperamentally and psychologically incapable of fulfilling. Not once, but twice, he made decisions, or was guilty of indecision, which robbed the Emperor of almost certain victory. And then his actual appointment had been such a chance, so thoughtlessly haphazard. On 12 June 1815, when Napoleon set out for the Northern Front, the army consisted of five corps, commanded by d'Erlon, Vandamme, Gérard, Reille and Lobau. The only Marshals with the army were Soult, Chief of Staff, Grouchy, commanding the Reserve Cavalry, and Mortier, who was taken ill and fell out at Beaumont. Ney, dressed in mufti, had accompanied the army, bitter and aggrieved at being left out; he acquired two of Mortier's horses and hung about near Napoleon's staff. By chance, while looking at a map outside a tavern by the Sambre, the Emperor happened to glance up, caught sight of Ney, and at once asked him to take command of two army corps and the regiments of cavalry, some 50,000 men in all, together with over seventy guns. 'It was,' observed A. G. Macdonnell, 'a strange and casual appointment.'[2] Apart from anything else, why did Napoleon not choose to command in person? He had in the past overseen the operations of more than two corps in a series of successful encounters with the Austrians, Russians and Prussians. Had he wished to outshine all those in subordinate positions, what more certain way of doing so? But the whole idea of his not wishing to share the credit for success may be dismissed by remembering his former instant and generous recognition of his corps and divisional commanders. His praise for Augereau at Castiglioni, for Lannes at Arcola, Masséna at Rivoli, when Napoleon greeted him as *l'enfant chéri de la victoire*, is enough to give the lie to such calumny. When we add the Emperor's acknowledgement of Davout's saving the day at Auerstädt, of his creating Macdonald a Marshal on the field of Wagram, of his unstinting commendation of Ney's rearguard action during the retreat from Moscow – Bravest of the Brave, Prince of the Moscowa – no more evidence is needed. But to have chosen Ney, who was suffering from what we would now call battle fatigue, and whose ability coolly to weigh the tactical odds, however unquestionable his courage, was sadly deficient, constituted the first of a series of blunders that Napoleon would never have made in his heyday.

Given that Ney was appointed, however, we now come face to face with perhaps the biggest If of all, for when Napoleon was engaging the Prussians at Ligny on 16 June, Ney, with a most unfortunate coalition of indecisive manoeuvring and petulant action, was undermining the Emperor's strategy – with the gravest consequences. Had Ney carried out Napoleon's orders promptly, that is, to seize Quatre Bras, he would have been in a position to threaten the Prussians' right flank and so enable Napoleon to finish Blücher's part in the affair. Because he had been slow and indecisive, Ney received orders from the Emperor to despatch d'Erlon's Reserve Corps to complete the business at Ligny. Again, had this been done, Blücher's army would have been so knocked about that it would not have been able to come to the aid of Wellington two days later. As it was, Ney, finding the fight for Quatre Bras becoming ever more severe because his own delay had allowed Wellington to bring up reinforcements, countermanded the Emperor's order and brought d'Erlon back towards Quatre Bras. In the event, d'Erlon took no part in either battle, so that the great If here is this: had Ney allowed d'Erlon to help finish off the Prussians at Ligny, there would have been no need to detach Grouchy with his 33,000 men, who would then have been available for Napoleon in his confrontation with Wellington at Waterloo. We will look further at Grouchy later on, but there is a further aspect of Quatre Bras to consider first.

An eagle is ascendant in spirit, swift in flight, sudden in decision and ruthless in deed. It was Napoleon's unique marshalling of these characteristics that made the eagle so aptly his symbol. His whirlwind tactics of rapid marching and vital concentration of force, which he employed in the Italian campaign of 1796/97, were what shook the European armies to their foundations. The astonishing way in which he redeployed the Grande Armée from the coastal areas near Boulogne to surround Mack's army at Ulm was a classic example of deception and rapid concentration, leading to the triumph of

Austerlitz. It was the speed and violence of his pursuit of the Prussian army after Jena and Auerstädt which utterly confounded what was left of Frederick the Great's legacy. And when the Emperor learned that Sir John Moore was threatening his communications with France by chasing Soult with his English leopards in Old Castile, he at once abandoned his idea of advancing into Portugal and hurled his force of 80,000 men northwards to entrap Moore's small army. *Vitesse* was always the watchword. Napoleon himself had once conceded that he might lose ground, but would never lose a minute. This great sense of urgency seems to have deserted him in the Waterloo affair. Not only did he lose countless minutes on 17 June, he threw away the best chance of winning the campaign. For a kind of lethargy seemed to overcome him. In spite of ordering Ney to take Quatre Bras that morning and, when surprised by Ney's wavering reluctance to act decisively, sending him a second order, couched in uncompromising terms – 'There is no time to lose. Attack with the greatest impetuosity everything in front of you' – Napoleon did not ensure that his orders were obeyed. Indeed, as Andrew Roberts has emphasized, if instead of wasting his time waiting for information as to Wellington's movements and hanging about near Ligny, Napoleon had joined Ney in a joint attack on Wellington, who had only some 50,000 troops at Quatre Bras, he would have won the campaign there and then. 'This loss of the initiative,' wrote Roberts,

was disastrous, and still worse was his decision at around 11 a.m. to split his forces by sending Marshal Grouchy off with 33,000 men and no fewer than ninety-six cannon to follow the Prussians in what at least initially turned out to be the wrong direction.

Concentration had been a cardinal principle of Napoleon's conduct of war, yet here he was breaking his own rules.

Now let us look at another aspect of chance – the intervention of fate and fortune.

'Can such things be,' demanded Macbeth, 'And overcome us like a summer's cloud, Without our special wonder?' It was the breaking of a summer's cloud, we might say, that overcame Napoleon on that night of 17/18 June 1815. Listen to Victor Hugo on the point:

It had rained all night, the ground was saturated, the water had accumulated here and there in the hollows of the plain as if in tubs; at some points the gear of the artillery carriages was buried up to the axles, the circingles of the horses were dripping with liquid mud. If the wheat and rye trampled down by this cohort of transports on the march had not filled in the ruts and strewn a litter beneath the wheels, all movement, particularly in the valleys, in the direction of Papelotte would have been impossible.

The battle began late. Napoleon was in the habit of keeping all his artillery well in hand, like a pistol, aiming it now at one point, now at another, of the battle; and it had been his wish to wait until the horse batteries could move and gallop freely. In order to do that it was necessary that the sun should come out and dry the soil. But the sun did not make its appearance. It was no longer the rendezvous of Austerlitz. When the first cannon was fired, the English general, Colville, looked at his watch, and saw that it was twenty-five minutes to twelve.[3]

Victor Hugo's conclusion is that if it had not rained in the night of 17/18 June 1815, Europe's fate would have been different. His reason? The battle of Waterloo could not be started until half past eleven and this gave Blücher time to come up. In support of this view we may note that Napoleon had set up his headquarters at Le Caillou and breakfasted there with his generals at eight o'clock on the morning of 18 June. Had the ground been completely dry, that is had there been no thunderstorm the previous night, his attack could have started at least four hours earlier than it did. We must note too that even when the French artillery did begin its bombardment at half past eleven, the ground was still wet, causing round shot to bury itself rather than ricocheting for many hundreds of yards with deadly effect. Moreover, shells were also robbed of their effectiveness by the sodden ground. But leaving this aside, it was *time* that would have been the crucial factor.

'Ask me for anything but time,' declared Napoleon. Had there been no thunderstorm, some precious hours would have been available to him. It was not until the climax of the battle, the evening of 18 June, that the Prussians intervened. This climax would have been reached well before that. Moreover there are subsidiary Ifs. An earlier start to the battle might have brought Grouchy on the scene; it might have revealed to Napoleon and Ney – and to Jérôme Bonaparte leading the attack on it – that the Château of Hougoumont had either to be taken, or screened and outflanked, if the principal assault on Wellington's position was to be successfully made.

The role played by Hougoumont will always arouse admiration and invite controversy. Victor Hugo went so far as to say that its conquest was one of Napoleon's dreams and that, had he seized it, it would have given him the world. Extravagant language, but perhaps not to be rejected out of hand. Hougoumont had two doors to its court, one to the château itself on the southern side, one belonging to the farm on the north. It was this latter door that was smashed open by a huge French officer who, followed by some of his jubilant men, rushed into the courtyard. They were instantly set upon by soldiers of the Coldstream Guards, who then succeeded in closing the doors and barring them with a vast wooden beam. Wellington was later to observe that his success at Waterloo had depended on closing these doors. It would perhaps be more accurate to say that a successful defence of Hougoumont was a crucial part of Wellington's strategy. It was because he appreciated its significance and had seen the scale of the French attack on it that he reinforced the garrison with four companies of the Coldstream Guards, thereby doubling its complement of Foot Guardsmen. Their remarkable achievement may be judged when we consider that, as Victor Hugo put it, they held out for seven hours against the assaults of vastly superior numbers.

After the initial failure of Napoleon's brother, Prince Jérôme, to take Hougoumont, neither he nor Napoleon himself took the decision to bypass this stubborn centre of resistance and get on with the main business of attacking Wellington's main line. Jérôme, in short, allowed what was a diversionary, albeit important, objective to take his eye off the main tactical purpose which was to pierce Wellington's centre. Instead of getting this principal attack under way, Jérôme poured more and more troops into the desperate struggle for Hougoumont. The divisions of Foy, Guilleminot and Bachelu hurled themselves against it; nearly all Reille's corps took their turn and failed; Bauduin's brigade was not strong enough to force

Hougoumont from the north, while Soye's brigade, although making the beginning of a breach in the south, could not exploit it. Jérôme had been making one of the classic errors of war – reinforcing failure – and on such a scale that he was robbing the French army of the strength to sweep Wellington aside before the Prussians came up to support him. Wellington, on the other hand, had reinforced success. Thus the contribution which Hougoumont's defenders made to victory at Waterloo was incalculable.

What would have happened if the gates had not been closed? For the purposes of speculation, we must assume that the French would have taken Hougoumont, for if, even though the gates were not closed, the British had still defied the French attacks and held on to the château, and if Napoleon had also permitted the same continued attempts to persevere, there would have been no change of circumstance. So we must ask ourselves what Napoleon would have done after capturing Hougoumont, had this happened; and in answering the question let us assume further that this capture was effected early on, in other words before Jérôme had dissipated his main forces against it. Napoleon then has two possible courses of action: to persist in the frontal assault on Wellington's centre, which in the event is what he did do, or try to outflank the Allied right and so roll up Wellington's position. This would have been the sure touch of Napoleon at his tactical best, as in former days when he instantly saw that the key to taking Toulon was to capture the Le Caire peninsula and so bring artillery fire to bear direct on the Royal Navy's ships; or when at Austerlitz he seized the fleeting opportunity to strike at and destroy the Austro-Russian centre, roll up their left wing and finish the thing off. In short, if the chance of closing the Hougoumont gates had not befallen, and the château had fallen early on into French hands, Napoleon's attack would not have been delayed or impeded. He would have been presented with great freedom of tactical choice, and provided he had taken a proper grip of the battle there and then, he must surely have prevailed. We will see shortly what might have come about had Napoleon defeated Wellington, but for the time being we may concede that the latter's comment about the closing of Hougoumont's gates, while an over-simplification as to what brought about success, does at least deserve serious consideration. Yet even given Hougoumont's retention in British hands, and the fact that Napoleon exerted himself far too late to rescue his army from the tactical blunders made by his subordinates, there was still one more chance, one more If which will always persist in the minds of those who ponder great battles.

'*On a perdu la France*' was Napoleon's comment to d'Erlon, referring to Ney's mistakes at Quatre Bras when he joined him there at midday on 17 June. The comment might equally well have applied to Grouchy. When on that same day Napoleon detached Grouchy and his 33,000 men to follow up and harass the Prussians, Grouchy himself and Soult tried to dissuade him, but the Emperor insisted. Not only was he giving himself too many objectives, he was dissipating his forces. A single aim – the defeat of Wellington – and a concentration of force to do so would have served him better. Moreover, his instructions to Grouchy were far from clear. Grouchy was required to pursue the Prussians and reconnoitre their movements so that Napoleon could determine their intentions. He needed to know what Wellington and Blücher meant to do. During the early hours of 18 June, Napoleon received a despatch from Grouchy announcing his intention to follow the Prussians towards Wavre and prevent their moving towards Brussels and Wellington's position. The Emperor's reply confounded confusion and contained these words: 'His Majesty desires you will head for Wavre *in order to draw near to us* [my italics] . . .' This in itself was contradictory for whereas Wavre was to the north of Grouchy, Napoleon was to the west. Had Napoleon's former Chief of Staff, Berthier, been there instead of Soult, he would never have permitted such sloppy phrasing. But Soult did at least press for the instant recall of Grouchy, only to have his intervention dismissed by the Emperor. The full impact of Grouchy's detachment was still to be felt.

In his most agreeable account of Marcellin Marbot's adventures as a cavalry *général de brigade*, based on Marbot's own memoirs, Vyvyan Ferrers suggests that these memoirs gave Conan Doyle the inspiration for writing his stories about Brigadier Gérard.[4] Ferrers also notes that the choice of the name Gérard was surprising, for as already recorded, one of the corps commanders at Waterloo was General Etienne Gérard, and on the fateful afternoon of 18 June he was with the newly appointed Marshal Grouchy, who was vainly attempting to follow up Blücher's army to Wavre and engage it. It was while Grouchy was pondering what to do that the thunder of guns at Waterloo was heard. If ever the initiative inherent to any great military commander needed to be employed, it was now. To march to the sound of the guns – at a time when your own force was contributing nothing to the battle's resolution – was so fundamental that Grouchy should have given instant orders to do so. Yet at this very moment General Gérard intervened and publicly told Grouchy that it was his duty to march upon the guns. Despite his own indecision, the one thing Grouchy was not prepared to tolerate was a lesson in command from one of his own subordinates, and after an ill-tempered dispute, the Marshal made it plain that his duty was to carry out the Emperor's orders and proceed to Wavre. And so he turned his back on the struggle which was to determine Europe's future. Had he marched to the guns with his 33,000 or so men, he would have intercepted the Prussian movement towards Waterloo and reinforced Napoleon at a moment when such reinforcement would have been decisive. Napoleon would not then have had to respond to Ney's plea for more troops with a petulant: 'Troops? Where do you expect me to find them? Do you expect me to make them?' They would have been to hand at the very moment when Ney was poised to execute the *coup de grâce*.

It is clear, therefore, that the various Ifs that we have looked at so far spring from mistakes made by Ney, Soult, Grouchy and Napoleon himself. Vincent Cronin names three blunders committed by the Emperor before the main battle had even begun: first, not crushing Wellington on the morning of 17 June, when the Prussians were retreating and the French could have brought overwhelming numbers against Wellington; second, his misjudgement both of the quality of British soldiers and the tactical skill of their commander; third, his gross overconfidence – had he taken the whole affair much more seriously, he would not have delegated Grouchy on his fruitless errand and ignored his subordinates' plea to get Grouchy back in time for the main attack.

A. G. Macdonnell finds fault not so much with Napoleon as with Marshals Ney, Soult and Grouchy. We have examined Grouchy's fatal indecision; Soult fell down by not stemming the tide of mistakes; Ney lost the battle by his ill-tempered countermanding of the Emperor's order on 16 June to send up d'Erlon's corps so that Napoleon could have destroyed Blücher's army rather than simply mauling it and pushing it back. Had this been done, Grouchy would have remained with the main body and Napoleon would have had an extra 33,000 men to dispose of Wellington, who in turn would have received no last-minute support from the Prussians. The mere fact that Wellington called it a close-run thing indicates how easily the scales might have been turned. Yet when all is said, we may be sure that Napoleon would have taken the credit for victory, and so must bear responsibility for defeat.

But what if he had won? In his essay 'Ruler of the World' Alistair Horne argues that victory at Waterloo would not have brought about Napoleon's ultimate success.

There were vast fresh forces of Russians, Austrians and Germans already moving towards France. A second battle, or perhaps several battles, would probably have followed Waterloo. But even if the ultimate engagement had ended in the likely defeat of Napoleon, with Britain out of the war, it would have been a *continental* and not a *British* victory. What followed would have, therefore, been a peace dominated by Metternich's Central European powers – by Russian, Austria and Prussia instead of Great Britain.[5]

I am not so sure. On hearing of Napoleon's escape from Elba and with the Allied resolution to outlaw him, Czar Alexander of Russia had told Wellington at the Congress of Vienna that it was for him to save the world again. With Wellington and Blücher beaten, would the resolve of the other powers have held firm? We have to imagine a triumphant Emperor entering Brussels at the head of his troops, frantic enthusiasm from the Belgians, who instantly declare for him, the Netherlands also changing sides, then Napoleon's return to Paris, acclaimed by all, even Talleyrand and Fouché – whose heads Napoleon might or might not have demanded – overtures for peace pouring out from the Tuileries, promises of democratic reform, the formerly circumspect Marshals rallying to their Commander-in-Chief, France jubilant, Napoleon overhauling the Grande Armée and preparing for the defence of the country's frontiers. In spite of the gathering Allied armies, their leaders might have recalled Napoleon's former ability to defeat them one by one or two at a time. They might have recalled the Emperor's pulling on his long boots in 1813 and 1814, winning battle after battle at Lützen, Bautzen, Champaubert, Château-Thierry, Vauchamp, Montereau – and these victories won with a small army of some 50,000 men. What he might now do with an army of four or five times that number, commanded by the most valiant and able set of lieutenants under his own unique direction, would surely have given the Allied sovereigns pause for reflection and compromise.

Besides, it is so agreeable to picture yet one more Congress of Vienna, convened by Metternich, who by then would have appreciated that Napoleon was not *un homme perdu* after all, a Congress at which not only did dancing gild the scene and amorous intrigue rule the plot, but at which Napoleon and Wellington finally met, with Talleyrand – whose cynical observation that treason was simply a matter of dates would have come full circle – hovering in the background, and Alexander once more falling under the spell of his brother Emperor. Would Marie Walewska have been there to consort with Napoleon, or would the wicked, dashing Hussar General, Count Neipperg, have been constrained to escort the Empress of France, Marie-Louise, to Vienna, bringing with them the King of Rome, Napoleon's son, destined six years later – if we assume that the Emperor still met his death in 1821 – to succeed his father as Napoleon II? If we are going to rewrite history, we might as well do it with a flourish.

There is perhaps one further diversion here. However insubstantial the Ifs of history may be, we must all applaud Stendhal's captivating suggestion that had Napoleon won at Waterloo, not only would there have been no liberals to be afraid of in the 1820s, but all the ancient sovereigns of Europe would only have kept their thrones by marrying the daughters of Napoleon's Marshals. Judging by the mettle of these

Marshals, the sovereigns in question could have done a great deal worse. There would have been one further benefit from Napoleon's winning – George IV would not then have boasted that he had been present on the battlefield.

And what if Napoleon had been killed at Waterloo – the 'good death' that he pondered on St Helena?[6] Why, the whole of France would have honoured him. Marshal Ney's comment as he gazed at Bessières' corpse on the field of Lützen, '*C'est notre sort. C'est une belle mort,*' would have echoed round the world in honour of the General, whom Wellington called '*un grand homme de guerre*', the greatest ever to appear at the head of a French army, and the magnificent ceremony, which took place in 1840, with Louis-Philippe on the throne of France, when Napoleon's coffin, returned from St Helena, was received by Marshal Moncey, Governor of Les Invalides, would have been enacted twenty-five years earlier.

There is one last If we may perhaps contemplate when we recall A. P. Herbert's delightful book, *Why Waterloo?*, in which he argues that Napoleon did not break out of Elba but was driven out. Had the French government honoured the treaty of Fontainebleau with regard to money, had Marie-Louise joined her husband on Elba, had Talleyrand been less malignant, or Colonel Campbell more vigilant, had Royal Navy frigates blockaded the island properly, there would perhaps have been no escape, no Hundred Days, no Waterloo. A. P. Herbert concludes that no single person could be arraigned for the tragedy that ensued. Yet he adds this: 'The Emperor of Austria, if he had had more humanity; Louis XVIII, if he had had more sense and honesty; Marie-Louise, if she had had more faith and fortitude, could have altered history and let one of the world's great men die peaceful and happy.'[7]

It was while Napoleon was still on Elba that his brother, Lucien, wrote to Masséna: '*Voilà donc enfin le drame terminé. Tant de gloire perdue par la plus lâche fin. Bon Dieu! Que de souvenirs. Que de regrets.*' It was when on that other island that Napoleon himself could not resist a resort to the 'what ifs' of history. Had he appointed some other general instead of Grouchy. Blücher would not have arrived in time to save Wellington from defeat. Yet we must recall that

Napoleon, who was so often to reiterate, 'Be clear and all the rest will follow,' broke his own rule in his confusing instruction to Grouchy. On St Helena the Emperor, like Lucien, has his regrets. He should have had Talleyrand and Fouché hanged. What a difference that might have made to the Hundred Days. Then again: 'To die at Borodino would have been to die like Alexander: to be killed at Waterloo would have been a good death; perhaps Dresden would have been better; but no, better at Waterloo. The love of the people, their regret.'[8]

He regrets, too, ever having left Egypt. He would have preferred to be Emperor of the East than of the West. The desert had always fascinated him and his own name meant lion of the desert. Besides, to have been master of Egypt would have been to be master of India. What rascals the English were! 'If I had been able to get to India from Egypt with the nucleus of an army, I should have driven them from India.'[9] Now the English would have to see what would come to them from Russia. 'The Russians, already in Persia, have not far to go to reach India.'[10] It was this last point of Napoleon's which some twenty years later was the cause of concern in the minds of the Englishmen who ruled India, and the cause also of their beginning to play the Great Game.

FOUR

Playing – and Losing – the Great Game

We shall never settle Afghanistan at the point of the bayonet.

SIR ALEXANDER BURNES

Yet settling Afghanistan at the point of the bayonet is precisely what the men who ruled India tried to do, not once, but twice. The second effort was somewhat more successful than the first. In this latter case the conduct of affairs was marred by a Governor-General who, with three courses of action open to him, chose the one most likely to lead to failure, and by a General who, for sheer dithering, incompetence and imbecility, outshone all his contemporaries. It was all part of the so-called Great Game, the moves and counter-moves by the Russians and the British in the not quite no-man's-land between the Czar's dominions and British India, the chess board formed by Central Asia, Persia, the Punjab and Afghanistan. The Governor-General in question was George Eden, Lord Auckland, and the General was William Elphinstone.

Auckland's immediate predecessor, Charles Metcalfe, was one of those men upon whom the success of British rule in India depended. He was a superb administrator, enlightened, magnanimous and wise. His understanding of his country's position in India is admirably summed up by the one of his pronouncements as Governor-General in the 1830s:

Our dominion in India is by conquest; it is naturally disgusting to the inhabitants and can only be maintained by military force. It is our positive duty to render them justice, to respect and protect their rights, and to study their happiness. By the performance of this duty, we may allay and keep dormant their innate disaffection.[1]

Not a bad recipe for any government of any people but, alas, too often overturned by dogma, prejudice and greed. Among Metcalfe's many achievements were abolition of slavery and *suttee*, the burning of widows, putting a stop to flogging and the teaching of a trade to petty criminals. Moreover, he was convinced that interfering in the affairs of native states was likely to do more harm than good and should therefore be avoided. When this policy is considered in relation to the Great Game, Metcalfe's clear-sighted wisdom is reinforced. With regard to Persia and Afghanistan he laid down that we should 'maintain our relations on the most friendly terms that will not involve us in stipulations likely to lead to an unnecessary war with Russia' and 'You may depend upon it that the surest way to draw Russia upon us will be by our meddling with any states beyond the Indus.'[2] It was just such meddling by his successor, Auckland, which brought about a signal catastrophe.

Auckland was a very different man from Metcalfe. Metcalfe was one who was usually found to be in control of events; Auckland was more inclined to allow events to carry him along willy-nilly. Metcalfe's character determined incident; incident influenced Auckland's character. Auckland was altogether too mild, too uncommitted, too amiable, too good-natured, too unconscious of being charged with the great task of controlling the lives of millions. He seemed incapable of taking the necessary steps to deal with famine. Yet when it came to dealing with Afghanistan, Auckland seemed to throw caution and common sense to the winds, refusing the friendship of the powerful and competent ruler, Dost Mahommed, and invading the country in order to place on the throne instead a pretender who had thrice been rejected and dethroned by his own people.

It must, however, be conceded that Auckland was subjected to much pressure by England's Foreign Secretary, Viscount Palmerston. Palmerston's policy was to keep any conflict between the various contestants for power and territory in those parts as far away from the frontiers of India as possible. Thus he would lend his support to Persia against Russia; to Afghanistan if threatened by Persia; to the Punjab if endangered from Afganistan. In so far as Palmerston's support for the Afghans against Persia's designs on Herat in persuading the Shah to accept the Czar's advice to abandon the idea, Britain's policy had prevailed. But Palmerston's direct interference in Afghanistan itself was to have dire consequences. Given the obsession of both Auckland and Palmerston with preserving Afghanistan's independence and warding off Russian notions of extending her influence there, it was not hard to find some pretext for interfering. Palmerston had always had a profound distrust of Russia. He and Auckland also had their suspicions that Dost Mahommed was not only plotting some association with the Russians, but – and here it was more than suspicion – planning to take back from Ranjit Singh, powerful ruler of the Punjab and firm ally of the British, the city of Peshawar, near the Khyber Pass and of great strategic importance, which Ranjit Singh had seized from Afghanistan thirty years before.

The only Englishman who really understood Afghanistan was Alexander Burnes, who knew the country well and had been sent as British envoy to the court of Dost Mahommed. Burnes's opinion, which proved to be correct, was that despite his flirtation with the Russians, Dost Mahommed would prove a trustworthy friend. But to support him would be to antagonize Ranjit Singh, whose aim was to overthrow Dost Mahommed and replace him with his predecessor, Shah Shuja, flabby, vicious, despised by the Afghans, whose only recommendation was that he was a pensioner of the British in India and might therefore, if restored to the throne, pursue a pro-British policy. Auckland rejected the advice of the man most qualified to give it, Alexander Burnes, and recommended to the British Government that Dost Mohammed should be ousted from the throne, that the rightful ruler should be restored and supported by a British military presence against any intervention, whether internal or external. Once Shah Shuja was securely established in power and Afghanistan's integrity and independence secure, the British soldiers could be withdrawn. It would have been difficult to imagine a recipe more likely to arouse the hostility of the Afghan people or more certain to result in this hostility being acted upon with sullen intrigue and treacherous violence.

At home the matter was discussed by Palmerston and the Prime Minister, Melbourne, together with other members of the Cabinet.

It was all done with great secrecy, and Palmerston made a point of concealing Burnes's favourable opinion of Dost Mohammed. The most surprising aspect of the whole affair is that Melbourne, who in general was most reluctant to take any action about anything unless absolutely obliged to do so, should have endorsed Auckland's proposals. In this particular case, however, the Cabinet's approval went for little, for Auckland had already taken action on his own authority. The expedition was doomed from the very outset, whatever initial success might have been achieved. It was founded on the totally false notion that Dost Mohammed was unpopular with his own people and that he could not be trusted. It further supposed, wholly erroneously, that the British candidate for the throne, Shah Shuja, would be welcomed back in power by his countrymen, and would turn out to be an effective ruler and a reliable ally. As if this was not enough, the policy absolutely ignored the nature of the Afghan tribes – savage, chauvinistic, treacherous, fiercely independent, murderous and unpredictable. They were as unlikely to accept an unwanted ruler imposed by the British as they were to tolerate the presence of a British army.

We have seen for ourselves in recent times how, to recall James Morris, 'uncompromisingly picturesque' the Afghans were.

The men wore huge turbans, or satin caps with gold brocade crowns, with leather boots buttoned up to the calf, huge sheepskin cloaks over their shoulders, and shirts with wide sleeves for the concealment of daggers or poison phials. The women were enveloped head to foot in the white cylinder of the *burkha*, with only a mesh at the eyes to demonstrate the human presence within.[3]

Apart from their innate bellicosity as far as foreigners were concerned, their innumerable tribes were constantly fighting among themselves. There were Tajiks, Hazarahs, Afridis, Khaibaris, Pathans, Tartars, Uzbeks, each with their own special brand of customs, traditions and qualities, making them not only more or less incomprehensible to foreigners, but, since even their own leaders could hardly govern them, still less manageable by an authority imposed from outside. The country itself, with its bleak, arid plains and savage mountain passes, was hardly hospitable, totally lacking in sustenance, and ideal for ambush or sniping. Indeed, as Lieutenant Mackinnon, 16th Lancers, observed on the line of march during the advance to Kabul: 'Not a soul to be seen . . . except when levelling a matchlock from some almost inaccessible crag.'

That Auckland faced a dilemma cannot be denied. The Persians, influenced by Russia, had besieged Herat in western Afghanistan. If the Perso-Russian menace persisted, it was conceivable that a threat to India might develop. There were thus three things that Auckland could do: leave Afghanistan alone, but make sure that British defences of the Indus were powerful enough to deter any would-be incursion; ally himself with the Afghan ruler, Dost Mohammed, and so present a formidable front against any misplaced Russian ambitions; or, if Dost Mohammed insisted on unacceptable terms for such an alliance, depose him and put a different ruler in his place. At the very moment Auckland made his decision to adopt the third course of action, the justification for doing anything at all disappeared, for the Persians, responding to diplomatic pressure from the British Government together with some troop movements from the Persian Gulf, raised the siege of Herat. What must strike us as extraordinary is that despite the expert advice of Burnes, Auckland allowed the influence of his chief political adviser, Sir William Macnaghten, to prevail, and having made up his mind for once, decided to stick to it. In short, he would finish off the Great Game there and then by despatching a British army to invade Afghanistan and set Shah Shuja on the throne. If Metcalfe had still been Governor-General, he would never have countenanced so hazardous and uncertain an expedition.

Yet to start with and from a purely military point of view, things went reasonably well. Towards the end of 1838 the army of the Indus, with some 10,000 British and East India Company troops, together with 6,000 of Shah Shuja's own soldiers, concentrated near Lahore. There they indulged themselves in partaking of Ranjit Singh's ill-organized and disreputable entertainments – 'a cabaret of dancing girls and bawdy buffoons' – the host himself, as was his custom, drinking too much. There were also military parades and reviews before the whole ponderous business of getting the army under way began. The plan was to cross the Indus towards Quetta with no fewer than 40,000 camp followers and 30,000 camels in order to approach Kabul via Kandahar and Ghazni. The nature of the supplies and commodities which accompanied the army reflected more the Sahibs' determination to do themselves well than the sinews of war. For although there were enough sheep and cattle to last for ten weeks and a month's supply of grain, literally hundreds of camels were required to transport the personal kit and creative comforts of senior officers. Cigars, soap, wine, crockery and preserves took pride of place as indispensable items of baggage, and every regiment had an enormous retinue of stretcher-bearers, blacksmiths, cobblers, saddlers, tailors, bhistis (water carriers) like Gunga Din, laundry-men, all the labourers necessary for looking after the horses and cattle, for erecting tented camps, supplying wood and cooking food. Entire families accompanied many of the camp followers. There were, James Morris tells us, even 'troops of prostitutes from half India, with fiddlers, dancing girls, fortune tellers'.[4] If the fortune tellers knew their business and dared to speak their minds, they must have had some gloomy predictions to make. There were thousands of horse-drawn vehicles,

and so all this great multitude stumbled away to war, each corps with its band playing, a regiment of Queen's cavalry, two of Company cavalry, nine regiments of infantry, engineers, gunners, Shah Shuja's hopeful sepoys and those splendid prancing banditti, the Yellow Boys [Skinner's Horse (1st Bengal Irregular Cavalry)].[5]

What was also remarkable was not so much that on arrival at Kabul things began to go wrong, but that most of this heterogeneous collection of soldiery and hangers-on got to Kabul at all. Although there was not much resistance to the invading army, the utmost vigilance was necessary every time there was a halt to ensure that the numerous bands of marauding horsemen were kept at bay. Yet before setting about an assault on the fortress of Ghazni, there was a determined attack on Shah Shuja's camp by a horde of Ghazni horsemen. It took the combined efforts of Shuja's own cavalry, the 16th Lancers and Bengal Light Cavalry, to repel them. When it came to the taking of Ghazni itself the Somerset Light Infantry (13th Foot) and the 36th Bengal Native Infantry were so impressed by each other's gallantry – and it was clear that both regiments excelled – that after the battle the men of the 13th went round the ranks of the 36th to shake them all by the hand. Thus far in the campaign, therefore, the British had shown themselves to be superior in morale and skill. This position of advantage would not last for long.

In August 1839 Shah Shuja re-entered his capital, Kabul, by courtesy of the British army. He was watched with sullen resentment by the people, who showed not the remotest sign of enthusiasm; indeed, they took little notice of him. General Keane, who had commanded the expedition, sensed the atmosphere and was quick to pass judgement on it. While reporting to Auckland with the hope that he had accomplished what the Governor-General had intended, his private view, confided to one of his subordinates who accompanied him on his return to India that autumn, was that before long there would be 'some signal catastrophe'. He could hardly have predicted the future more accurately.

Despite all Auckland's concern and Palmerston's fears, there were no Russians in Kabul. Yet no city could have seemed more ominous. James Morris's description of it at that time is hauntingly relevant to our own times:

Kabul lay deep within the mountains at 6,000 feet, clustered at the foot of a mediaeval citadel, the Bala Hissar, on a desolate gravel plain: a foxy, evasive kind of city, riddled with xenophobia and conspiracy, and living it seemed always on its nerves. All around were unmapped, bald and inhospitable highlands, pierced by narrow ravines and deep river-beds, traversed only by rough tracks. The kingdom made its living by plunder and agriculture, for the Muslim Afghans thought trade an ignoble occupation, and left it to foreigners. The general character of the people was at once savagely independent and desperately unpredictable. The Afghans could be lively, humorous, courageous, even warm-hearted; but they could also be bigoted, sly, and murderous.[6]

Into this den of uncertainty, then, came the British in support of their imposed and despised ruler, Shah Shuja. The former ruler, Dost Mohammed, whom Burnes had so positively championed, was gone. Burnes himself was there as British Resident and as assistant to the

Envoy and Minister, Sir William Macnaghten, who had distinguished himself as a learned, fire-eating Indian civil servant. The soldiers, now reduced in numbers, for much of the original force had returned to India, got down to the business of enjoying themselves. There were two brigades of infantry, one cavalry regiment and a battery of horse artillery. As was customary in those parts, equestrian sports played a large part in the troops' entertainment, together with cricket and band concerts. There were in addition the subjects of Kipling's poem, 'The Ladies': 'the things you will learn from the Yellow an' Brown, They'll 'elp you a lot with the White!' The Kabul women were tall, handsome, lithe and athletic, and, as many Afghan men had more of a taste for painted youths, they were eager and hungry too. Despite the concealing and modest *burkha*, they were, like the Colonel's Lady an' Judy O'Grady, sisters under the skin. This may have been all very well for the British officers but it hardly endeared them to the Afghans. Nevertheless the British felt secure, and in 1840 took the incalculably unwise step of moving their garrison from the Bala Hissar, the citadel within Kabul which dominated the city and could have been made more or less impregnable, to an almost inconceivably unsuitable cantonment on a low, swampy piece of ground about a mile to the north-east of Kabul, virtually indefensible, overlooked by hills and forts from all sides, with, between it and the city, orchards and canals which would effectively inhibit rapid deployment of horses and guns, with a perimeter far too lengthy to be manned. As if all this were not a sufficient display of military mismanagement, it was then crowned by one more gigantic act of folly. The commissariat stores were positioned several furlongs *outside* the cantonment!

It is time for some Ifs. If Metcalfe or almost anyone with an understanding of India and its neighbouring states had still been the Governor-General, the idea of imposing an unpopular, incompetent and dissolute has-been like Shah Shuja on a people as proud, inconstant, vengeful and warlike as the Afghans would not even have entered the British calculations in considering what to do about the supposed Russian menace. Metcalfe would have been shrewd enough to appreciate that Burnes knew what he was talking about, would have shrugged off any earnest pleading by civil servants, and would have resisted any ill-conceived direction from Melbourne's Government at home with the confident certainty that he knew best. Dost Mohammed would have been assured of British support and Burnes would have been despatched to Kabul with a suitably impressive retinue to negotiate terms by which the British in India would guarantee the continued independence of Afghanistan, together with vague assurances as to the future of Peshawar. At the same time Ranjit Singh, ruler of the Punjab, whose support and friendship was so important to the British position in India, would have been soothed by the customary coalition of bribes, flattery and veiled threats. There would in short have been no invasion of Afghanistan, but simply a British envoy and adviser positioned in Kabul, keeping an eye on the encroaching intrigues of Persia and the expansionist policies of Russia. Such assurances to Dost Mohammed, backed by the diplomatic activity of Palmerston, would have been adequate to preserve Afghanistan's integrity.

Yet, even given the mistakes of policy and the negligence of the consequent military deployment, there would still have been an even chance of, if not reconciling, at least coercing the Afghans into acceptance of the British presence, even though it was only this presence which maintained the position of Shah Shuja as their ruler. But to do so, three conditions would need to be fulfilled: the continued occupation, strengthening and reinforcement of the Bala Hissar; secure lines of communication back to India; and the choice of a bold, efficient and respected general officer in command at Kabul. We have noted the indescribable folly of abandoning the citadel. The British now took two further steps most likely to turn a dangerous situation into an irretrievable one.

In the first place Auckland, getting his priorities wrong as usual, elected to cut the subsidies to the Ghilzai tribes who controlled the mountain passes back to India. He would have done better to have doubled them. His wholly false economies simply added to the magnitude of the disaster that his policies were leading to. Yet he still had one more trick up his sleeve to make the assurance of this impending calamity double sure. In April 1841 Auckland appointed a friend of his, Major-General William Elphinstone, to the command at

Kabul. Elphinstone had last been in action at Waterloo, twenty-six years earlier. He was wholly inexperienced in warfare in India or Afghanistan. He knew nothing of oriental languages, and in spite of coming from an East India Company family, did not even speak Urdu. He was so afflicted by gout that he could hardly hobble along. He had absolutely no desire for the command he was now presented with, and was totally aware of his own unfitness for it, acknowledging that he was 'done up in body and mind'. Perhaps the most memorable comment on Elphinstone was put into the mouth of that poodle-faking yet somehow irrepressibly dashing bounder Flashman by George MacDonald Fraser:

I still state unhesitatingly, that for pure, vacillating stupidity, for superb incompetence to command, for ignorance combined with bad judgement – in short, for the true talent for catastrophe – Elphy Bey stood alone . . . Elphy outshines them all as the greatest military idiot of our own or any other day.[7]

Even Elphinstone noted the hazardous siting of the cantonment and the perilous lines of communication to Jalalabad and the Khyber Pass, but he did nothing to lessen these dangers other than to urge his subordinates to clear the mountain passes quickly if anything untoward occurred, so 'that I may get away', hardly an inspiring call for decisive action. And all the time discontent among the tribes and in Kabul was growing, and would eventually come to a head in November, when the Kabul mob surged round and attacked the British Residency. Burnes courageously tried to calm the Afghans, but in vain, and in trying to escape was seized by the mob and hacked to pieces. This was the moment when instant, daring, decisive and ruthlessly punitive action was called for, the sort of action which would have been taken by Clive, John Lawrence, John Nicholson or Lord Roberts,[8] the kind of men whose deeds would live in men's memories and never perish as long as the Raj itself endured.

And now we come to another great chance that was missed. If Elphinstone and his army had stormed Kabul, retaken the Bala Hissar citadel, shot a few dozen rebels, established an iron grip on the city and then despatched some fast-moving columns to sort out the Ghazis and Ghilzais – with both the sword and the purse – it is just possible that some kind of accommodation might have been reached, permitting reinforcements to move from India to strengthen the garrison at Jalalabad and organize a secure withdrawal of the army through the mountain passes, thus allowing Elphy Bey to crown an otherwise totally undistinguished career with one successful action and earn himself a knighthood.

But apart from two or three pathetically inadequate sorties from the cantonment, which resulted in rapid defeat and ignominious retreat, nothing was done. The Afghan rebels grew stronger and bolder by the day. They seized the commissariat, blocked the roads and virtually besieged the British in their wholly indefensible cantonment. If only the British had been secure in the Bala Hissar with their supplies, they could have laughed a siege to scorn. But as it was they were in a hopeless position, with inadequate food, winter coming, low morale, a commander destitute of ideas, willpower or energy, no likelihood of reinforcement, a host of terror-stricken camp followers, and an Envoy, Macnaghten, obliged to witness the policy he had recommended in absolute ruins, who now decided to do the one thing that could only make matters worse – negotiate from a position of weakness. He negotiated with Dost Mohammed's son, Akhbar Khan, recently returned to Kabul with a formidable band of Uzbeg horsemen, and he could hardly have chosen a more devious or treacherous agent with whom to form an agreement. On 11 December 1841 the two men reached an understanding that the British would leave Afghanistan, restoring Dost Mohammed to the throne, while the Afghans in their turn would provide safe conduct and supplies. Had things been left like this, it might just have been possible to salvage something from the dreadful mess that Macnaghten had got himself into. It might have been thought that no further blundering could be imagined, yet the supreme misjudgement was still to come. Macnaghton responded to a secret proposal from Akhbar Khan that Akhbar would become Vizier to Shah Shuja and be handsomely rewarded by the British, while the British themselves would remain in Afghanistan until August 1842 and then voluntarily withdraw, having successfully executed their policy. That Macnaghten should have given credence to a secret arrangement by Akhbar Khan, which betrayed not only other Afghan leaders but Akhbar's own father, must strike us now as astonishing. Yet he did so, only to learn shortly afterwards that it was he who had been betrayed, for when he met Akhbar Khan again on 23 December and expressed his willingness to accept the secret agreement, Akhbar ordered his Ghazis to seize him. Macnaghten was bundled away, shot and hacked to pieces. His severed head was then paraded through the streets of Kabul.

Once again Elphinstone was presented with a reason for taking violent action and exacting vengeance for treachery and murder. Once again he did nothing so necessary and justifiable. Instead, and still from a position of pitiable weakness, he renewed negotiations with Akhbar Khan. Indeed the very word negotiation exaggerates a process which was one of submission to the terms imposed by the Afghans. The British army was to withdraw forthwith, forfeiting most of its money and – another stupefying concession – its guns. Hostages would be held in Kabul to guarantee Dost Mohammed's safe return. One further condition puts us in mind of Wellington's reply to the gentleman who believed he was Mr Brown: 'If you believe that, you'll believe anything'; it was to the effect that the Afghans would escort the army with its followers through the mountain passes to the frontier with India. Everything was now in place for final disaster.

We may once again recall Flashman's comment on the whole affair. After a lifetime of contemplation, he could not recall a greater shambles in the chronicles of warfare. Even he, one of the smoothest-talking anti-heroes of fiction, was at a loss to describe the sheer scale of stupidity, incompetence and irrationality exhibited by Elphinstone and his staff. If a general officer of real ability had been set the task of bringing the army to utter ruin, he could not have bettered the performance which now took place. On 6 January 1842 the army of about 4,500 soldiers, accompanied by 12,000 camp followers, set off from Kabul. Before them was a 100-mile march – redcoats, sepoys, horses, mules, bullocks and camels by the thousand – in order to reach Jalalabad. The route would be over mountain passes some 5,000 feet high, in icy weather, with snow everywhere, no guarantee of supplies, inadequate clothing, and, despite all the Afghans had promised, no protection from the numerous defiles which might have been designed for ambush. Even if there had been no interference by the treacherous and vengeful Afghan tribesmen, indeed, had the heterogeneous column been aided by them, to have reached Jalalabad in any sort of order would have been a miraculous achievement. But given that they were subjected to continuous, merciless harassment, ambush and attack, it was hardly surprising that of the entire army, only one man reached Jalalabad – a surgeon, Dr Brydon. All the rest were killed, dispersed, starved, captured, or horribly wounded and left to die. Even after four days the fighting strength of the army was down to less than 1,000. Two days later those still left approached the worst of defiles, the Jugdulluk, to find barriers across the track. Then, as the soldiers tried to struggle through, the Gilzai horsemen fell upon them, slashing with their swords and knives. Twenty officers and forty-five British soldiers finally reached the village of Gandamack. They were surrounded by Afghans, who called for a parley. The parley turned into a slaughter of all but a few soldiers made prisoner, including Captain Souter of the 44th Regiment, who had wrapped the colours round his waist to preserve them, and because of his colourful appearance appeared to the tribesmen to be of ransomable value. Dr Brydon, however, had bypassed Gandamack and did reach Jalalabad, thus fulfilling the prophecy of Colonel Dennie, 13th Foot, who had predicted a year earlier that one man would get to Jalalabad from Kabul to tell the garrison that the rest of the army had perished.

The greatest irony was still to come. Later in 1842 Ellenborough succeeded Auckland as Governor-General and despatched General Pollock to force his way through the Khyber Pass with another army, to find that Jalalabad under General Sale had successfully withstood its besiegers. Meanwhile, General Nott was secure at Kandahar and, when ordered by Ellenborough, withdrew via Ghazni, destroyed its fortress and went on to take Kabul where he blew up the bazaar. He finally joined Pollock's force and with him succeeded in quelling Afghan resistance, releasing all British prisoners and generally restoring the prestige of the Raj. And then, as if to show that the whole of Auckland's ill-fated endeavour had been for nothing, after the British armies had returned to India, Shah Shuja was murdered and Dost Mohammed was restored to his throne where he reigned for a further thirty years.

So we are left with two great Ifs. If only Metcalfe or Ellenborough had been Governor-General in 1838, instead of Auckland, the ghastly misappreciation of the situation would not have been made; there would have been no invasion of Afghanistan, no humiliating submission to Akhbar Khan, no retreat from Kabul and no massacring of an army and its camp followers. The one redeeming feature of it all was that during that dreadful retreat, many individual acts of heroism and sacrifice by those taking part in it still excite our admiration and wonder today.

The second great If is that had almost any general other than Elphinstone – Keane, Pollock, Nott or Sale, say – been chosen to command in Kabul in 1841, faulty deployment, ineptitude, vacillation, absolute military folly, lassitude and criminal inactivity would, we may confidently suppose, have been replaced by security, strength of purpose, boldness, speed of reaction, total confidence in the superiority and invincibility of British arms – in short, the sort of leadership shown by Roberts during the Second Afghan War in 1878–80, when the British, still intent on playing the Great Game,[9] and losing a few tricks here and there, including the disaster of Maiwand, called by the Marquess of Anglesey the worst defeat suffered by the Anglo-Indian army when Ayub Khan routed a force under Burrows,[10] once again interfered in the affairs of Afghanistan. It was Roberts who, in what was perhaps the finest achievement of his career, marched from Kabul, covering over 300 miles at summer's height in scarcely more than three weeks, with 10,000 men and as many camp followers, over almost roadless country and mountain passes, and at the end of it utterly defeated Ayub Khan's army which was positioned strongly in the hills outside Kandahar. Roberts had cleared up the problem of Afghanistan. Abdul Rahman was confirmed as Amir of the country. He agreed to British control of his foreign policy in exchange for a subsidy and support against aggression from elsewhere.

For the time being the British were holding the best cards in the Great Game. Neither then, nor during the First Afghan War, did Russian and Great Britain come to blows in the hills and valleys of

Afghanistan. But in between the two Afghan campaigns and just before the game went tragically wrong in India itself with the so-called Mutiny, the two great European powers did come to blows in the hills and valleys of the Crimea.

FIVE

Balaklava: 25 October 1854

Lord Raglan is utterly incompetent to lead an army through any arduous task. He is a brave good soldier, I am sure, and a polished gentleman, but he is no more fit than I am to cope with any leader of strategic skill.

WILLIAM HOWARD RUSSELL[1]

We are commanded by one of the greatest old women in the British Army, called the Earl of Cardigan. He has as much brains as my boot. He is only to be equalled in want of intellect by his relation the Earl of Lucan . . . two such fools could not be picked out of the British Army to take command.

CAPTAIN PORTAL, 4TH LIGHT DRAGOONS[2]

'You have lost the Light Brigade!' It was thus that Lord Raglan bitterly reproached Lord Lucan on the evening of 25 October 1854. As a simple statement of fact the words were not unfounded. Before the charge, according to Captain Portal who rode in it, the Light Cavalry Brigade had mustered on parade some 700 men; after it they numbered a mere 180.[3] But was it Lucan who lost it? Controversy as to who was to blame has featured in many an analysis of the battle. The truth is, of course, that many people were to blame, Lucan among them. It was a combination of personal ill-feeling, general mismanagement and peculiarly bad orders which led to so great, yet glorious, a blunder. Given the circumstances which prevailed, however – a Commander-in-Chief who had no clear idea of how to conduct a battle, and who, unlike his former chief, Wellington, was in the habit of expressing himself with ambiguity rather than precision; a Commander of the cavalry, Lucan, who was at odds with Raglan's handling of the campaign and with his subordinate, Cardigan, in charge of the Light Brigade; and given too that the aide-de-camp who delivered the fatally misconstrued order was half insane with impatience and injured pride, so much so that he actually seemed to indicate the wrong objective – then it was perhaps not so remarkable that things went awry, although why General Airey, Raglan's Chief of Staff, should have pronounced the Light Brigade's charge as 'nothing to Chilianwala' may still puzzle us.[4] It was after all a feat of arms recalled for courage and discipline rather than for foolhardiness and waste.

But if by chance Raglan had shown the same sort of drive and initiative at the first battle of the campaign as Wellington did at Salamanca, then the charge of the Light Brigade, indeed the entire affair at Balaklava, need never have taken place at all. And even if he had behaved as he did during that first encounter and the British army had still found itself at Balaklava in October 1854, it only required the Light Brigade's commander, Cardigan, to display some spark of military daring, some inkling of the cavalry spirit, even some modicum of tactical know-how for the charge of his brigade, to have been a very different matter with a possibly decisive outcome. We must go back to the start of the campaign to see how things might have developed.

In spite of all the fuss about custody of the Holy Places,[5] the Crimean War came about because Czar Nicholas I believed the time had come to expel the Turks from Europe and divide up the property of 'the sick man'. At the same time Emperor Napoleon III of France was possessed of an ardent desire to cut a figure in the world and add to the military glory attained by his uncle. Moreover, Britain was determined to maintain Turkey's integrity and put a stop to the extension of Russian power in the East. Thus a relatively trivial dispute was used to justify a struggle for supremacy in the East.

The Czar could hardly have chosen an envoy more likely to provoke Turkey's ire than Prince Menschikoff, who went to Constantinople in March 1853 and demanded that the Sultan should recognize both the Greek Church's claim to custody of the Holy

Places and – much more significantly – Russia's right to protect the Sultan's Greek Orthodox subjects. Menschikoff was both tactless and insolent, but these disagreeable qualities were largely offset by the diplomatic skills of the highly regarded British Ambassador at the Sublime Porte, Lord Stratford de Redcliffe, who had been there for ten years, had encouraged reform and who, in spite of his hostility to the Czar, persuaded the Sultan to satisfy the Greek Church with regard to the Holy Places, at the same time lending his support to the Sultan in rejecting Russia's claim to be protector of Turkey's Greek Christians. Whereupon in June 1853 Russia invaded the principalities of Moldavia and Wallachia, and after the failure of the Great Powers to reach some compromise, Turkey declared war in October. An extension of the war swiftly followed. Turkey defeated a Russian army at Oltenitza, the Russian fleet destroyed a Turkish squadron at Sinope, the French and British fleets passed the Dardanelles and entered the Black Sea in January 1854. Two months later France and Britain declared war on Russia.

Thus France, Great Britain and Turkey were Allies. For centuries in the past the British had been fighting the French. With the exception of the Vichy episodes in the Second World War, they were never to do so again. Yet Lord Raglan could not get out of his head that the enemy – even when in this particular war they were fighting side by side with him – were the French, and would frequently refer to them as such during the campaign. This was not the only difficulty encountered by the Allies.

It was all very well to declare war on Russia, but where was it to be waged? The Allies wished to ensure that the Russian armies evacuated the principalities and did not reach Constantinople. But what strategy should they adopt to realize these aims? By the end of May 1854 both the French and British armies had arrived at Gallipoli and Scutari, and the striking difference between their administrative arrangements was at once evident. The French were properly equipped with tents, medical services and a transport corps. The British were hopelessly ill prepared in all these respects, although Raglan had requested proper transport, only to be refused by the War Office. When the two armies made their way to Varna in order to deal with the Russians in the principalities, they found they had gone. It was now August and both malaria and cholera devastated the Allied soldiers. But at least some strategic idea emerged, and it was decided that the Allies would attack and take Sebastopol, thus removing this base of Russian power in the Black Sea and its threat to Turkey. This decision was made, not by commanders on the spot, who opposed it, but by the Allied Governments, hardly an auspicious beginning. None the less, in September the British and French armies – composed respectively of 26,000 men, 66 guns and 30,000 men, 70 guns – landed in the bay of Eupatoria, north of Sebastopol, and began their advance.

We have already observed that Lord Raglan was not distinguished for either his fitness to command or the clarity of his direction. His counterpart, General St Arnaud, was gravely ill – he was shortly to die – and was in no condition to provide bold leadership or offensive spirit. Moreover, Raglan's subordinate commanders hardly inspired confidence. Lucan and Cardigan, leaving aside their sheer incompetence, were at loggerheads, and were soon to demonstrate their absolute inability to handle the cavalry properly. The two infantry divisional commanders, Sir George Cathcart and the Duke of Cambridge, were not as useless as the cavalrymen – no one could have been – but they had none of the experience or dash of men like Craufurd, Picton, Pakenham and Hill who had served under Wellington. Raglan's Chief of Staff was General Airey, who should have been aware that apart from giving sound advice, his main purpose was to ensure the clarity of his Commander-in-Chief's orders, which he singularly failed to do.

Happily for the British army this weakness of leadership at the top was more than counterbalanced by the strength of the regimental system. It was Humphrey Ward who praised Kipling for discovering Tommy Atkins as a hero of realistic romance. No army, said Ward, had so strong a sense of regimental unity and loyalty as our own. Arthur Bryant too was eloquent in emphasizing regimental pride:

the personal individual loyalty which each private felt towards his corps gave to the British soldier a moral strength which enabled him to stand firm and fight forward when men without it, however brave, would have failed. To let down the regiment, to be unworthy of the men of old who had marched under the same colours, to be untrue to the comrades who had shared the same loyalties, hardships and perils were things that the least-tutored, humblest soldier would not do.[6]

Raglan was fortunate therefore in having under his command regiments of the Light Division, the Highlanders and the Brigade of Guards when it came to tackling the enemy. What would these famous regiments have to fight?

Opposing the Allied advance towards Sebastopol was a force of some 40,000 Russian soldiers under the command of Prince Menschikoff, who had positioned his men and about a hundred guns on the high ground overlooking the river Alma, fifteen miles north of Sebastopol. The battle of Alma was fought on 20 September and was characteristic of most Crimean encounters as far as the Allies were concerned. There was no proper reconnaissance, no clear plan, no thought about exploitation of success, no coordination between armies, no control or direction by Raglan, and the outcome was determined by the sheer courage and endurance of the British infantry. This dereliction of duty by those who were supposed to be directing the battle may be gauged by the fact that the Great Redoubt, key to the whole Russian defence, had to be taken twice, first by the Light Division and 2nd Division, and then again – because the reserve divisions were not moved forward quickly enough to consolidate its capture, thus allowing the Russians to reoccupy it – by the Guards and Highlanders. Its initial capture shows us the mettle of the British infantry:

The first line of the British army, the Light Infantry Division and the 2nd Division, rose to its feet with a cheer, and, dressing in a line two miles wide, though only two men deep, marched towards the river. Under terrific fire – forty guns were trained on the river, and rifle bullets whipped the surface of the water into a bloody foam – the first British troops began to struggle across the Alma, the men so parched with thirst that even at this moment they stopped to drink . . . During the terrible crossing of the river formation was lost and it was a horde which surged up the bank and, formed by shouting, cursing officers into some ragged semblance of a line, pressed on up the deadly natural glacis towards the Great Redoubt. It seemed impossible that the slender, straggling line could survive . . . Again and again large gaps were torn in the line, the slopes became littered with bodies and sloppy with blood, but the survivors closed up and pressed on, their officers urging, swearing, yelling like demons.

The men's blood was up. The Light Division, heroes of a dozen stubborn and bloody battles in the Peninsula, advanced through the smoke, swearing most horribly as their comrades fell . . . suddenly, unbelievably the guns ceased to fire . . . the British troops gave a great shout, and in a last frantic rush a mob of mixed battalions tumbled into the earthwork. The Great Redoubt had been stormed.[7]

But, alas, the Duke of Cambridge's division with a brigade of Guards and the Highland Brigade, which should have been following up, had not moved from its position north of the river, allowing large numbers of Russians to take advantage of their own artillery bombardment, move forward and reoccupy the Great Redoubt. Thereupon the Guards and Highlanders, under terrible fire from cannon and rifles, advanced with the same steadiness as if taking part in a Hyde Park review. So heavy were the casualties suffered by the Grenadier and Coldstream Guards that one officer suggested to Sir Colin Campbell that they should retire or risk destruction. He received the magnificent reply that it would be better for every man of Her Majesty's Guards to lie dead on the field than for them to turn their backs on the enemy. Neither course of action was necessary, however, for not only did the Guards and Highlanders retake the Great Redoubt, they successfully repelled a further Russian infantry attack. As they charged forward the enemy fled, leaving the Allies in triumphant possession of the battlefield.

Now we come to the first great If of the Crimean campaign. If at this point the British cavalry, who were poised ready for pursuit, had been launched against the fleeing enemy, they could have inflicted frightful loss. Lucan and Cardigan were aching to do so. It was one of those rare opportunities which when seized lead on to triumphant success, but when neglected deliver only frustration and guilt. Yet Raglan positively forbade the pursuit. There could be but one reason for his doing so – the French refused to go further and Raglan dared not go on alone.[8] Had he been more forceful or decided to act with British troops only, he might have ended the campaign there and then, by capturing Sebastopol. As it was, the defeated Russians, totally unmolested, streamed into the city.

When we consider that the whole purpose of the Crimean campaign, as directed by the Allied Governments, was to take Sebastopol – and here as a result of the very first battle of the campaign, an absolutely heaven-sent chance of doing so presented itself, yet was not taken – we may perhaps sympathize with the outraged sentiments of Captain Nolan, 15th Hussars. A passionate advocate of cavalry's proper and aggressive use, Nolan burst into William Howard Russell's tent and gave vent to his sense of outrage – a thousand British cavalry contemplating a beaten, retreating army, complete with guns and colours, with nothing but a few wretched, cowardly Cossacks, ready to gallop away at the mere sound of a trumpet call, to dispute their passage, and nothing done: 'It is enough to drive one mad! It is too disgraceful, too infamous.'[9] The generals should be damned. We shall meet Captain Nolan again when another great chance, another great If, and another gross mishandling of cavalry occurred.

Having omitted to take this tide at the flood, Lord Raglan was obliged to put up with the shallows and the miseries of what was left of his life's voyage. It would not be for long and would lead to his humiliation and death. Instead of seizing Sebastopol the Allied armies made their ponderous way to the east and then the south of the city, giving the Russians time both to reinforce its defences and indeed to pour more troops into the Crimea. This new deployment of the British army emphasized the strategic importance of Balaklava, through whose port all the sinews of war had to come. It was the Russian attempt to capture it that resulted in the battle of Balaklava. On the morning of 25 October the British army was singularly ill deployed to meet and defeat this Russian attack. Apart from the 93rd Highlanders and about 1,000 Turks, the only troops between the port and General Liprandi's advancing force of 25,000 horse, foot and guns were the two brigades of the Cavalry Division, positioned some two miles north of Balaklava at the foot of the Fedioukine Heights.

The idea that chaos is a good umpire and chance a well-known governor of battles was well illustrated at Balaklava, for nothing could have been more chaotic or chancy. During the action of 25 October, Lord Lucan received four orders from Lord Raglan. Not one of them was either clear or properly understood. Each one was either too late to be executed as intended, violently resented by Lucan, ignored or so misinterpreted that the outcome was calamitous. We may perhaps comfort ourselves with the reflection that there was nothing unusual about this. Even today, with superlative communications when orders are transmitted from one level of command to another, their purpose and emphasis are subject to very different translation into action, for each commander has his own view of a battlefield, broad or narrow. Each has his own intention. No wonder they seldom coincide.

Raglan's first order to Lucan was: 'Cavalry to take ground to left of second line of Redoubts occupied by the Turks.' To execute the order, although he did so, was not merely distasteful to Lucan, for the very last thing cavalry was designed for was to take or hold ground, but, much more important, it was tactically dangerous, since moving to the Redoubts on the Causeway Heights, the cavalry would further isolate Sir Colin Campbell's small force of 500 Highlanders, the final defence of Balaklava itself. Thus at the very beginning of the action, we find Lucan totally unable to comprehend what his Commander-in-Chief had in mind. Indeed, from his point of view Raglan was guilty of a gross tactical error. We may perhaps discover the reason for this absolute discord when we remember that being in very different positions on the ground, the two men had very different conceptions of what was taking place. This perilous disparity of view was magnified by what happened next.

To those coolly sitting on their horses with Lord Raglan on the Sapouné Heights, the incident must at first have appeared to be an instance of that insolent indifference to danger which characterized many a British military operation in the nineteenth century. Later, it must have seemed more like culpable inactivity, and indeed it was only comprehensible when the contours of the ground beneath these onlookers were properly appreciated. A substantial body of Russian cavalry advancing to attack the Highlanders had seemed to pass within a few hundred yards of the British cavalry, now stationed where Raglan had ordered them, to the left of the second line of Redoubts. Yet although the Russian cavalry passed so close to Lucan's division, the two formations could not see each other, were not in fact aware of each other's proximity, simply because of the high ground between them, screening each from the other's view. Yet to Raglan and his staff looking down upon them, this mutual unawareness was not apparent. When the Russian cavalry then set about attacking the 93rd Highlanders, 'the slender red line' proved more than a match for the enemy squadrons. Three times the Russians came at then; three times they were repulsed by the disciplined steadiness and accurate fire-power of the 93rd. At one point Campbell had to quell his men's eagerness to charge with some fitting oath, but they had done the trick. The enemy withdrew.

Yet these half-dozen or so squadrons were but the vanguard of a much larger body of Russian cavalry which had followed them across the Causeway Heights. Perceiving this further threat, Raglan had issued his second order – indeed, had done so before the Highlanders' gallant action had been fought – and this order, 'Eight squadrons of Heavy Dragoons to be detached towards Balaklava to support the Turks who are wavering,' arrived too late to be executed in the way that Raglan had intended. In command of these Dragoon squadrons was Brigadier-General Scarlett, whose face was as red as his tunic, a brave and competent cavalryman who had won the respect and affection of his men for his unassuming and good-natured ways. He was now about to bring off 'one of the great feats of cavalry against cavalry in the history of Europe'.[10] As he led his eight squadrons, two each from 5th Dragoon Guards, Scots Greys, Inniskillings and 4th Dragoon Guards, towards Balaklava, with the Causeway Heights on their left, he observed on the slopes of these heights a huge mass of Russian horsemen. There were three or four thousand of them. Yet Scarlett with his mere 500 or so Dragoons was quite undismayed and coolly ordered his squadrons to wheel into line. It was at this point that Lucan arrived on the scene and ordered Scarlett to do what he was about to do anyway – charge the enemy. It was fortunate that the Russian cavalry came to a halt with the intention of throwing out two wings on their flanks in order to engulf and overwhelm

Scarlett's force. Thereupon Scarlett ordered his trumpeter to sound the charge.

Although the Light Brigade's action at Balaklava is more renowned, it was the Heavy Brigade's charge which was truly remarkable as a feat of arms.[11] In spite of the appalling disparity of numbers, the British cavalry enjoyed one great advantage. The Russian hordes were stationary, and it is an absolute maxim that cavalry should never be halted when receiving a charge but should be in motion. By remaining stationary, the Russians would sustain far more devastating a shock. For those surveying from the heights, what now transpired was breathtaking. Scarlett and his first line of three squadrons seemed to be positively swallowed up by the mass of grey-coated Russian cavalry, and although this enemy mass heaved and swayed, it did not break. Indeed, their two wings, in motion again now, began to wheel inwards to enclose and crush the three squadrons. But now Scarlett's second line took a hand in the game. The second squadrons of the Inniskillings and 5th Dragoon Guards flung themselves wildly into the fray on the left, while the Royals, who had not received orders to do so, but rightly acted with timely initiative, charged in on the right. There was further heaving and swaying by the Russians, but no sign yet of breaking.

No such initiative as that of the Royals was displayed by Lord Cardigan, who was about to be presented with the chance of a lifetime. He and his Brigade were a mere few hundred yards from the flank of the Russian cavalry, observing the action, most of them consumed with impatience, yet no thought of joining in the fray even occurred to Cardigan. The best he could do was to declare that 'These damned Heavies will have the laugh of us this day.' Any commander possessed of the real cavalry spirit would have been longing for the moment to arrive when his intervention would have been decisive. And this moment was about to come. Despite his dislike and contempt for his superior commander, Lord Lucan, Cardigan took refuge in his contention that he had been ordered to remain in position and to defend it against any enemy advance. It would have been far more in keeping with his custom to have ignored Lucan's order. Indeed, Lucan himself maintained that his instructions had included a positive direction that the Light Brigade was to attack 'anything and everything that shall come within reach of you'. There could be no gainsaying that the Russian cavalry, already reeling from the Heavy Brigade's assault, came within this category.

Action by the Light Brigade was about to become even more opportune and necessary, for it now became apparent that the Russian cavalry mass was recoiling, being pushed back, swaying uphill. Now was the moment for the *coup de grâce* and it was delivered by the 4th Dragoon Guards, who had been held in reserve and were now ordered to charge by Lucan. Crashing into the Russian right and charging head on, the regiment went right through the enemy force. 'The great Russian mass,' wrote Cecil Woodham-Smith, 'swayed, rocked, gave a gigantic heave, broke, and, disintegrating it seemed in a moment, fled.'[12] If ever there was a moment for pursuit to finish the thing off and write *finis* to the battle of Balaklava, it was now. If only Cardigan had seized this moment and charged then, the victory would have been complete and the Russian cavalry would not have been allowed to escape. But Cardigan was not a man to act without specific orders. Initiative, except in designing bizarre uniforms or ogling pretty women, was foreign to his nature. What Cardigan could not or would not see, others did, and urged him to act. Captain Morris, commanding the 17th Lancers, urgently pressed his brigade commander: 'My lord,' he said, 'it is our positive duty to follow up this advantage.'[13] Cardigan insisted that they must remain put. Morris further implored him to allow his own regiment to charge the enemy who were in such disorder. Cardigan was adamant. Furious and frustrated, Morris appealed to his fellow officers: 'Gentlemen, you are witnesses of my request.'[14] Cardigan's refusal to act was even more reprehensible than Grouchy's inactivity at Waterloo for he could at least see what was going on.

The moment passed, and the Russian cavalry, unmolested further and complete with their artillery, were allowed to establish themselves at the eastern end of the North Valley, guns unlimbered and ready for action. They would not have long to wait. Yet if the Charge of the Light Brigade had been enacted during the Russian disorder and flight, no such controlled movement would have been possible by the enemy. In short, the Russians would have been unable to redeploy at the eastern end of the North Valley, and thus there would have been no such objective for Raglan to concern himself with and about whose capture he was now to issue further wholly confusing orders. We may perhaps conclude this particular speculation by observing that had the Light Brigade charged when it should have done, the two actions of the Heavy and Light Brigades would have become one, and Alfred, Lord Tennyson would have had to confine himself to one poem rather than two.

Lord Raglan now set about the business of making confusion worse confounded. His third order was given when, as a result of the Heavy Brigade's action, the Russians recrossed the Causeway Heights and were to the north of them. Raglan determined to recapture the Redoubts, the Causeway Heights and the Woronzoff Road. To take and hold ground would, of course, demand infantry. The 1st Division was at hand, but the 4th Division, under command of a disgruntled, almost insubordinate Sir George Cathcart, was taking its time to get forward. Not wishing to lose his chance, Raglan conceived the idea of recovering the Heights with cavalry, who would then hand over to the infantry divisions. But Raglan's third order was once more a master-piece of ambiguity. Moreover, the version of it retained by him differed from that which reached Lucan. What Raglan had intended was that the cavalry should advance at once, recapture the Redoubts and control the Heights until the infantry came up. But the order which reached Lucan implied that he should wait until the infantry were there to support him before advancing. In other words Lucan's reading of the order – not to advance until supported by infantry – was the exact opposite of what Raglan intended. It was therefore with mounting impatience that Raglan gazed down at the action which Lucan did take – to mount the Cavalry Division, positioning the Light Brigade at the western end of the North Valley, while the Heavy Brigade was drawn up behind them on Woronzoff Road. Thus deployed, Lucan waited for the infantry.

Raglan, in his certainty that an advance by the cavalry would oblige the enemy to withdraw from the Redoubts, could not understand why Lucan made no move, and when he saw that parties of Russian artillerymen were preparing to take their guns away from the Redoubts, his agitation knew no bounds. It was then that Raglan sent out the fatally misunderstood fourth and last order to Lucan. It read: 'Lord Raglan wishes the Cavalry to advance rapidly to the front – follow the enemy and try to prevent the enemy carrying away the guns. Troop Horse Artillery may accompany. French cavalry is on your left. Immediate.' This order had been written out by General Airey from Raglan's instructions. We have seen that lack of precision in the third order resulted in its not being carried out. If it had been clear and executed as intended by Lucan, the fourth order would never have been needed. Yet here with this fourth order we see again that a precise word or two substituted for an imprecise phrase would have removed all ambiguity. What 'to the front' means to one man is very different from what it means to another. Had Raglan so phrased the order that it clearly complemented his previous one, the one relating specifically to the Causeway Heights, as he meant it to, how differently Lucan would have read it. Had it said, 'Cavalry to advance to the Causeway Heights to prevent enemy carrying away the guns from the Redoubts,' Lucan would have been in no doubt as to what his Commander-in-Chief wanted.

This is the first great If which could have prevented the Noble Six Hundred from riding into the Valley of Death. The second is that if only any aide-de-camp other than Captain Nolan of the 15th Hussars had carried the order to Lucan, there might have been some chance of Lucan's realizing what Raglan actually intended. As it was, Nolan, who had endured agonies of humiliation and frustration at the Light Brigade's inexplicable inactivity when so splendid and classic an opportunity following the Heavy Brigade's charge had presented itself, was given the task. Moreover, Raglan aggravated both the imprecision of his order and the furious impetuosity of Captain Nolan by calling out to him as he rode off, 'Tell Lord Lucan the cavalry is to attack at once.'

To Lord Lucan this new written order, which he regarded as quite unrelated to the previous one, was not merely obscure, it was crazy. The only guns that he could see were those at the eastern end of the North Valley – *to his front*. For cavalry to attack batteries of guns frontally and alone was to contravene every tactical principle and to invite destruction. As Lucan read and re-read the order with mounting consternation, Nolan, almost beside himself at Lucan's apparent reluctance to take immediate and decisive action, repeated in tones of arrogant contempt the Commander-in-Chief's urgent postscript that the Cavalry should attack at once. Small wonder that Lucan should have burst out angrily, 'Attack, sir? Attack what? What guns, sir? Where and what to do?' It was then that Nolan threw away the last chance of the operation going according to plan. With a furious gesture but, alas, one fatally lacking in proper direction, he pointed, or appeared to point, at the very guns that Lucan could see, those at the end of the North Valley, accompanying his gesture with words full of insolence and empty of precision: 'There, my lord, is your enemy, there are your guns!'

Here we may pause for an instant and insert another If. If only, at that very last moment, Nolan had curbed his frantic impatience and calmly explained to Lucan that the guns in question were those on the Redoubts and that therefore the Light Brigade must advance to the Causeway Heights, all might yet have gone well.[15] But after this ill-tempered exchange, Nolan rode over to Captain Morris, 17th Lancers, and asked if he might ride with the Regiment. Morris agreed. Meanwhile, Lucan had passed on the order to Lord Cardigan. Even Cardigan felt obliged to point out that the valley was commanded by guns not only to the front, but to the right and left as well. Lucan acknowledged his objection, but insisted that it was the Commander-in-Chief's wish and that there was no choice but to obey.

Thus the position when Cardigan deployed his brigade in readiness to advance was that the Russians occupied the Fedioukine Heights with horse, foot and guns, and the Causeway Heights including the 1st, 2nd and 3rd Redoubts with infantry and guns. At the head, that is, the eastern end, of North Valley were twelve Russian guns and behind them their main body of cavalry. About a mile and a half away, at the western end of the valley, was the Light Brigade. By this time the British infantry had come up, the 1st Division occupying ground held by the 93rd Highlanders, while the 4th Division was in the area of the 4th Redoubt. After receiving his orders from Lucan,

Cardigan rode over to speak to Colonel Lord George Paget, commanding the 4th Light Dragoons, who was to command the second line of the brigade. Cardigan told Paget that he would expect his best support. Paget had been enjoying a 'remarkably good' cigar while Nolan and Lucan had their angry exchange, and when he heard Colonel Shewell of the 8th Hussars reprimanding his men for smoking their pipes – in Shewell's words, 'disgracing the Regiment by smoking in the presence of the enemy' – he could not but wonder whether he was disgracing his regiment with his cigar. 'Am I to set this bad example?' he asked himself. A good cigar, however, was no 'common article in those days' and he determined to keep it. The 4th Light Dragoons had a reputation to maintain. They were known as 'Paget's Irregular Horse', and the cigar lasted until the charge was over.

It might be supposed that Lucan had already contributed enough to the day's work, but even now he interfered further. Cardigan had placed three regiments, the 13th Light Dragoons, 17th Lancers and 11th Hussars, in the front line, while the second line had the 8th Hussars and 4th Light Dragoons. Lucan ordered Colonel Douglas, commanding 11th Hussars, Cardigan's own regiment, to drop back to a position supporting the front line. As the charge proceeded Paget, conscious of Cardigan's insistence on his best support, had brought the 4th Light Dragoons up to the left of the 11th Hussars, thus forming a new second line, with the 8th Hussars to the right rear. 'Walk march. Trot:' Cardigan gave the order. His trumpeter sounded 'March'. The charge was on. Captain Portal, 4th Light Dragoons, recalled later that they had ridden only a quarter of a mile, galloping now, when the most fearful fire opened on them from both sides, dealing death and destruction in the ranks. They kept going, did their work among the enemy guns, which with support – of which there was none – they could have brought back with them, and then retired in good order, still at the gallop and again through murderous crossfire. Neither Portal nor anyone else seeing what had to be done thought that those still alive after the charge would ever get back.

One of the 8th Hussars, Lieutenant Calthorpe, who was serving on the staff and did not take part in the charge, observed it all, his own regiment and the others thundering along the valley at an awful pace, unchecked by the fearful slaughter, disregarding all but their objective, rendering havoc amongst the enemy's artillery. This was the time, Calthorpe recorded, when the brigade commander should have rallied his men, gripped the situation and given the necessary orders. But according to Calthorpe, Cardigan's horse took fright, wheeled round and galloped back down the valley. Calthorpe was mistaken here. Neither Cardigan nor his charger had taken fright. Indeed, perhaps the most remarkable aspect of the whole affair was Cardigan's absolute indifference to the hazards of the charge or the fate of his brigade once it had charged. He evaded some threatening Cossacks by galloping back through the enemy guns, and judging his duty now done, calmly rode back down the valley.

It was left to the combined efforts of Paget and Shewell to take control and salvage what was left of the Light Brigade. As the Brigade charged home, the leading lines of the 13th Light Dragoons and 17th Lancers suffered terrible casualties as the guns in front of them opened fire. Those surviving, about fifty, galloped through the guns, sabres and lances at work, and on to rout some Russian Hussars, until they were checked by numerous Cossacks. Then the 11th Hussars came right through the guns in pursuit of fleeing enemy Lancers. Paget was leading the 4th Light Dragoons at full gallop on to the enemy gunners, and to their right the 8th Hussars under the iron hand of Colonel Shewell went through the battery and pulled up on the far side. Now the survivors faced a double threat, from a huge body of enemy cavalry in front and from six squadrons of Russian Lancers who had descended from the Fedioukine Heights, endangering their withdrawal. In the absence of Cardigan, Paget rallied the 4th Light Dragoons and 11th Hussars, charged towards the enemy Lancers and brushed past them. Shewell did the same with seventy troopers, and the retreat, worse by far than the charge itself, began. Mrs Duberley, wife of the 8th Hussar paymaster, observing pitiful groups of men making their way back down the valley and realizing who they were, exclaimed: 'Good God! It is the Light Brigade.'

One of Paget's comments on the bearing of riderless horses during the charge itself is revealing and shows what terror these noble creatures could feel without the reassuring presence of their riders:

They made dashes at me, some advancing with me a considerable distance . . . cringing in on me, and positively squeezing me, as the round shot came bounding by them, tearing up the earth under their noses . . . I remarked their eyes, betokening as keen a sense of the perils around them as we human beings experienced . . . The bearing of the horse I was riding, in contrast to these, was remarkable. He had been struck, but showed no signs of fear . . . And so, on we went through this scene of carnage, wondering each moment which would be our last.[16]

'Then they rode back, but not Not the six hundred', wrote Tennyson. Someone had blundered all right, but who was it? Was Lord Raglan justified in accusing Lord Lucan, 'You have lost the Light Brigade'? When things go right in a battle, there is no shortage of those claiming credit for it. When things go awry, the number who step forward as candiates for recognition tends to be smaller. We may recall that during the battle of Balaklava, Raglan issued four orders. None of them was precise. None of them was properly understood. None of them was executed in the way that had been intended. The whole affair may be regarded as a series of unfortunate chances, preceded, however, by one golden chance, one unique opportunity, one classic moment for decision, which if taken, seized and exploited would have ended the battle on a note of triumph for the British cavalry in particular and the British army in general. This moment was, of course, when the Russian cavalry was fleeing from the Heavy Brigade's charge, and the Light Brigade failed to turn the dismayed enemy flight into absolute rout. Then, with the aid of the advancing infantry divisions, Raglan could have inflicted such a defeat on the Russian forces at Balaklava that they might have lost stomach for a continued campaign there and then. Sebastopol would have fallen and the Crimean War would have been over.

But given that this chance was lost, we must remember the other less welcome chances – the chance position of Raglan from which he and his staff were quite unable to appreciate what Lucan could or could not see; the chance of his totally inadequate orders, which did not define either line of advance or object of attack; the further chance of Raglan's not making it clear that the cavalry was to move at once, not to wait for the infantry to arrive; and the chance of choosing

Nolan of all men to deliver both the written order and the further urging of Lucan to attack at once. If all or any of these blunders had not been committed, the Light Brigade would have prevented the guns from being removed from the Redoubts and the battle could have proceeded with the infantry's arrival. It was not only Lucan who had lost the Light Brigade, although he must bear heavy responsibility. Between them all – Raglan, Airey, Lucan, Cardigan, Nolan – they saw to it that chance governed all and that chaos umpired the whole sorry business.

It is to the Noble Six Hundred that we must give the accolade. Riding back down the valley at the rear of what was left of the 4th Light Dragoons and the 11th Hussars, Paget noted the last mile strewn with dead and dying, all of them friends, some of them limping or crawling back, horses in agony, struggling to rise, only to flounder again on their mutilated riders. It had been, in Cardigan's words, 'a mad-brained trick', but all the regiments of the Light Brigade had covered themselves with glory. Even in 'the jaws of death' discipline had been superb in completing the business of 'sabring the gunners there'. Some of those who rode back even told Cardigan that they were ready to go again.

Honour the Light Brigade! Magnificent, but not war. This was a French observer's judgement. The French were reliable and competent Allies in 1854. Not so in 1940.

SIX

May–June 1940:
Disaster and Deliverance

Of course, whatever happens at Dunkirk, we shall fight on.

WINSTON CHURCHILL, 28 MAY 1940

I have said earlier that those of us fortunate enough to have fought in a major battle – and survived – know only too well how chance can turn the scales and chaos can gild the scene. We know too that when it comes to combat, its essential elements do not change. Throughout the history of war they have been and still are fire-power, movement and signalling. The need for those involved in battle to move about, control and apply agents of violence in order to dismay or dismember an adversary persists. What does change is method, for method is conditioned by the change in agents of violence. The Führer of the Third Reich and Commander-in-Chief of the Wehrmacht, Adolf Hitler, understood this, and as early as 1932, before coming to power, declared:

The next war will be quite different from the last world war. Infantry attacks and mass formations are obsolete. Interlocked frontal struggles lasting for years on petrified fronts will not return. I guarantee that. We shall regain the superiority of free operations.[1]

In the event Hitler more than lived up to that promise. That he did so was in large measure due to the efforts of two men – von Seeckt and Guderian.

General von Seeckt was Commander-in-Chief of the 100,000-strong Reichswehr from 1920 to 1926, and during these years he imbued it with two priceless qualities concerned essentially with the winning of battles. The first was leadership, the second tactical doctrine. In forming and training the Reichswehr, he set out to create an army not of mercenaries, but of leaders. He trained his majors and colonels so that later they could command divisions, his lieutenants and captains so that they could command battalions and regiments. Each sergeant and corporal was ready to become an officer, each private and trooper an NCO. At one time, out of the total 100,000 men, nearly half were NCOs. Seeckt's great achievement was to preserve the kernel of a greatly expanded army within the nutshell of a tiny restricted one. Moreover, he virtually outflanked and evaded the Allied purpose of doing away with the great German General Staff, which had been specifically outlawed by the Treaty of Versailles.

He did even more. All the military training pamphlets were rewritten not merely so that they could serve a rearmed and powerful German Reich, but in accordance with a principle which had in the past shown itself to be fundamental to successful military operations, and was to do so again with even greater effect. This principle laid down that all the important fighting arms must be closely integrated. Here was the seed which later gave birth to the mixed panzer groups and teamwork so indispensable to mobile warfare, and which proved so invincible in action. There was nothing really new in it. Co-operation of horse, foot and guns had long been a principle of tactics. At Marengo in 1800, as we have recorded, the timely, point-blank discharge of cannon by Marmont at the Austrian grenadiers, coming almost simultaneously with Desaix's advancing infantry and Kellermann's flank charge with a handful of heavy dragoons, had turned defeat into victory. Yet the lesson had been forgotten or submerged in the mud of Flanders. In spite of piecemeal tank, infantry and artillery cooperation in the First World War, the need for this process to be a continuous one had been neglected. Seeckt restored this battle technique to its rightful place, and insisted that mechanized cavalry, infantry and artillery should not merely work as one, but should enjoy the intimate support of new weapons such as anti-tank guns and aircraft as well.

This system of mixed groups, of highly trained teams, which brought together the three elements of combat, fire, movement and signalling in the most effective and most rapidly exploitable way, was to be a consistent thread in the creation of a new Wehrmacht, and was to pay high dividends. It was in fact to form the basis of all Hitler's great battles of conquest, and would prolong his capacity for resistance far beyond what a simple comparison of numbers might have been expected to produce. Seeckt's vision was based partly on his own experience of the Great War, partly on influences from abroad and from within his own Reichswehr. Indeed, the development of his ideas by some of his subordinates was such that they themselves were later to lead the Panzergruppen to their most spectacular successes. Seeckt believed ardently in mobility, rapid movement and the need to restore superiority of the attack by grand, sweeping operations which would engulf, paralyse and annihilate the defending forces. What would matter in future warfare, he argued in 1921, was the use of relatively small but highly skilled mobile armies in cooperation with aircraft.

The fertility of his ideas was not wasted on barren soil. Among the officers who took up Seeckt's ideas and developed them further was the man who later became a panzer leader of the first order – Guderian. Unlike some other great tactical commanders, he was generous in acknowledging the source of his principal designs. He paid tribute to the writings of Fuller, Martel and Liddell Hart, in particular the latter's emphasis on using armoured forces for long-range strokes, operations against the opposing army's communications, and creating a type of division which contained panzer and panzer-infantry units. To get the most out of tanks, Guderian insisted, you had to use them in mass and move them so fast that they reached the enemy's main defence zone before the guns there could effectively intervene; in the same way the enemy's tanks, attempting to counter this penetration, must be stopped, either by overwhelming them with superior armoured forces or by using tactical air forces, which must provide close support for the armour. The secret of the whole concept lay in expanding initial depth on a relatively narrow front to a combination of depth and width, thus disrupting the entire enemy defensive zone. Guderian summed up the essentials of decisive panzer attack as being 'suitable terrain, surprise and mass deployment in the necessary width and depth'.[2]

In short, Guderian's ideas were revolutionary and as such instantly appealed to Hitler when he saw Guderian's tank prototypes and heard him expound his tactical theories. A single gigantic attack on a demoralized enemy who would succumb at the first stroke: this was Hitler's way of waging war. Not only would he hurl himself upon the enemy 'like a flash of lightning'[3] but both force and fraud (the cardinal virtues in war) would be on unprecedented scales. In the air they would be supreme. A single blow would do the business, overwhelming attacks on every weak point, stupendous in their effect, a 'gigantic all-destroying blow'.[4] Such was the theory of Blitzkrieg. In September 1939 it was put into practice, and its principles – surprise, speed, concentration – were totally vindicated. The campaign in Poland was over in a matter of weeks. Now Hitler could turn his attention to the West. Indeed, no sooner was the Polish affair over than he began goading his generals to prepare for an all-out attack on the Western Allies. His directive read: 'An offensive will be planned on the northern flank of the Western front, through Luxembourg, Belgium and Holland. This offensive must be launched at the earliest possible moment and in the greatest possible strength.'

Hitler's confidence in the success of such an offensive was reinforced by his placing, as he put it, 'a low value on the French Army's will to fight . . . After the first setbacks it will swiftly crack up.' This view was shared by one of the British Expeditionary Force's corps commanders, Alan Brooke, who was later to become so staunch and sound a CIGS. Brooke found little comfort in the security of the Maginot Line. If it broke, he suspected, the French fighting spirit might break too. Brooke's confidence was unlikely to be restored by contemplating the command arrangements and tactical ideas of the French Commander-in-Chief, General Gamelin: Gamelin was incapable of exercising command from his remote headquarters at Vincennes, which did not even have radio communications. Moreover, he completely ignored what had happened in Poland, believing that it could not possibly happen in France. The whole concept of Blitzkrieg was dismissed or miscomprehended. Having thus closed their eyes to tactical realities, the French High Command proceeded to do the same with the strategic ones. A German attack was most likely to come through Belgium. The invasion must therefore be met there. When General George, commanding the North-eastern Front, realized that Gamelin intended to commit the bulk of his strength to the Low Countries, he protested strongly that to do so would dangerously weaken the central part of the front.

Then in January 1940 an event occurred which proved decisive, one of those chances on which the fortunes of war depend. On 10 January Hitler had given orders that the plan to invade Belgium and Holland, Fall Gelb, should be launched one week later. The following day, however, it was made known that a Luftwaffe major in a light aircraft had strayed across the Belgian frontier at Mechelen, and documents giving details of this operation had been captured by the Belgians. This event had the effect of putting Gamelin's doubts to rest and confirmed his proposed deployment to meet just such a threat. Initially the effect on Hitler was rather surprising – he did not change his plans, but a bad weather report made him decide to cancel the whole offensive until the spring. Meanwhile, other influences were at work. Given that there was now time for the German General Staff to think again, the ideas of von Manstein, then Chief of Staff to von Rundstedt, Commander of Army Group A, began to gain ground. Von Manstein's proposals sprang from his conviction that a main thrust in the north against what was expected to be a powerful Allied defence could not lead to decisive victory. By shifting the main weight further south, however, it might be possible to penetrate *behind* the Allied defences in Belgium. It was the difference between pushing against maximum opposition and cutting it off at the roots, as a sickle does with corn.[5] Quite apart from the capture of the top-secret documents at Mechelen, which gave him cause for further reflection, Hitler had been thinking along similar lines, and when he listened to von Manstein's theories, which coincided with his own penchant for surprise, boldness, risk, sudden, unexpected, hammer-like blows, paralysing in their strength and velocity, he seized upon them with rapt enthusiasm. Thus with the Allied deployment based on a strong right flank formed by the Maginot Line, a strong left flank for the Dyle-Breda position, and a weak centre opposite the Belgian Ardennes, with nothing much behind it, everything was set for a change of plan.

'What a standing temptation,' observed Alistair Horne, 'the spectacle of this French line, so weak in the centre, might present to an opposing captain of audacity and genius.'[6]

But what if the documents had *not* fallen into enemy hands? Two questions emerge. First, would this have made any difference to Hitler's plans? Second, would it have changed Gamelin's? In Hitler's case it may be doubtful, for bad weather alone had obliged him to call off the offensive until the spring, so that there were months of rethinking ahead and plenty of time for the far bolder, imaginative, potentially decisive plan of von Manstein to work its magic on the Führer. The sheer beauty of the notion of bursting like a thunderbolt through the French centre and thereby destroying their entire Army had an irresistible appeal to the Führer's vision of Blitzkrieg, of a 'gigantic all-destroying blow'. And as the plan matured from the broad ideas of its architect, von Manstein, with the fervent backing of von Rundstedt, whose Army Group A would be required to execute it, even Halder, Chief of General Staff, once he was convinced – and this took some time – of its soundness brought all the thoroughness and excellence of his organizing powers to its support. Above all, Hitler, as Supreme Commander of the Wehrmacht, was the ultimate arbiter and accepted full responsibility for it. So it seems likely that whether the documents had been lost or not, *Sichelschnitt* would have gone ahead.

What about Gamelin? Capture of the documents merely confirmed his preconceived belief that the German attack would be a kind of repetition of the Schlieffen Plan, a violation of the neutrality of Belgium and Holland, then sweeping through to northern France. What may surprise us today is that it did not apparently occur to Gamelin that sudden possession of the German operational plan might not constitute part of a gigantic piece of bluff and that a German attack on the Low Countries might be no more than a secondary affair, a mere diversion to facilitate a main thrust breaking out in the French centre between the Meuse and Moselle. It was this very possibility that was of such concern to General Georges, who feared that by committing so much strength to the Low Countries, there would be no adequate reserves left to deal with a German attack in the centre. Georges might have been reiterating Hamlet's cry at his father's ghost's revelation, 'O my prophetic soul!'

Without the captured documents, which seemed to remove Gamelin's doubts, the question therefore becomes: would Georges have been able to persuade his Commander-in-Chief to strengthen the French centre, perhaps making use of the British Expeditionary Force, whose fighting spirit, despite lack of really effective tanks and anti-tank guns, was not in doubt? Let us say that there was fundamental reassessment of Allied strategy and that instead of stringing out their forces along the front, with no depth, no proper reserves, no plans for counter-penetration and all the means to go with it – movement, concentration, coordination, a substantial armoured counter-attack force of all arms with powerful air support – the French and British High Commands had anticipated the dangers of a powerful armoured attack supported by the Luftwaffe with its *Schwerpunkt* in the centre and amongst other contingencies have prepared for it. Then we get the fascinating picture of a German offensive which bogs down, is halted and subjected to all the fire-power from both ground and air weapons which the Allies can bring to bear. In turn doubts arise as to the Führer's intuition, his *Vorhersehung*, his military and political genius, in short his leadership and right to hold the position of Supreme Commander of the Wehrmacht. Then, if ever, would have been the time for the German army's generals, many of whom had long opposed Hitler's policies but had been silenced by his string of blood-less victories, to have turned against him and brought off some kind of *coup*. A largish If, but not wholly inconceivable. As it was, how-ever, *Sichelschnitt* succeeded beyond all expectations, and we must now turn to the Ifs arising from its success. For although this success brought with it the fruits of victory – no more doubts by the generals as to Hitler's strategy, his tactical instinct, political intuition or inexor-able will-power – even *Sichelschnitt* revealed a major tactical error and contained a fatal strategic flaw. It all began on 10 May 1940.

In essence, of course, the plan worked. The main thrust of Army Group A to the Meuse and beyond was overwhelmingly successful. Guderian's corps poured through a hole made in the French line, demonstrating how peerless were panzer and Stuka in harness. In ten days German spearheads reached Abbéville, and Boulogne three days later. On 27 May Belgium capitulated. British forces, sandwiched between Army Groups A and B, fell back on Dunkirk. The Germans set about finishing off the French, who surrendered on 16 June. Yet the campaign had not been without its hiccups. On 16 May, when Guderian, having crossed the Meuse, was preparing to expand his bridgehead into a huge gap and flood through with his panzers to the Channel, he was astonished and dismayed to receive orders from von Kleist – orders which had originated with Hitler – to halt the advance until the infantry came up. Hitler had become concerned about Guderian's flanks and the danger of a counter-attack against them from the south, and his behaviour at Münstereifel, Führer HQ, was hardly that of a commander confident in his own orders and in those subordinates carrying them out. Excitable, talkative and always ready to blame others, it seemed that the self-styled 'hardest man in centuries' had lost his nerve, not because things were going wrong, but at a time when they were going superlatively well. Halder recalled the Hitler was terribly nervous, frightened by his own success, afraid to take chances, and worried about the south flank, accusing his staff of ruining the whole campaign. He would not countenance a continuance of the operation westwards.

In taking this line Hitler was missing the central point of all that Guderian had for so long been trying to persuade the sceptics – that once a panzer thrust had got going, it must maintain momentum day and night. It must never halt, to be located, checked, counter-attacked. The enemy must be continuously subjected to unexpected, ever-deepening, ever-broadening thrusts, disrupting reserves, communications, headquarters, supply areas, a never-ending yet ever more paralysing flow of integrated panzer, motor infantry and artillery groups, with the Stukas and transport aircraft to keep them supported and supplied. All this was fundamental. Fortunately for the progress of the campaign, after a good many threats, 'resignations' and interventions, Guderian was permitted to carry out further reconnaissance in force, and this was all he needed. Such reconnaissance is open to all sorts of interpretation, and by 18 May his panzers reached St-Quentin; the following day they were forcing the

Somme; on 20 May Guderian himself was on the outskirts of Amiens, watching 1st Panzer Division's attack; the day after that units of 2nd Panzer Division were at the Atlantic coast.

What General Gamelin had said could not happen had caused the complete disintegration of the French 9th Army under General Corap, which was unfortunate enough to find itself in the path of von Rundstedt's *Schwerpunkt*. The French resistance leader and author, Vercors, summed it all up when he described the sombre epic of a wholesale retreat towards Dunkirk as an immeasurable disaster: 'The French Army was smashed to pieces, cut to shreds by the tanks, nailed to the ground by the enemy's Stukas. A hundred miles from the front dazed soldiers were streaming back.'[7] Why had this happened? The truth was that the German superiority, not in numbers where they were slightly inferior, but in leadership, training, tactics and morale, was overwhelming. The Allied forces were no match for, simply had no chance against, fast, integrated, Luftwaffe-supported and Luftwaffe-supplied armoured columns which struck hard and deep into Allied territory.

It was fortunate for Hitler that his interference in the tactical handling of von Rundstedt's Army Group by giving orders on 16 May to halt Guderian's panzers did not have serious consequences. Later that month, however, his influence on the battle was to have a profound effect. There has always been much controversy concerning the halting of von Rundstedt's panzers on 24 May, at a time when the British Expeditionary Force was still vulnerable to encirclement and capture. There are in fact several versions of the story. The key to it all is Hitler's hand in the game. On 23 May von Kluge, Commander of 4th Army, with the bulk of the Panzer Divisions, proposed to von Rundstedt that his formations should halt and close up. Von Rundstedt, convinced that the Allied armies were trapped, with his own Army Group well placed to be the anvil and von Bock's, from the north, the hammer, agreed. 4th Army's War Diary records that the Army 'will, in the main, halt tomorrow [24 May] in accordance with Colonel-General von Rundstedt's order'. If this were so, it is clear that the order was given by the Army Group Commander, not by Hitler, who, it was maintained, endorsed the order when he visited von

Rundstedt on 24 May. Yet as Chester Wilmot has asserted,[8] the records kept by Halder and Jodl at Supreme HQ contend that the halt order originated with Hitler, a point later confirmed by von Rundstedt himself. Amidst this controversy one thing was clear – the various generals concerned disagreed widely.

Von Brauchitsch, Army Commander-in-Chief, protested that von Bock's nearest forces were thirty-five miles from Dunkirk, whereas von Rundstedt's were a mere fifteen miles away. It was therefore for von Rundstedt to continue the advance and close the trap. Wait for von Bock and the British army would escape. But Hitler had his eye on defeating the French army. Destroy it and he would be master of Europe. Thus von Brauchitsch's recommendation that 4th Army should be put under the command of von Bock, who would then continue the attack from east, south and north, was not taken up. Neither Halder nor von Rundstedt supported the idea. Whether Hitler *initiated* the order to halt or not is thus less important than his failure to see that in this instance the immediate military objective, Dunkirk, was of far greater ultimate significance than the political prize of Paris. Hitler was overlooking Guderian's great lesson that the one thing he, as Supreme Commander, must not allow to happen was for the panzers to halt. The command arrangements were secondary. He should have made certain with the supreme tactical powers he wielded that the drive went on until the enemy's annihilation was complete. No matter what other orders had been given, he should have overruled them. As it was, the British army escaped to fight again.

But what if Hitler had insisted on a continued drive to cut off the British army, resulting in no evacuation from Dunkirk? As it was, 337,000 British and French soldiers escaped. What would we have done without them? It was all very well for Churchill to say with characteristic defiance that no matter what happened at Dunkirk, we would fight on. What with? The Royal Navy and Royal Air Force would no doubt have continued to defend our shores and skies, but how would the army have fared? We will do well to recall what Churchill himself was doing and saying at this critical time.

Well before the extent of the Dunkirk evacuation's success was known, Churchill was giving tongue to both his defiance and his confidence. On 28 May, after the Belgian surrender and when only some 14,000 men had got away from Dunkirk, he reported the gravity of the situation to the House of Commons, and then declared:

I have only to add that nothing which may happen in this battle can in any way relieve us of our duty to defend the world cause to which we have vowed ourselves, nor should it destroy our confidence in our power to make our way, as on former occasions in our history, through disaster and through grief to the ultimate defeat of our enemies.

After this speech, Churchill held two meetings in his room in the House of Commons, both gatherings remarkable for the effect that he had on his colleagues. At the first, attended by just the other four members of the War Cabinet, they discussed the question of whether negotiations with Germany should even be contemplated. Chamberlain and Halifax suggested that they might, while Churchill himself emphatically disagreed, as indeed did Attlee and Greenwood. That Britain, under Churchill's leadership, should fight on no matter what happened was powerfully endorsed by the meeting which immediately followed, and which was attended by all other ministers, twenty-five of them. Having explained that Germany would probably take Paris and then offer some terms for peace, and that Italy would be likely to join in the war on the German side, also offering terms, Churchill stated that there was no doubt that they must decline anything like that and fight on. The Prime Minister's performance was regarded by those present as magnificent. Churchill next gave an account of all that was happening, explaining that the British Expeditionary Force would fight its way to the coast and evacuate as many of its men as possible. Fifty thousand should certainly get away; twice that number would be better than anyone dared hope. Dunkirk was the only port left. Churchill would now have to prepare the British people for bad news. The war would come to these islands; the enemy would attempt an invasion, although that would be difficult, made more so by British defensive measures. He went on to say that having thought carefully about the question of negotiating with Hitler, he had concluded that we should not get better terms now than if we fought it out. German terms would rob us of our fleet and naval bases. A British Government would be a puppet. On the other hand, Britain had immense reserves and advantages.

Who can doubt therefore that even if only 50,000 British soldiers, or fewer, had been evacuated from Dunkirk, Churchill, whose words had been greeted with the most enthusiastic acclaim by his ministers, and who went on to inspire both the House of Commons and the nation with his 'Finest Hour' speech, would have lived up to his pledge delivered to the French Prime Minister, Reynaud, and his colleagues on 11 June: 'Whatever happens here, we are resolved to fight on and on for ever and ever and ever'?[9] Even given that in the event, most of the British Expeditionary Force was saved, there was no disguising the magnitude of the disaster – nearly all the BEF's guns, tanks and other equipment had been lost. Their replacement and the reorganization and training of the British army would take time. But happily, time in this particular instance sided with the British, for the catastrophe of the battle for France had revealed a major flaw in Hitler's strategy.

Apart from the tactical error of halting the panzers on 24 May, *Sichelschnitt* was strategically incomplete, for it made no provision for finishing off England after defeating the French army. We may perhaps understand why. Hitler seemed to have convinced himself that because he had no quarrel with Britain – provided he was given a free hand in Europe – Britain would make peace. If this were not so – again he was deluding himself – he had outlined air and sea measures which would strangle the island. One thing was quite plain. It would be impossible to plan for total victory without first arranging to destroy the Royal Navy and the RAF. Thus, quite apart from Churchill's resolution and what he called 'a white glow, overpowering, sublime, which ran through our island from end to end', there were further more practical reasons for arguing that even if a substantial part of the British Expeditionary Force had been captured by a continued panzer drive, there would have been strong military reasons for continuing the struggle. British naval and air forces would presumably have been even stronger, not having sustained the losses they did at Dunkirk, during which the RAF had lost nearly 500 aircraft and the Royal Navy six destroyers, with a further nineteen damaged. Why should a Battle of Britain fought in June 1940 have been lost, when the Luftwaffe was at the limit of its operational and administrative resources, when it was so convincingly won three months later after the Luftwaffe had had time to recuperate and reorganize?

From Britain's point of view it was one thing to avoid defeat, another to inflict it. Churchill had made it known that wars are not won by evacuations. Where then could British forces best inflict damage on the Axis? The answer was not hard to find. No sooner had Italy declared war on Britain than Britain, taking the declaration more seriously than the country which had made it, began to employ her forces in the Mediterranean and Middle East to harass Italy. The Mediterranean Fleet soon established its ascendancy over the Italian Navy, while the Desert Rats began to plague Graziani's 10th Army. This activity did not greatly harm the principal foe. Only the Royal Navy and Royal Air Force could do that. But North Africa was at this time the only theatre of operations where Great Britain could engage the enemy on land, and before long she would be engaging the panzers and Stukas too.

Churchill therefore began to build up Wavell's forces in the Middle East, particularly with armoured formations. Whether he would have been able to do so quite so soon or in such numbers had the Dunkirk affair not gone so well must be in question, but his boldness in doing it at all when the threat of invasion still hung over our islands must be applauded. Initially Churchill saw his Middle East forces' strategic use as defensive, at any rate to start with in view of Italy's huge numerical superiority of ground troops, whereas Wavell was thinking far more boldly and was contemplating 'such measures of offence as will enable us and our Allies to dominate the Mediterranean at the earliest possible moment; and thereafter take the offensive against Germany in Eastern or SE Europe'.[10] Herein lay the kernel of the entire Mediterranean strategy, which Churchill was to embrace so fervently and which was to have so profound an effect on the strategic policy of the Grand Alliance.

Napoleon, it will be recalled, had jibbed at the idea of a direct assault upon England. Too risky. Instead he would go to Egypt and there strike a shrewd blow. It was something that Hitler never quite saw, even though some of his advisers pressed him hard to understand how vital the Middle East was. If it may be said that Hitler missed his first chance of winning the war outright by not planning the overthrow of France *and* Britain in 1940, he was to be presented with a second chance, and then even a third, to paralyse British resistance and opportunity in 1941 and 1942.

SEVEN

The Peg on Which All Else Hung

When Göring was asked by Ivone Kirkpatrick[1] in June 1945 what Germany's greatest mistake was, he replied: 'Not invading Spain and North Africa in 1940.'

There are two great rules of strategy which have endured throughout history. Each is dependent on the other. The first is to select your primary object correctly. This is the master rule. The second rule is so to concentrate and deploy your forces that you achieve the object. From 1941 onwards these rules were honoured by Hitler more in the breach than in the observance. That Hitler was faced with a strategic dilemma after his direct attack on England had failed is not to be denied. It was in failing also to comprehend where the war's centre of gravity had shifted to, where the true line of operations lay, that Hitler contravened the two great strategic principles. Had he considered the whole situation, not only from his own point of view, but from the British position too, he might have come to a different conclusion.

Even before the Battle of Britain, whereas Churchill with, of course, a much simpler strategic aim – that of survival – was clear as to what had to be done, Hitler was confusing the issue with reasoning, which might be politically comprehensible but was militarily flawed. Thus we find Churchill making one of his most memorable speeches in the House of Commons, a speech which was later broadcast to the nation. It was 18 June 1940:

Hitler knows that he will have to break us in this island or lose the war. If we can stand up to him, all Europe may be free, and the life of the world may move forward into broad, sunlit uplands . . . Let us therefore brace ourselves to our duty and so bear ourselves that if the British Empire and its Commonwealth lasts for a thousand years men still will say. 'This was their finest hour.'

Look here upon this picture and on this. Hitler was certainly conscious of the need to subdue Britain. Yet in his arguments to his Commanders-in-Chief a month after Churchill's peroration, in July 1940, the Führer turned the priorities upside down:

In the event that invasion does not take place, our efforts must be directed to the elimination of all factors that let England hope for a change in the situation . . . Britain's hope lies in Russia and the United States. If Russia drops out of the picture, America, too, is lost for Britain, because the elimination of Russia would greatly increase Japan's power in the Far East . . . Decision: Russia's destruction must therefore be made a part of this struggle . . . The sooner Russia is crushed the better . . . if we start in May '41, we will have five months in which to finish the job.

Of course there are those who have argued that Hitler's primary object was always clear – to defeat Russia – and that he concentrated his forces to do so, thereby conforming to the two great strategic rules. The argument falls down when set against the strategic circumstances of the time. In late 1940 and early 1941 he was not at war with Russia, and either would not or could not see that England's subjection was not subsidiary to an attack on Russia. It was an indispensable condition of victory.

Whether Hitler could see it or not, there were others who did. One of them was his Naval Commander-in-Chief, Admiral Raeder. He had produced and went on producing reasons why Germany should concentrate on war against England, particularly in the Mediterranean, which, he maintained, was the pivot of their world empire. Since Italy was weak, Britain would be bound to try to strangle her first, and to make her attacks on Italy easier would aim to get control of North-west Africa. Therefore Germany must take steps to forestall any such move. In cooperation with Spain and Vichy France, Gibraltar must be seized and French North Africa secured. Then, together with the Italians, German forces should capture the Suez Canal and advance through Palestine and Syria to Turkey. 'If we reach that point,' Raeder concluded, 'Turkey will be in our power.

The Russian problem will then appear in a different light. Fundamentally Russia is afraid of Germany. It is doubtful whether an advance against Russia in the north will then be necessary.'[2]

In short, conquer Egypt, get control of the whole North African coast and Middle Eastern oil, strike a blow at British sea power, which enabled Britain to preserve a degree of initiative, and how would she be able to conduct offensive operations, other than by air? It is just as well that Hitler did not take this view for his failure to do so allowed British forces to build up a new centre of gravity of their own. From this would develop a Mediterranean strategy, essentially subsidiary, it is true, to the defeat in Europe of the German armies – which alone could bring the war to an end – but providing none the less a stepping-stone to this eventual undertaking.

Michael Howard summed the whole matter up when he wrote that

if there were no prospect of a successful decision against Germany herself there was a subsidiary theatre where British forces could be employed to harass the enemy and perhaps inflict serious damage. Italy's entry into the war had turned the Middle East into an active theatre of operations. As a centre of gravity of British forces it was second only to the United Kingdom itself.[3]

Although Hitler was contemplating his attack on the Soviet Union as early as July 1940, it was clear from his War Directive No. 18, dated 12 November 1940, that he had not altogether overlooked other theatres of strategic importance, for this directive included references to French North Africa, Gibraltar, Libya and Greece. The French must secure their African possessions against Britain and de Gaulle's forces, while the actual participation of France in the war with Britain might develop. Measures to bring Spain into the war would be pursued with a view to capturing Gibraltar and driving the English from the Western Mediterranean. Even more significant, German forces would be prepared to assist the Italian offensive against Egypt. A Panzer Division would stand by ready for service in North Africa and the necessary shipping would be positioned in Italian ports. The Luftwaffe would make plans for attacks on Egypt and the Suez Canal. This directive, however, was soon overtaken by two more. War Directive No. 21, issued in mid-December, might be said to have determined the outcome of the whole war. Its opening sentence must have sent a shiver down the spines of those who read it at Hitler's HQ and the three Service HQs, in fact of all those who remembered a former war on two fronts: 'The German Armed Forces must be prepared, even before the conclusion of the war against England, to crush Soviet Russia in a rapid campaign.' Operation *Barbarossa*, as it was called, would start on 15 May 1941.

But there was another factor to be considered which to some extent thwarted the Führer's planned timetable, yet paradoxically presented him with an opportunity which, despite the other strategic distractions, might, if seized, have spelled out a war-winning formula. The armed forces of his ally, Mussolini, were not doing well either in Tripolitania or on the Albanian-Greek front. Accordingly German support for battles in the Mediterranean area would be forthcoming. Rommel's Afrika Korps went to Libya, X Fliegerkorps remained in Sicily, and an entire Army Corps would assist the Italians to break through the Greek defences. This move in turn caused Churchill to support Greece, and in doing so gravely weakened Wavell's winning hand in his campaign in the Western Desert, which up until then had been triumphantly successful. Not strong enough either in Greece or Tripolitania, British forces were obliged to evacuate the former and withdraw from the latter. Yet amidst all these defeats, one glimmer of comfort could be discerned. Hitler had declared in November 1940 that the Mediterranean question must be liquidated during that winter, so that he would get his German troops back in the spring, not later than 1 May. In fact, he did not get them back then and *Barbarossa* did not begin until 22 June 1941, more than a month later than Hitler had intended. Although the effect of this delay was not felt immediately, it was a different story in November 1941, with the drive on Moscow bogged down and the icy winter threatening to turn this particular version of Blitzkrieg into another retreat from Moscow. It was the turn then of the Wehrmacht to experience something like despair and paralysis.

It was also in May 1941, well before the attack on Russia, that Raeder renewed his proposal for a 'decisive Egypt-Suez offensive for the autumn of 1941 which would be more deadly to the British Empire than the capture of London'.[4] Raeder and his staff accepted Hitler's priorities but insisted that while the attack on Russia 'naturally stands in the foreground of the OKW [*Oberkommando der Wehrmacht* (High Command of the Armed Forces)] leadership, it must under no circumstances lead to the abandonment of, or to delay in, the conduct of the war in the Mediterranean'.[5] Rommel and his panzers had brought a new set of rules to desert fighting and in March and April 1941 had bundled the British right out of Cyrenaica back into Egypt, leaving only Tobruk in their hands, and Rommel too was clear as to what Germany should have done – keep her hands off Greece and concentrate on North Africa to drive the British right out of the Mediterranean area. Malta should have been taken, thus robbing the British of the base from which they harassed Rommel's supply lines. Capture of the whole British-held coastline would have isolated south-east Europe. It could all have been done for no more than the cost of the Balkan campaign. The prize would have been not just the Balkans but oil and bases for attacking Russia. When we think what Rommel was able to do with a mere handful of German divisions, the prospect of his having, say, an extra Panzerkorps from the huge force which attacked Russia, must give us pause.

Churchill himself was in no doubt about the grave consequences of losing Egypt and the Middle East. In a telegram to Roosevelt earlier that same month he did not endorse the President's view that such a loss would be 'a mere preliminary to the successful maintenance of a prolonged oceanic war'. Even if the United States entered the war, exclusion of the Allies from Europe and much of Africa and Asia would mean that a war against this mighty agglomeration would be a hard, long, and bleak proposition. Therefore the British would fight 'to the last inch and ounce for Egypt'. The desert flank was in Churchill's view 'the peg on which all else hung' and he was soon to urge Wavell to return to the attack there once more. But Wavell and his fellow Commanders-in-Chief were harder pressed and more stretched in their resources at this time than perhaps at any other. The East African campaign was not quite finished; Greece and Crete had taken their toll of men and material; Malta must be maintained,

Tobruk turned into a fortress and supplied; Rashid Ali's pro-German revolt in Iraq had to be suppressed; Syria, where the Vichy French were being difficult, had to be invaded and occupied, and Rommel attacked. What might not have been achieved by the Wehrmacht if they had been allowed to concentrate their might against the British at this moment?

Churchill had surely been right in his prognostication to Roosevelt. If British forces had been turned out of the Middle East, by what means – no matter how defiant our spirit and staunch our leadership – would we have prosecuted the war against Germany? We were still virtually alone. Any attempt to engage German armed forces on land in Europe was out of the question. No doubt the growing strength of the Royal Air Force would have permitted the bombing of German targets. No doubt the Royal Navy would still have preserved integrity of the British Isles. But what would our strategy have been if we had been turned out of the Mediterranean and the Middle East? As the war progressed, with Germany so involved in Russia that the stuffing of the Wehrmacht was gradually knocked out of it, our entire strategic posture was based not merely on strengthening our Middle East position but reinforcing it – first, by taking on Rommel's Panzerarmee and eventually inflicting severe losses on it; second, in conjunction with the United States and the Free French, by occupying North-west Africa and so becoming masters of the North African shores and of the Mediterranean; third, by using Africa as a stepping-stone to Sicily and Italy, thus knocking Italy out of the war, and by sheer attrition, as opposed to free manoeuvre, tying down sufficient German forces to enable Anglo-American armies to invade north-west Europe. All this was feasible only because the bulk of the Wehrmacht was engaged in a titanic struggle with the Red Army. None of it would have been possible if Hitler had paid more attention to Raeder.

Yet Hitler had not put the idea out of his mind. War Directive No. 30 read:

Whether, and if so how, it may be possible, in conjunction with an offensive against the Suez Canal, finally to break the British position between the Mediterranean and the Persian Gulf is a question which will be decided only after *Barbarossa*.

Raeder's whole point was that had it been done first, *Barbarossa* in the form it took would not have been necessary. Even as late as eleven days before *Barbarossa* was launched on 22 June 1941, Hitler issued one more Directive relating to this matter, No. 32, remarkable not for its execution but for its conception. It laid down how the war was to be conducted after Russia had been conquered. Hitler was actually planning to fulfil his former promise to Raeder to finish Britain off. The British position in the Middle East would be strangled by converging attacks from Libya through Egypt, from Bulgaria through Turkey, and from Transcaucasia through Iran. In addition, the Western Mediterranean would be closed by seizing Gibraltar. Planning was to begin 'so that I may issue final directives before the campaign in the east is over'. It may sound like an exercise in 'making pictures' – as Marmont commented on Napoleon's unrealistic imaginings – yet there was to be one more opportunity, one more chance, for Hitler to have struck a deadly blow to the British position in the Middle East, and this was to come when the campaign in Russia was already a year old.

By this time the whole course of the war had been altered by the Japanese attacks on Pearl Harbor and Malaya. Britain and the United States at once became Allies against Japan, and within a few days – because of Hitler's almost incredible blunder of declaring war on America – Allies against Germany and Italy. Some weeks later the Allies agreed a broad strategic policy to concentrate first on Germany's defeat, tightening the ring round her by sustaining Russia, strengthening the Middle East and getting hold of the whole North African coast. Curiously enough, at the Führer Naval Conference four days after Pearl Harbor Hitler asked Raeder whether it was likely that the United States and Britain would abandon East Asia for a time in order to crush Germany and Italy first. At times Hitler's strategic vision was acute. Raeder, while assuring him that the British could not put India at risk and the Americans would not abandon the Pacific to the Japanese Navy, took the opportunity to press his former strategy. While the Allies were preoccupied elsewhere, he argued, now was the time to seize Malta and the Suez Canal and prepare for a great linking-up with the Japanese in the Indian Ocean: 'The favourable situation in the Mediterranean, so pronounced at the present time, will probably never occur again.' In fact it did occur again as a result of Rommel's great offensive which began in January 1942, and as a result of poor generalship and a greatly weakened 8th Army, which had been robbed of promised reinforcements by the demands of the Far East, culminated in the fall of Tobruk on 21 June. Rommel's Order of the Day was a stirring and triumphant document:

The great battle in the Marmarica has been crowned by your quick conquest of Tobruk. We have taken in all over 45,000 prisoners and destroyed or captured more than 1,000 armoured fighting vehicles and nearly 400 guns . . . you have through incomparable courage and tenacity dealt the enemy blow upon blow. Your spirit of attack has cost him the core of his field army . . . Now for the complete destruction of the enemy. We will not rest until we have shattered the last remnants of the British Eighth Army. During the days to come, I shall call upon you for one more great effort to bring us to this final goal.

The loss of Tobruk was a great blow to Churchill, although it enabled him to extract from Roosevelt 300 Sherman tanks and 100 105-mm self-propelled guns, weapons which were greatly to influence future battles in the desert. Churchill must have longed for a general of Rommel's character and ability, who brought Blitzkrieg to the desert and had the uncanny tactical awareness, the *Fingerspitzengefühl*, which enabled him time after time to wrest the initiative from his slower-thinking and slower-moving adversaries. He insisted on the mixed Panzergruppen of tanks, armoured infantry, anti-tank guns and artillery, supported by Stukas, whose lightning manoeuvres so bewitched, bothered and bewildered the 8th Army. Besides, he led from the front, something which seemed to have little appeal to British generals.

Yet it was the very magnitude of his achievement in June 1942 which blinded Rommel to the true priorities. Having Tobruk in his hands, with all the fuel, trucks and stores his Panzerarmee so badly needed, he closed his ears and mind to the absolute necessity of having Malta too, if his supply and reinforcement prospects were to have even a chance of matching those of the British, so much closer to their well-nigh invulnerable lines of communication. Thus the tiny fortress of Malta, the key to mastery in the desert, was chucked aside at the very moment when its possession might indeed have opened the gates of Egypt, the Suez Canal, and the Persian Gulf with all its oil, so priceless to the Axis. When we consider that a few months later Hitler poured his troops and aircraft into Tunisia in order to counter the Anglo-American invasion of French North Africa, it is clear enough that the resources to exploit Rommel's capture of Tobruk and defeat of the 8th Army existed, if only the strategic opportunity to reinforce success had been seized. As it was, Auchinleck took a grip on the 8th Army which was being steadily reinforced, and Rommel's attempt to win the first battle of Alamein with inadequate resources failed. The last chance of bringing off Raeder's great plan had gone, and shortly Churchill would appoint a battle-winning team, composed of Alexander and Montgomery, who with an even more powerful 8th Army and Desert Air Force would see to it that Rommel, the Desert Fox, would no longer be in search of quarry. He himself would be the quarry.

In his essay 'How Hitler Could Have Won the War', John Keegan asks this question: 'What if, in the summer of 1941, Hitler had chosen to make his major attack not into Soviet Russia but across the Eastern Mediterranean, into Syria and the Lebanon?'[6] He goes on to refer to War Directive No. 30 and No. 32, which, as already shown above, referred to operations that would be considered *after Barbarossa* had been launched, and would deal with potential offensives to break the British position in the Middle East. He then poses the further question as to what might have happened if a thrust from Bulgaria and Greece had been chosen as the principal one *instead* of *Barbarossa*. Keegan then puts forward two variants. The first envisages making use of the Dodecanese islands, other Greek islands and Cyprus as stepping-stones to land in Syria and Lebanon. The 7th Airborne Division would be employed in, say, capturing Cyprus instead of being wasted, as it was, in an assault on Crete. Once established in the Levant, panzer columns would set about conquering Iraq, Iran and Saudi Arabia, thus solving Hitler's oil problem. Furthermore, success in this way would enable Germany to threaten Russia's Caspian Sea oil resources. One advantage of this plan was that it respected Turkish neutrality, but on the other hand was so dependent on adequate shipping and protection from British naval and air attack that it might well have foundered. It certainly takes little account of the British potential to interfere.

Keegan's second option involves the violation of Turkish territory, in short, an invasion first of European Turkey from Bulgaria and Greece, to be followed by seizing Istanbul, crossing the Bosphorus and gaining control of Anatolia: all this would not have involved the same demand for shipping and command of the sea, and could have led to a powerful strategic advantage whereby German forces could both secure Turkey's frontier with Russia at the Caucasus and advance into Iran and Iraq to menace Arabia. Keegan concludes that had Hitler exploited his Balkan victories by plumping for this second option and so threatening Russia's southern flank, as well as her western one, a pincer-type *Barbarossa* might have succeeded, thus robbing Britain, and later the United States, of the one ally who seemed to have inexhaustible supplies of time, space and manpower. Moreover, Britain's hold on the Middle East could have been fatally damaged.

Yet there is both a third and a fourth option, as already implied above. In the first place, had Hitler listened to Raeder in 1941, seized Malta with his airborne forces and deployed even a part of the huge panzer and Luftwaffe forces that he was assembling for his attack on Russia; in short, if the Afrika Korps in February 1941 with Rommel still in charge had been a much more powerful one, supported by all the air and naval strength that Germany and Italy between them could have mustered, it is difficult to see how Wavell and his fellow Commanders-in-Chief, with their resources already overstretched, could have resisted a full-scale assault on Egypt, the Canal and beyond. But this is to suppose, as John Keegan did, that Hitler could have been persuaded to abandon or postpone his great strategic and ideological aim – to crush the Soviet Union with a direct attack from the west.

We shall therefore let this hypothesis slip, and turn instead to the actual circumstances of June 1942, with 8th Army at bay and Rommel and the Afrika Korps riding in triumph, not through Persepolis,[7] but through the surrendered Tobruk garrison, when a major switch of the Wehrmacht's power could have turned the scales in the battle for North Africa, and so allowed Rommel's veterans to have enjoyed both the spoils of opportunity and Egyptian daughters of the game: what then? The answer is provided for us by our own *Official History* of the Middle Eastern campaign:

Had the Eastern Mediterranean arena not been successfully held during the lean years (in which case, for want of bases, no British fleet or air forces could have even disputed the control of the Mediterranean sea communications) the task of the Allies in gaining a foothold in Europe would have been rendered immensely more difficult; indeed it might well have proved to be beyond their powers.[8]

Thus we may perhaps endorse Churchill's emphasis on the importance of the desert flank as 'the peg on which all else hung'. This last opportunity of seizing the Middle East may justly be thought of as the tide in Hitler's affairs which should have been taken at the flood if his dream of *Weltmacht*, world power, were to be realized. If Rommel had taken Egypt and surged on from there, there would have been no Anglo-American invasion of French North-west Africa. Indeed, it is not easy to imagine what the Western Allies' strategy for challenging the Axis would have been. But Rommel and his men were not to savour the delights of Cairo and Beirut. At the Cairo conference of August 1942 Churchill had made known his passionate concern with winning the desert war: 'Rommel! Rommel! Rommel! Rommel! What else matters but beating him?' It is to the beating of Rommel that we must now turn our attention, and by doing so introduce another 'if by chance'.

EIGHT

Master Plan Manqué

Of course, you realize, don't you, that is was your husband who won the battle of Alamein!

NIGEL NICOLSON TO LADY MCCREERY

We have noted that Napoleon called for lucky generals. He would have been more than happy with Montgomery, whose luck knew no bounds. Montgomery was lucky to get command of 8th Army in the first place. Churchill, supreme arbiter of such matters, wanted someone else – Gott – and only Gott's death in an aeroplane crash gave Montgomery his chance against Rommel. He was lucky that Rommel was at the end of his tether – emotionally, physically, and above all logistically. He was lucky to take command at a time when the pendulum of supplies and reinforcements had swung so completely in favour of the British. During August 1942 Rommel's Panzerarmee consumed twice the amount of supplies he received. He was short of 1,500 trucks, 200 tanks, several hundred troop-carriers and 16,000 men. In the same month the British received 400 tanks, 500 guns, 7,000 vehicles and 75,000 tons of stores. During the six months ending in August their reinforcements in all services totalled a quarter of a million men, roughly two and a half times the size of Rommel's army and five times the number of his German soldiers.

Nor was Montgomery's luck confined merely to material and numbers. The Desert Air Force was at the peak of its strength and skill. Ultra – the cipher-breaking device which enabled the British to read the German High Command signals – gave Montgomery complete and continuous information about Rommel's supply position and his intentions. As if this were not enough, Montgomery enjoyed immense freedom – freedom to choose his own subordinates, freedom to plan the nature and timing of the battle, freedom from interference. Alexander backed him absolutely and left him alone: even Churchill let him have his own way. And Montgomery's knowledge that the great Allied armada, Operation *Torch*, was to land in North-west Africa about two weeks after his own planned attack on the El Alamein line must have been a comfort.

A. G. Macdonnell described Wellington's task in the Peninsula as the easiest that has ever faced a general. Whilst we may demur, we might say that he would perhaps have revised this judgement had he written about the North African campaign. Incomparably good intelligence of what the enemy was up to, overwhelming strength, an imminent landing by an Allied army to his opponent's rear, this opponent's critical lack of supplies and mobility, meant that short of some cardinal error of disposition or deployment – and Montgomery was far too cautious and calculating for that – he was practically bound to win.

Yet in spite of all this, there came a point in the battle when it seemed that the master plan – Montgomery was very fond of referring to the need to have a master plan and deploring other generals' failure to have one – met with a snag, and it is speculation as to what might have happened if this snag had been tackled differently that will present us with this particular chance. But first we must set the scene more fully. It must be conceded that Montgomery made good use of all his luck. With his victory, a legend was born. The nation, indeed the whole Western world, was avid for a victory, any victory, and Montgomery made sure that the need was satisfied. He thereupon made the best of it. He was the finest public relations officer in the whole British army, and soon the country had a new name to play with, a hero, a battle-winner, and justifiably so, for as Fred Majdalany put it: 'At a moment when the future of the Western world was in the balance and history held its breath, he [Montgomery] rallied his country's soldiers as Churchill had rallied his people.'[1] This, we may conclude, was Montgomery's greatest achievement; he made the 'brave but baffled' 8th Army, and thereafter the other armies and Army Group he commanded, believe in their capacity to win and go on winning.

Shortly after his arrival in Cairo on 4 August 1942, Churchill decided on 'drastic and immediate' changes in the Middle East command arrangements. Alexander would replace Auchinleck as Commander-in-Chief and Gott would take over 8th Army. Gott's death resulted in Montgomery's appointment, and he arrived on 12 August and almost at once took over command of 8th Army. Alexander was just the man to exercise high command while leaving it to Montgomery both to plan and fight the forthcoming battle, and to bask in public esteem. Whereas Montgomery courted and relished adulation, Alexander shunned it. Besides, 8th Army should identify itself with its own commander. So, as Nigel Nicolson put it, 'Alexander gave Montgomery his chance, never countermanding his orders, rarely suggesting an element in his plan, and supporting him by every possible means, political, administrative and psychological, to achieve their common object, the defeat of Rommel.'[2]

It was to Alexander that on 10 August 1942 Churchill gave a directive notable for its clarity and simplicity: 'Your prime and main duty will be to take or destroy at the earliest opportunity the German-Italian Army commanded by Field-Marshal Rommel, together with all its supplies and establishments in Egypt and Libya.' The earliest possible moment turned out to be some nine months later, for it was not until May 1943 that Alexander was able to report that he had fully discharged this prime and main duty.

In preparing for this great task, Montgomery was highly successful in restoring high morale in 8th Army. That eminent historian, Ronald Lewin, recorded how quickly Montgomery imposed his will on his officer corps and his personality on the troops. He created the impression that it was *his* army and that under his command things would go well. This injection of a new sense of purpose and confidence was so striking that when Churchill paid another visit to the desert on 19 August and listened to Montgomery's analysis of the situation and plans to deal with it, he found

a complete change of atmosphere . . . the highest alacrity and activity prevail . . . it seems probable that Rommel will attack during the moon period before the end of August . . . The ensuing battle will be hard and critical, but I have the greatest confidence in Alexander and Montgomery, and I feel sure the Army will fight at its best.[3]

We may perhaps look more closely at the two principal actors in what was to be a curtain-raiser for the final phases of the Desert War: the one more or less at the end of his tether, the other at the outset of a career which was to take him to unimagined heights of public popularity and self-stimulated aggrandizement. In the forthcoming duel between them, we see once more how character determines incident and how incident illustrates character. David Irving's assessment of the two men touches on their similarities and differences alike.[4] Both Rommel and Montgomery had more enemies than friends among their fellow generals; both could be high-handed and arrogant, awkward, even insubordinate, when subjected to what they regarded as incompetent direction, yet in sole command they shone; they had no intellectual interests, but enjoyed winter sports; both had a flair for public relations. Yet in their style and exercise of command they differed absolutely. Rommel's whole attitude to war was chivalrous; Montgomery simply wanted to kill Germans. Rommel led from the front; Montgomery retired to his caravan. Rommel relied on his *Fingerspitzengefühl* to outmanoeuvre and confound his enemy; Montgomery used other people's brains and in the end won by sheer weight of numbers.

As the days of August 1942 advanced, the shadows were lengthening for Rommel and the Afrika Korps. They still had not received the fuel and ammunition necessary for a successful operation, while Montgomery's force was daily growing stronger and more confident. On the eve of the coming battle, the last time that he would attack 8th Army, except for a half-hearted affair at Mededine in March 1943, Rommel confided to his doctor that this decision was the hardest he had yet taken: 'Either we manage to reach the Suez Canal, and the army in Russia succeeds in reaching the Caucasus, or . . .' He indicated with a gesture that the alternative could mean only defeat.

The irony of it all was that only two months earlier Rommel had been riding high, with the Afrika Korps exulting in its victory, its capture of Tobruk relieving immediate logistic needs, 8th Army reeling from the shock, still disorganized, still lacking reinforcements which were to arrive in the coming weeks, desperately trying under the firm leadership of Auchinleck to stabilize some sort of defensive barrier at El Alamein: if Rommel could have then persuaded Hitler to neutralize Malta and send him additional panzer and Stuka power and supplies, what might not have been achieved? There would have been no doubts then. Even Hitler's fellow dictator, Benito Mussolini, not exactly famed for exploiting victory, strongly supported the idea of one more decisive push to the Suez Canal and beyond, picturing himself riding into Alexandria on a white horse at the head of his troops. That all this could have been done in July is clear enough when we remember that later that year, in order to counter the Anglo-American descent on French North-west Africa, Hitler acted with lightning speed and despatched to Tunisia sufficient strength to delay the Allied advance to Bizerta and Tunis for months.

The Allied landings in Morocco and Algeria had taken place on 8 November. By the end of that month there were 15,000 German soldiers in Tunisia, including Parachute and Glider Regiments, Panzer Grenadiers, reconnaissance companies, and several Panzer Regiments, some of which were equipped with the Tiger tank, mounting the famous and deadly 88-mm gun. Soon the whole of 10th Panzer Division would follow, plus two more German and two Italian divisions. That the Germans had been able to reinforce so strongly and rapidly was a tribute to Hitler's prompt reaction and use of German transport aircraft and his ally's shipping, all supported by a strengthened Fliegerkorps II with no fewer than eighty-one fighters and twenty-eight dive-bombers. What could Rommel not have done with even half this addition to his Panzerarmee? Indeed, had Rommel broken Auchinleck's defences in late July or early August 1942, Operation *Torch*, the invasion of North-west Africa, might itself have been put in question. The whole strategic balance of the war against Germany might have been turned inside out.

But we cannot call back yesterday or bid time return. Rommel did not wait or demand instant, powerful reinforcement. Instead he pushed on with inadequate strength and was met at El Alamein by 8th Army, which under Auchinleck, well advised by his Chief of Staff, Dorman-Smith, was concentrated, fought in integrated battle groups, massed its artillery, husbanded its armour, formed a light armoured brigade for flank reconnaissance and wore down the Italian divisions.

Rommel himself conceded that Auchinleck was handling his forces with great skill. He commanded with great coolness, was not going to be rushed, and had the huge advantage of a Desert Air Force which dominated the battlefield. In a word, Auchinleck was keeping *balance*, a requirement which Montgomery was later to make so much of. By maintaining this balance and by refusing to be thrown off it, Auchinleck was able to make decisive use of the advantage inherent to his position – important ground, assured supplies, superior fire-power, ready reinforcements. He beat the Afrika Korps at its own game, and succeeded in drawing its panzers on to his own armour and artillery fire posted firmly on ground of his own choosing.

If Auchinleck was able to check Rommel in July 1942, how infinitely more likely it was that Montgomery would be able to repeat the performance at the end of August when he enjoyed even greater strength. 'The more one examines the record of the Alam Halfa battle,' wrote Ronald Lewin, 'which Rommel launched during the night of 30/31 August, the more clearly one sees that it was doomed from the start.'[5] The Afrika Korps was given an immensely difficult task – a night move through a major minefield whose depth and density were far greater than expected, and unfamiliar going over thirty miles to be accomplished by dawn the following day, in order to charge off to the north and the coast. Even at the height of its powers and confidence, with adequate supplies and an unsure enemy, the Afrika Korps might have found the task too much. But the Afrika Korps was no longer at the peak of its form; its supplies were nig-gardly; its two Panzer Divisions were down to less than 100 miles of petrol. Moreover, Rommel launched his attack against an adversary who not only knew what he was going to do, but how and when he was going to do it, an adversary who had sufficient strength in hand to defeat forces more powerful than those at Rommel's disposal.

It was not therefore surprising that Montgomery's 8th Army was able to win the battle of Alam el-Halfa. Nor was it surprising that Montgomery made the best possible copy out of his victory:

My first encounter with Rommel was of great interest. Luckily I had time to tidy up the mess and to get my plans laid, so there was no difficulty in seeing him off. I feel that I have won the first game, when it was his service. Next time it will be my service, the score being one-love.[6]

Montgomery made much use of such sporting metaphors. He was less inclined to give credit to others, however, and made no mention of the point that fundamentally 8th Army's plan for defence at Alam el-Halfa was the same as the one previously outlined by Auchinleck and his staff. Now would come the real test, the game when it was Montgomery's service. He had spoken of hitting Rommel for six out of North Africa. How did he propose to do it?

There were three things that 8th Army had to do if it were successfully to carry out the task set by Churchill, to take or destroy the Panzerarmee: first, to punch a hole in the enemy position; second, to pass 10 Corps with all its armoured mobility through the hole; third, to develop operations so as to destroy Rommel's forces. In the end this last requirement meant encircling the Panzerarmee, and to have done so with sufficient strength and speed was probably always beyond 8th Army's powers. None the less Montgomery made plans to do so. His first idea was to launch his main attack with Leese's 30 Corps in the north, break the enemy's defences, cut two lanes in the minefields, and allow Lumsden's 10 Corps – what Churchill called 'the mass of manoeuvre' – to pass through, position itself on ground which controlled the enemy's supply routes and so oblige the Panzer Divisions to attack Lumsden's armour under conditions favourable to the British, both in terms of ground and numbers. Then, with the enemy armour neutralized, his infantry would be rounded up. Meanwhile, Horrocks's 13 Corps would attack in the south in order to prevent Axis concentration against 8th Army's main northern thrust and also to crack about behind the enemy's positions and advance towards El Daba.

Although in broad terms the plan remained the same – to break through in the north while making a secondary attack in the south – the method of doing so changed. As Montgomery himself explained, whereas his initial idea was to destroy Rommel's armour first and then deal with the infantry, his revised plan reversed the process. He would hold off or contain the enemy armour while methodically destroying infantry holding the defensive system. Montgomery referred to this latter operation as a 'crumbling' process, arguing that as enemy armour would be unlikely to remain inactive while this crumbling was going on, and would launch counter-attacks, this very reaction would enable his own armour to take on the enemy's from positions of advantage. The whole thing depended on 30 Corps' ability to establish corridors through the minefields quickly so that 10 Corps could pass through, but if this did not happen, the armoured divisions would have to fight their own way through. This notion, as experienced armoured commanders knew to their previous cost, was a recipe for disaster when troops were up against the mixed panzer groups of the Afrika Korps. And in the end a second great infantry effort became necessary, after the first one faltered, before the mass of manoeuvre broke clear. It is with this faltering and the controversy which arose as to how it was to be overcome that our 'if by chance' of this particular battle has to do.

But first we may note that even at the relatively late stage following Rommel's repulse at Alam el-Halfa, one member of the German Naval staff made an appreciation of the situation, dated 8 September, remarkable for its brevity and perspicacity:

In order to safeguard our position in the Mediterranean, to protect Italy, to prevent a planned British offensive, to frustrate the enemy's plans for a defensive front and to create the prerequisites for a direct connexion between Germany and Japan, the Naval Staff believes that the following requirements must be met:

1 North Africa must be held, if at all possible, from the Alamein position.
2 The Luftwaffe must be greatly reinforced.
3 Malta must be seized.
4 The plan of an offensive against Suez at a later date must be adhered to.

No one would have endorsed this proposal more ardently than Rommel himself, although he was all too well aware that while being required to fulfil the first and fourth requirements, there was little likelihood of OKW's agreeing to provide the resources without which the second and third ones could not be met. Even so, while on leave Rommel tried once more to persuade Hitler during a meeting at the

Berlin Chancellory on 1 October to provide at once powerful Luftwaffe forces and at least 30,000 tons of supplies each month if he were to conduct a successful defence against a forthcoming British attack on the Alamein position. Hitler made promises. Tiger tanks, self-propelled guns, rocket launchers and all the fuel the Panzerarmee would need. But no arrangements were made for the indispensable conditions of providing sufficiently powerful air and sea forces which would enable such reinforcements to get to North Africa.

The actual battle of El Alamein had five parts: the break-in on the night of 23–24 October; the so-called crumbling operations of 24 and 25 October, when Rommel returned to the desert, operations which did not clear the way for 10 Corps; Rommel's counter-attacks and Montgomery's change of plans from 26 to 28 October; Operation Supercharge on the night of 1–2 November which wore down the Panzerarmee to the point when it could no longer prevent a break-out; finally, the break-out itself, from 3 to 7 November. It is the third of these five parts which mainly concerns us here.

After the battle of El Alamein, Montgomery was fond of declaring that it had been fought exactly in accordance with his master plan. In saying this he did scant justice to 8th Army, Rommel's Panzerarmee, his closest advisers and his own flair for managing a battlefield. Quite apart from von Moltke's contention that no plan survives contact with the enemy – and this was notably true of El Alamein – by suggesting that he had to change nothing, Montgomery detracts from one of his strongest faculties as a commander, the trick of remaining 'balanced'. What he might have said with more accuracy about his master plan is that the broad idea of it – feint in the south, breakthrough in the north – was adhered to, but that it succeeded by virtue of his having adequate reserves at the outset and creating more later, thus allowing him to adapt the master plan in detail and emphasis. This was what is meant by balance. You are then able to adjust your dispositions, concentrations and intentions without serious enemy interference, while ensuring that the enemy is himself constrained to respond to your movements and activities and cannot therefore develop his own influence on the course of the battle in the way he would like to. He dances to your tune. His plans are 'cabin'd, cribb'd, confin'd, bound in To saucy doubts and fears'. Yours are 'Whole as the marble, founded as the rock, As broad and general as the casing air'.

Yet there came a point during the battle of El Alamein when it must have seemed to Montgomery that even his plans were subject to saucy doubts and fears. On 26 October he needed to practise his balancing act, for although 8th Army had driven a deep and wide wedge into the Axis defences, and crumbling was proceeding, there appeared to be no immediate prospect of getting right through these defences and finishing off the job. To do this would require a major rethink and a major redeployment. And the choice of place for the *Schwerpunkt* of this second attack would be critical. It is ironic that Rommel guessed correctly where Montgomery would be inclined to do it. If there had not been a change, the attack might have failed. As it was, counsels other than Montgomery's prevailed.

One of the most priceless commodities which may be possessed by a general in charge of a battle is calm. Montgomery had it. He was able to shut himself off from the hurly-burly of a battle, to stand back and contemplate the next step without being unduly swayed by the happenings of the moment, to insulate himself from the heat of activity. He would withdraw to his caravan, trusting his subordinate commanders to conduct operations as he had directed, and quietly make up his mind what to do next. Realizing that the impetus of his offensive was waning, he decided to regroup his forces in order to create a reserve with which to restore momentum to the battle. What this amounted to was that 13th and 30th Corps would adjust their formations in such a way that he could draw into reserve the New Zealand Division, including 9th Armoured Brigade and two armoured divisions, the 7th and 10th. All this reorganization was to be completed by 28 October. Meanwhile Rommel, who judged that the British were 'operating with astonishing hesitancy and caution', mustered what reserves he could and began to launch a series of counter-attacks, which the British anti-tank defences and tanks were able to contain.

Rommel was not the only one to misjudge Montgomery's pause for reorganization. Churchill too, on reading reports of withdrawals of troops from the front, concluded that the battle was petering out, and on the morning of 29 October levelled a storm of reproach at the CIGS, General Brooke. 'What was *my* Monty doing now, allowing the battle to peter out?' was the way Brooke later recorded Churchill's complaints. Monty was always Brooke's Monty when things were not going well. 'Why had he told us he would be through in seven days if all he intended to do was to fight a half-hearted battle? Had we not got a single general who could even win one single battle?' At a Chiefs of Staff meeting later that day Brooke, supported by Smuts, succeeded in persuading Churchill that the battle was proceeding satisfactorily. It might not have done so without the intervention of some of Montgomery's advisers.

Having further strengthened his reserves by withdrawing 1st Armoured Division, Montgomery's initial intention was that the final infantry attack would be made in the north by 30 Corps, while 10 Corps HQ would prepare to take charge of the subsequent break-out. The idea was for the 9th Australian Division to assault on the axis of the coast road and make way for the reinforced New Zealand Division to launch itself westward along the coast, making a hole for 10 Corps to break out. Rommel had guessed correctly where Montgomery wanted to make his final, decisive effort and had consequently reinforced the northern sector with 90th Light Division, part of 21st Panzer Division and the Italian Trieste Division. During the morning of 29 October, however, while the Australian attack was still under way, Montgomery was conferring with Richard Casey, Minister of State for the Middle East, accompanied by Alexander and his Chief of Staff, General McCreery. During their conference, some new battle information came in which prompted an instant review of the situation. This in turn led to a dramatic change of direction for the final offensive.

Up until then Montgomery had resisted suggestions from his staff that it was a mistake to persist in attacking the strongest part of the enemy defences. But now McCreery strongly recommended an alternative – to attack at the point where German and Italian forces joined up, just north of Kidney Ridge. Brigadier Williams, Montgomery's chief of Intelligence, emphatically supported this view, and

Montgomery allowed himself to be convinced, no doubt further influenced by the opinion of own Chief of Staff, de Guingand, who also backed McCreery's insistent voice. Alexander, well aware of the contribution to victory made by his Chief of Staff, wrote later: 'There is no doubt at all in my mind that this was the key decision of the Alamein battle.' Even Montgomery himself, never lavish with praise for others, remarked that the change of thrust-line for *Supercharge*, as the operation was called, proved most fortunate. It is a view reinforced by many of those who did the actual fighting and achieved the actual break-out. One of them points out that when Dick McCreery was asked for his opinion as to where the attack should go in, and gave it, it was accepted reluctantly by Montgomery, 'and was successful after severe fighting . . . I really believe that had we gone further north as Monty wanted, we should never have got out of the minefields. It was therefore Dick McCreery's decision that won Alamein for Monty.' Allowing always for hyperbole, there is a germ of truth in Nigel Nicolson's observation on first meeting Lettice McCreery: 'Of course, you do realize, don't you, that it was your husband who won the battle of Alamein!'

Supercharge did succeed: Rommel withdrew and 8th Army followed. It was 4 November 1942. Four days later Anglo-American forces landed in French North Africa. While it was clear that El Alamein had been a great victory for the British, whether it was strategically desirable *at that moment* may be questioned, for we only have to imagine in what a precarious position Rommel and his Panzerarmee would have been if Rommel's lines of communication had still stretched all the way to the Alamein defences at the time of the Anglo-American landings in Algeria and Morocco. This leads us in turn to a further strategic If. It was by chance that McCreery was at Montgomery's HQ on the morning of 29 October. If he had not been, would the decision to change the thrust-line for *Supercharge* have been taken? And if Montgomery had persisted in his original choice of *Schwerpunkt*, what would the outcome have been?

Let us take two hypotheses, either of which might have had a profound effect on the battle for North Africa and the Mediterranean, and in order to be even-handed, one case will on the face of it be advantageous to the Axis, the other to the Allies. We must bear in mind that Churchill was insistent that the timing of Montgomery's offensive at El Alamein should be such that its successful conclusion, that is, beating Rommel, would precede the planned Anglo-American landings in French North Africa, whose D-Day was to be 8 November. Montgomery's second bite of the cherry, *Supercharge*, began on 2 November and two days later had succeeded in opening the door for British armoured regiments to break out. Thus Rommel became preoccupied with extraction of his forces and withdrawal to another defensive position. Now comes the first hypothesis. There is no change of thrust-line for *Supercharge*, Montgomery sticks to his original plan of attacking in the north, 8th Army does *not* get through the minefields, Rommel's defences remain firm, there is once more stalemate. Moreover, this further loss of momentum while Montgomery has to think yet again, regroup yet again and plan a further attempt to break through all lasts for the best part of a week, that is, until after 8 November. The situation that Churchill hoped for – Rommel beaten and on the run – has not come about.

The second hypothesis presupposes a decision of strategic boldness relatively rare in Allied counsels but which nevertheless might have paid high dividends in one way while robbing the Allies of substantial gains in another. Operation *Torch*, the landings in French North Africa, was first discussed and agreed in principle when Churchill conferred with Roosevelt in December 1941 soon after America's entry into the war. Although the American military men wanted a direct assault on Europe, it became clear after Roosevelt's undertaking to Russia that a second front would be opened in 1942, that this could not be done in Europe. It was then that Churchill renewed his proposal about French North Africa, and despite opposition from General Marshall and General Eisenhower, who regarded the idea as a dissipation of resources away from the decisive area of Europe itself, Roosevelt overruled his generals and gave orders that *Torch* would take place in 1942. There were still disagreements between the Allied countries, first as to the strategic consequences of executing *Torch*, second as to the actual method of doing so. Marshall, Army Chief of Staff, saw the operation as part of creating a defensive circle round

Europe. The British saw it rather as a means both of securing the Middle East, its oil and the Mediterranean sea routes, and of closing the ring, not to stand defensively on it but by tightening it, to throttle the Third Reich. The second disagreement revealed that although the Americans were keen to get to grips with the German armies, they were thinking circumspectly and wanted to land only on the Atlantic coast of Africa, then move eastwards, whereas the British were aiming to capture Tunis and the straits there quickly, so proposed to land as far east as possible.

General Eisenhower's appointment to command the operation was both timely and beneficial, as he proved a splendid coordinator, and once converted to *Torch* embraced it wholeheartedly. Like the British, he too wanted to land as far east as Bône. Churchill added his weight to the argument for landing as far east as possible. In signalling Roosevelt, he insisted that to land too far west would be to rob *Torch* of all its strategic promise, that Algeria must be occupied, that landings at both Oran and Algiers were essential, so that Bizerta and Tunis could swiftly be taken, even if the Allies had to fight the Germans for them. It would all be a necessary prelude to subsequent attacks on Italy. In the end it was agreed that there would be simultaneous landings at Casablanca, Oran and Algiers.

It was a bold enterprise considering the risks being run: an amphibious operation with largely untried troops; a gauntlet of U-boats; the danger of enemy air attack; the uncertainty of French reaction – welcome or resistance? Yet the Axis was taken completely by surprise, so much so that there is a lot to be said for Admiral Cunningham's subsequent comment to the effect that bold as the plan had been, it had not been bold enough, for had the Allies landed forces as far east as Bizerta and Tunis, with among other tasks that of capturing the airfields there, the Axis would have been forestalled and success complete. With the principal airfields and ports of Tunisia in Allied hands, together with powerful air and naval forces, no German and Italian divisions would have been transported there, the French would have swung completely to the side of the Allies, and Hitler would have been presented with a very different problem.

Given, then, the situation in the second week of November 1942 as we have now depicted it – the Allies established in Algeria and Tunis; Rommel and his Panzerarmee still defiantly hanging on at El Alamein – what would Hitler have done? There would have been two broad options – to continue to put up some sort of resistance in North Africa or to have abandoned it. Given the first of these, it would no doubt have been possible with a supreme effort to transport troops, weapons and supplies by sea and air via, say Tripoli, to reinforce Rommel and guard against a further Allied advance from Tunis eastwards. But to have done so would almost certainly have meant that such reinforcements would prove to be hostages to fortune in view of Allied air and naval superiority, together with their ability to win the race for which side could build up more quickly. Sooner or later Montgomery, assuming he did not get the sack from Churchill, would again have mustered sufficient reserves to mount yet another assault on Rommel's defences, supported by overwhelming artillery and air power.

Yet what strategic advantage could Hitler have hoped to wrest from further resistance in North Africa, other than that of time? If he were to choose the second option and abandon the campaign there, and at the same time rescue Rommel and his army to fight again another day, it would involve another huge air and sea effort, with all the dangers of counter-action by the Allies, to embark and ferry the troops and their weapons back to Italy or Greece; it would moreover allow the Allies time to prepare for an earlier assault on what Churchill had described as 'the soft underbelly of Europe'. We may perhaps judge Hitler's likely action in these hypothetical circumstances by recalling his actual orders to Rommel when the Desert Fox had urged withdrawal from the Alamein position on 2 November 1942: 'in your situation there can be no thought but of persevering, of yielding not one yard, and of hurling every gun and every fighting man into the battle'. After promises of air reinforcements and supplies, Hitler assured Rommel that the enemy must be at the end of his strength. It would not be the first time in history that the stronger will had triumphed over stronger battalions. 'To your troops therefore you can offer no other path that than leading to Victory or Death.' In the event Rommel conducted a skilful withdrawal, even though slowly but surely being pushed further west by 8th Army, and won one spectacular battle against the Americans at Kasserine in Tunisia in February 1943; but even he could not prevail against the combined Allied advances from east and west. He handed over command of Army Group Africa to von Arnim on 9 March 1943 and flew to Rome. The battle for Tunisia went on until May 1943 when the Axis forces capitulated with the loss of all their equipment and nearly a quarter of a million men, a number comparable with German losses at Stalingrad when von Paulus's 6th Army – Hitler had vetoed his request for permission to break out before it was too late – surrendered to the Red Army. Hitler's battles of conquest were over. Those of resistance were about to begin.

We may therefore conclude that of these two hypotheses, one – that of a further setback for Montgomery at El Alamein – would probably have made little difference in the end, whereas the other – a bolder *Torch* which rapidly took possession of Tunisia – would have had benefits for both sides: for the Allies because they would have obtained control over the whole of North Africa and the Mediterranean earlier; for the Axis because the reinforcements poured into Tunisia would have been available to contest the next Allied strategic move – the assault on Italy. Churchill had referred to Europe's soft underbelly. When this belly was attacked, however, it turned out to be somewhat harder than expected.

NINE

The Hard Underbelly of Europe

Britain's prime and capital foe is not Italy but Germany.

WINSTON CHURCHILL, HOUSE OF COMMONS, 27 JULY 1943

In 1980 that distinguished and, alas, late historian, John Grigg, published a book called *1943: The Victory That Never Was* in which he put forward one of the more interesting Ifs of the Second World War. His book attempts to show that the cross-Channel invasion, which was at length mounted in 1944, should have taken place a year earlier. Grigg argues that the four prerequisites for landing successfully in France – air superiority, enough troops, shipping to carry them, and some means of preventing the Germans from concentrating against and eliminating an Allied beach-head – either existed or could have been created in 1943. In making this claim, bearing in mind the strategic circumstances of early 1943, he may be said to have overlooked the very commodity which he is trying to save – time.

In order to gauge these circumstances, we must go back to the Casablanca conference of January 1943 at which, as Michael Howard put it, the Mediterranean strategy was legitimized. To prepare for this crucial meeting between Churchill and Roosevelt, together with their military advisers and commanders, the British Joint Planning Staff had produced a paper remarkable for its prescience and persuasion. The central point of their deliberations was how to exploit the strategic advantage which possession of the whole of North Africa would present to them. In debating how to knock Italy out of the war, they reasoned that bombing alone would not induce the Fascist regime to sue for peace, and even if such a move were on the cards, the Germans would not permit it, but simply occupy Italy. Yet a combination of bombing together with the capture of Sicily and Sardinia might destroy Italian morale and bring about an internal collapse. In this event the Germans might be compelled to take over Italy in order to defend it and be obliged to assume all the other Italian commitments in the Balkans. Despite Churchill's misgivings, he agreed with the US policy of attempting to divide the Italian people from Mussolini's government. The Joint Planning Staff therefore produced a report which outlined how the Allies could achieve a dual aim of inducing the Italians to give up and force the Germans to occupy Italy, so stretching their resources still further. This would be done by continuing bombing, raiding the coasts and shipping, capturing either Sicily or Sardinia, threatening Crete and the Dodecanese, and stepping up subversion in the Balkans. Their report thus concluded:

The prizes open to the Allies in the Mediterranean in 1943 are very great. They include the severe reduction of German air-power, the reopening of the short sea route, the denial to Germany of oil, chrome and other minerals, the elimination of one of the Axis partners and the opening of the Balkans.

If we decide to exploit the position which we have gained, our first object should be to induce the Italians to lay down their arms everywhere; our next should be directed against the Balkans.

Unless Italy collapses far more quickly than we expect, this exploitation must, however, be at the expense of *Round-Up*[1] in 1943.

We are therefore faced with the alternative of:

(a) Concentrating resources in the United Kingdom for a *Round-Up* which may, in any event, be impracticable for 1943; and this at the cost of abandoning the great prizes open to us in the Mediterranean and of remaining inactive for many months during which the Germans would recuperate;

or

(b) Pursuing the offensive in the Mediterranean with the knowledge that we shall only be able to assault Northern France next year if there is a pronounced decline in German fighting power.

We cannot have it both ways. In our view (b) is the correct strategy and will give the Russians more certain, and possibly even greater relief.

The British Chiefs of Staff endorsed this paper and it was the policy recommended in it which Churchill and his advisers advocated at the Casablanca meeting with Roosevelt and his team. The decisions taken there, which included giving high priority to the security of sea communications, in other words defeat of the U-boat and the taking of Sicily at the earliest possible moment, clearly set the pattern for future Allied strategy. Although the British were content that taking Sicily conformed with their ideas of wringing every advantage from exploiting Mediterranean success, the Americans were far from convinced that this was the way to win the war. Only by engaging major German forces in north-west Europe, they maintained, could this be done. But, as there were so many Allied forces in the Mediterranean, it would be sensible to use them there. To go from North Africa to Sicily in order to increase pressure on Italy and distract the Germans from Russia was all very well, provided this was recognized as being merely opportunistic and not part of some master strategic plan. But what about the invasion of north-west Europe? What effect would these Mediterranean operations have on what the Americans regarded as the most important goal of all? It was beginning to be acknowledged by those at Casablanca that the Mediterranean option would delay the other, crucial invasion for at least a year. Was such a delay acceptable? The British answer was that even if there were no further Mediterranean operations, it would still not be possible to invade north-west Europe in 1943. Better therefore to exploit success now in the south and guarantee proper action in the west in 1944. Churchill had expressed what he referred to as two-handed flexibility, that is, a strategy of pushing right-handed now, left-handed later, and finally both-handed 'as our resources and circumstances permit'. But in any case, looking at it all in January 1943, the battle for North Africa had to be finished off first.

And so we return to John Grigg's claim that the cross-Channel invasion could and should have been undertaken in 1943. Yet once the decision to invade Sicily had been taken at Casablanca in January 1943 – *four months before* the capitulation of the Axis forces in North Africa – there could be no possibility of a mid-1943 assault on Western Europe. For such a notion to be taken seriously it would have been necessary at the beginning of that year, while Montgomery was still chasing Rommel, to decide not to invade Sicily, indeed not in any way to exploit the clearing of North Africa by moving north into southern Europe. Even with all the troops available to them, it took Alexander and Eisenhower until May 1943 to finish off the business in North Africa and capture Tunis. Thus there would have been no time to move, train, equip and prepare for a cross-Channel invasion in mid-1943. Certainly there would have been wholly inadequate resources in the United Kingdom to mount an assault on Europe without major reinforcement from the Mediterranean area. The fiasco of the Dieppe raid in August 1942 had shown what sort of disaster was in store for any ill-prepared descent on France.

Quite apart from the Allies' difficulties with time, the other great weakness of Grigg's argument turns on the power of the Wehrmacht and its ability to concentrate against a 1943 landing in France. If there had been no invasion of Sicily and thus, we may assume, no fall of Mussolini or an Italian defection from the Axis, there would have been no serious distraction of German divisions in the south. Furthermore, a June 1943 invasion of France would have preceded Hitler's great Kursk offensive in Russia in July. Such would have been the noise of preparations in the United Kingdom that Hitler's Western Front would not have been milked for offensives in the East. Furthermore, the battle of the Atlantic had still to be won, hence the high priority given to it by the Allied leaders at Casablanca. Until the safety of convoys bringing all the men and material necessary for the great cross-Channel venture from the United States to Britain could be guaranteed, it was unlikely that the necessary build-up, or indeed security of the invasion fleet itself, would justify so vital a strategic venture.

Yet there is one variation of Grigg's idea which merits examination. Let us say that one of the Ifs in the last chapter – that is, a much bolder *Torch*, landing further east and swiftly capturing Tunis, thus pre-empting Hitler's reinforcement of it, together with a successful third bite of the cherry by Montgomery resulting in Rommel's Panzerarmee being eliminated from the scene – presents us with the whole North African coast in Allied hands by November 1942.

Would an invasion of Western Europe in 1943 then have been on the cards? At that time the Atlantic Wall was infinitely weaker than it was a year later and there were far fewer German divisions stationed in the west. It was not until the end of 1943 that Rommel began his inspection of the Wall. Two months later he set to work to bring its defences up to such a standard that they would, in his view, hold up against the strongest attack. Every ingenious device for defending the coastline with obstacles underneath the water, minefields on the beaches, coastal batteries reinforced with steel and concrete to immunize them from air and naval bombardments, wire, pillboxes with machine-guns, 88-mm guns – all these would contest landings from the sea, while airborne troops would have to encounter flooded low-lying ground and booby-trapped posts driven into the earth of likely landing zones. Rommel's drive and dynamic leadership transformed the whole sector where in the event the Allies did land in 1944.

None of these extensive defensive measures had been taken by the summer of 1943. Yet when we recall that the first draft plan for the invasion of Normandy was made in August 1943 and the actual operation did not take place – fundamentally altered and strengthened by this time – until ten months later; when we note that Montgomery, appointed to command 21st Army Group at the end of 1943, found that the proposed plan was 'simply not an operation of war' and demanded and got drastic amendments and additions to it, which would involve doubling the assault frontage and increasing the sea landings by 40 per cent and the air landings by 200 per cent; when we appreciate that Admiral Ramsay, commanding the Allied navies, required double the number of minesweepers, an additional 240 warships and an extra 1,000 landing craft in order to carry out the revised plan; and when we consider too the assembly, equipping, training and briefing of thousand upon thousand of Allied soldiers, together with a complex and lengthy deception plan which aimed to take the Germans' eyes off Normandy and on to the Pas de Calais – when all these factors are taken into account, we may perhaps conclude that even with a much earlier winding up of the North African campaign, a descent on Western Europe in the summer of 1943 would not have been a practicable proposition. And we have only to imagine the consequences of a 1943 invasion which failed, thus allowing Hitler to bring his entire strength to bear upon the Soviet Union, to endorse Michael Howard's judgement that the Mediterranean campaign, as it was in fact carried out, was a proper part of the overall Allied grand strategy, and that it still has to be shown that there was a better way of winning the war.

But even given this judgement there are still some persistent Ifs about the conduct of the Italian campaign. On 10 July 1943 the Allies had landed in Sicily. Eight days later Mussolini telegraphed Hitler asking for a meeting 'to examine the situation together attentively, in order to draw from it the consequences conforming to our common interests and to those of each of our countries'. The following day the two dictators met at Feltre, near Treviso. Their discussion was not fruitful. Hitler spoke for two hours about how to conduct war. None of the Italians understood a word except Mussolini, who later tried to make Hitler appreciate the danger of Italy being crushed by the combined weight of Britain and the United States. Italy's power of resistance and morale had been badly damaged. In reply Hitler promised air and army reinforcements to defend Italy, which was in Germany's interest too. The crisis, Hitler made plain, was one of leadership. Indeed it was, and immediately after his meeting with the Duce, when he was back at the Berghof, the Führer was shown a report from Himmler, which not only predicted a *coup d'état* to get rid of Mussolini and instal Marshal Badoglio, but also stated that Badoglio would then initiate peace talks as soon as the Allies had completed the conquest of Sicily. Within a few days the first of these predictions had become a fact. On 25 July King Victor Emmanuel III dismissed Mussolini and appointed Badoglio as head of government.

When the news reached Hitler at his headquarters, he flew into a rage, but did not allow anger to cloud his judgement. Rightly suspecting that Badoglio would opt for surrender of one sort or another sooner or later, he began to make plans to prevent the military situation in Italy from getting out of hand. Even though it might be necessary to wait for further information before taking action, the planning could be done here and now – on the very evening of Mussolini's fall. If only the Allies could have taken a leaf out of

Hitler's book, and had both plans to exploit a possible surrender by Italy and the forces to implement them. One of the difficulties here, of course, lay in the Americans' reluctance to commit themselves too heavily to a campaign in southern Europe, when their eyes were firmly on the principal task of getting to grips with the main German armies in Western Europe. But as Churchill was to observe, there was only one thing worse than having Allies and that was not having them.

No such inhibitions troubled the Supreme Commander of the Wehrmacht. Hitler's political intuition, so cold, calculating and clear, was matched by the sheer efficiency, thoroughness and foresight of his military staff. Hitler's comments on the likely reaction of his Italian Allies as a result of the change in government were very much to the point. They would conceal what amounted to treachery by proclaiming their loyalty. But of course they would not be loyal. Therefore Germany would play the same game, while making preparations to take over the whole country and 'capture all the riffraff'. Four plans were made and the forces necessary to execute them nominated. Mussolini would be rescued – as indeed he later was in a daring airborne raid by Otto Skorzeny; Rome would be occupied and a Fascist Government restored; Italy would be occupied by German forces; and the Italian fleet would be seized or destroyed. No one could accuse Hitler of not thinking in bold and broad terms.

In order to be ready to establish a proper grip on the whole peninsula when the time of the Italian collapse came, Army Group B under Rommel began to concentrate with its headquarters at Munich and would contain no fewer than eight divisions, drawn mainly from France, while General von Vietinghoff would take command of a newly formed 10th Army consisting of all German divisions in the south of Italy. What a contrast there was therefore between Hitler's correct interpretation of likely developments and his rapid, ruthless action in order to control them, and the slowness and feebleness of the Allied reaction to an opportunity – that of 'knocking Italy out of the war' – which they had longed for and yet were totally ill prepared to exploit when at last it was presented to them. What might have been achieved if they had made realistically bold plans and earmarked the forces to carry them out?

It was not, in Churchill's case, for want of trying. At a meeting in Algiers with Eisenhower, Marshall and Brooke on 31 May 1943 – prior to which the Prime Minister had issued a note stressing the advantages of knocking Italy out of the war, for instance German withdrawal to the Alps, which would only be brought about 'by bold and vigorous use of the forces at our disposal' – Churchill reiterated his passionate desire to see Italy out of the war and 'Rome in our possession'. To achieve this he would be willing to send eight additional divisions, together with extra anti-aircraft units for use in post-Sicily operations. General Marshall on the other hand was reluctant to make any decision until after the attack on Sicily had started. Only then, he argued, would it be possible to determine whether the Germans intended to defend southern Italy or withdraw beyond the river Po. Yet such a way of thinking was a pitiful example of 'letting I dare not, wait upon I would, Like the poor cat i' the adage'. This was no way to win campaigns or wars. To wait to see what the enemy would do before deciding upon your own action was to surrender the initiative. The whole business of war – especially when you did hold the initiative, as the Allies did in the summer of 1943 – was to surprise and confound the enemy by striking hard and daring blows, obliging him to dance to your tune, not the other way round. Churchill was well aware of this and strongly disagreed with Marshall's view that the Allies should be cautious in their choice of what to do after conquering Sicily. Thus in the event the Sicilian campaign was launched without any clear notion of what to do next!

Shortly before the actual invasion – D-Day was 10 July – Churchill and the British Chiefs of Staff returned to the charge. The latter urged the Americans to exploit the forthcoming capture of Sicily by taking offensive action on the mainland of Italy and eliminating her from the war. This would hold down more German divisions. Churchill went further and exhorted Eisenhower to 'put your right paw on the mainland as soon as possible. Rome is the bull's eye.' As the Sicilian campaign got under way and seemed to be going well, he followed up this exhortation with further suggestions to the Chiefs of Staff as to how to proceed: 'Why should we crawl up the leg like a harvest-bug from the ankle upwards? Let us rather strike at the knee.' Once air power was firmly established on the island, we should use both that and sea power to land as far north in Italy as air cover could be provided. Plans should be prepared at once to seize Naples, march on Rome and cut off German forces further south. 'Tell the planners to throw their hat over the fence; they need not be afraid there will not be plenty of dead weight to clog it.'

It was just such bold and imaginative ideas that the Germans feared. They need not have worried. The Sicilian campaign was not going as quickly as had been hoped, but at least Churchill obtained Allied agreement to the invasion of the Italian mainland. He was determined that

the powerful British and British-controlled armies in the Mediterranean [would not be allowed] to stand idle . . . Not only must we take Rome and march as far north as possible in Italy, but our right hand must give succour to the Balkan patriots . . . I shall go to all lengths to procure the agreement of our Allies. If not, we have ample forces to act by ourselves.

If only Churchill's earlier plea in May to seize opportunity when it presented itself, or the joint planners' suggestions in that same month to exploit an Italian collapse *before* the Allies invaded or the Germans established a grip on the country had been taken up – plans made, forces earmarked, with a number of options selected to fit varying circumstances, so that if and when Italian feelers for an armistice were detected, a rapid descent on Rome with airborne and seaborne forces, seizure of airfields, establishment of air mastery and a complete switch of Italian military resources to the Allied side would result, what a dividend would have been forthcoming.

Hitler had always been concerned that the Allies would take full advantage of Italy's 'treachery'. He overestimated both their inclination and ability to act quickly and their strategic boldness when at last they did act. Six weeks were to pass between the time of Mussolini's overthrow and the declaration of an armistice between Badoglio's Government and the Allies. During those six weeks Hitler had not only deployed sixteen German divisions in Italy and taken control of the country; he had also disarmed and immobilized the Italian army. The Allies had talked much and done little.

The Sicilian campaign had, however, been brought to a successful conclusion by 16 August – the same day that Hitler ordered Rommel to move his troops across the Italian frontier. The Allies had gained much valuable experience in conducting airborne operations and amphibious assaults, directing Anglo-American armies with all the logistical problems involved, but they had perhaps failed to grasp one great strategic lesson. The courageous and skilful way in which the Germans had conducted their defence and shown themselves to be masters of delay and withdrawal should have given them pause when contemplating the ideal defensive country which abounded in Italy. All the more reason, we might say, for making plans earlier to land in Italy as far north as possible from the word go.

When the Allies did launch their invasion of the Italian mainland, it had two parts: Montgomery's 8th Army crossed the Straits of Messina on 3 September 1943 and Mark Clark's 5th Army landed at Salerno six days later. Any fears Hitler had had that the Allies would make maximum use of their air and sea power to seize Rome and force the Germans to establish their defence of Italy as far north as the Pisa–Rimini line astride the Apennines were put to rest. The Italian campaign was now to become a slow, slogging and bloody contest whose strategic value could be summed up by saying simply that it kept a large number of crack German divisions busy and therefore unable to add their weight to the decisive battles which were to be fought in Russia and Normandy. So slow was the Allied advance in southern Italy that when by the end of 1943 the Allies were still only seventy miles north of Salerno, Hitler agreed that Kesselring should establish the Winter Line across the peninsula only just north of Naples. The so-called Gustav Line, with its almost impregnable core, Cassino, was to give the Allies many months of struggle, frustrations and bloodshed. Yet the very persistence of Cassino's defenders gave rise to another opportunity and another If.

Cassino! The very name sounds like a knell, and it summoned a good many soldiers to heaven or to hell. The battle lasted for more than four months, from 15 January 1944, when Allied shells first fell on Monastery Hill, until 18 May when the Poles occupied the Abbey itself. It began too soon and went on for too long. The great irony of the whole affair was that Allied attacks on the Cassino defences began early in order to help bring about success for the planned landings at Anzio, south of Rome. On Christmas Day 1943 Churchill sent a telegram to Roosevelt explaining that Alexander was preparing to land two divisions at Anzio on or about 20 January (in the event 22 January), which should decide the battle for Rome. The idea was that by the Allies landing behind the Cassino defences, the Germans would have to react, weakening these defences and so allowing a breakthrough and a linking up of the two thrusts. Although the landings themselves were completely successful, what followed was so much the reverse that in the end it was further assault on the Gustav Line itself which came to the rescue of the beleaguered Anzio beach-head.

When the US 6th Corps landed at Anzio on the morning of 22 January they met virtually no opposition. Apart from a few coastal batteries there were only two German battalions in the neighbourhood. A few hundred enemy soldiers were rounded up, and by the end of that day the best part of two divisions, nearly 40,000 men with 3,000 vehicles, were safely ashore. 'The road to Rome', wrote General Westphal, Kesselring's Chief of Staff, 'was open. No one could have stopped a bold advance-guard entering the Holy City.'

The American commander, General Lucas, though instructed by Alexander to push forward boldly with strong mobile patrols and to make contact with the enemy – instructions which Churchill vigorously endorsed – did nothing of the sort, but simply sat down, occupied the beach-head and built up troops and supplies. He made no attempt to exploit surprise and initial success. If ever there were a moment to make assurance double sure and take a bond of fate, it was now. Indeed, Lucas had every reason for rushing on inland to seize important ground from which he could have threatened the German lines of communication to the Gustav Line. By the end of a week he had four divisions ashore, but was merely occupying an area about fifteen miles long and eight miles deep. Alexander should have given positive and unequivocal orders to push on, particularly as intelligence sources indicated that substantial German reinforcements could not arrive on the scene until a week had passed. Yet by the end of that week the reaction of the Germans had been such that they were not just containing Lucas's divisions, they were preparing for counter-attacks to eliminate them. We may sympathize with Churchill's frustration and disappointment that what he had regarded as so splendid an opportunity had been thrown away. His comment that what he had hoped would be a scalded cat had turned into a stranded whale was a just one. If the whole enterprise had gone differently and the Germans had been forced to abandon the Gustav Line in January 1944, instead of four months later, what a different complexion the Italian campaign might have had. Yet as things turned out, with a prolonged and bitter struggle at both Cassino and Anzio still to come, one more opportunity to change the course of the campaign was to be created by Alexander's strategy.

One of the best and most enduring books about the battle of Cassino, *The Monastery*, was written by Fred Majdalany, whose battalion (2nd Battalion XX The Lancashire Fusiliers) was so fiercely engaged. In it he explains the psychological aspect of the whole struggle whereby the Monastery itself became an enemy in the eyes of the soldiers:

Because of the extraordinary extent to which the summit of Monte Cassino dominated the valleys: because of the painful constancy with which men were picked off by accurately observed gunfire whenever they were forced to move in daylight within its seemingly inescapable view: because of the obvious obsessive theatrical manner in which it towered over the scene, searching every inch of it, the building set upon that summit had become the embodiment of resistance and its tangible symbol.[2]

Hence the controversial bombing of the Abbey, which the Allied commanders suspected was occupied by German soldiers as their main observation post. This bombing, which preceded the second main battle for Cassino, did not have the required effect. 'It achieved nothing,' wrote Majdalany, 'it helped nobody.' The first attack, as we have seen, was launched prematurely in order to assist the Anzio landings, but failed. The second battle, fought by the 4th Indian Division and the New Zealand Division, began on 15 February 1944. The experiences of a company of the 1st Royal Sussex do much to explain the sheer horror and peril of trying to capture a knoll between their own positions on Snakeshead Ridge and Monastery Hill.

They had to advance silently at night over difficult ground against an alert enemy only seventy yards distant. Their leading platoons had moved only fifty yards when they came under withering machine-gun fire and showers of grenades. Having gone to ground, small groups then tried to wriggle over the stony ground to work round the flanks to an objective which was so near, yet so inaccessible. The hill was too steep, the Germans' supply of grenades seemed unlimited, while their own, despite replenishment from other companies, soon ran out. The position was, in short, untenable, and orders were given for them to withdraw before first light. Three officers and sixty-three men had taken part in this fruitless endeavour. Two officers and thirty-two men had been killed or wounded. If the remainder had not been withdrawn, they would all have been accounted for.

Such was the flavour of battles for Cassino, and just as the 4th Indian Division, all its valour and perseverance notwithstanding, failed to take Monastery Hill, so did the gallant and determined New Zealand Division. It must be understood, however, as those of us who argued the toss with the German army in Italy know, what brave, skilful and dedicated soldiers the defenders of Cassino were. Their tactical improvisation in defence and counter-attack, their superb fieldcraft and concealment, brilliant use of mortars and their perfected practice of fighting with the all-arms team taught the Allies, too apt to rely on ironmongery and weight of fire-power, lesson after lesson.

So there was once more deadlock in Italy: the Allies unable to break through at Cassino, the Germans unable to push the Anzio forces back into the sea. Hitler was in no doubt about the importance of holding on in the Gustav Line. The longer they could hold the enemy off at the periphery, he told Kesselring, the better. The gaining of time was vital. What Hitler had in mind here was the development of jet aircraft and the V weapons, in which he placed great faith. Therefore, despite Kesselring's concern that if he held on too long in his present position it would be breached and he would therefore prefer to fall back on the Apennine line, Hitler ordered postponement of such a move for as long as possible. For the time being it seemed that Hitler was right, for on 15 March Alexander tried once more to breach the Gustav Line. Once again bombing was tried, this time with the aim of obliterating the German defences in the town of Cassino itself. Once again the Allies overestimated the effect that 1,000 tons of bombs and an even greater weight of artillery shells would have on the hardened 1st German Parachute Division, whose fanatical bravery and unshakeable morale, together with exceptional fighting ability, held firm. The battle lasted for a week, and although the New Zealand Division and 4th Indian Division succeeded in capturing part of the town, Monastery Hill was still not taken. The German line held. One more effort would be required.

Before it was made, another great controversy arose with regard to the respective claims of the Italian campaign and the forthcoming invasion of France. This concerned the projected landing in southern France, Operation *Anvil*, which was designed to assist the forthcoming battle for Normandy. It would mean robbing Alexander of six divisions, including the skilled French mountain troops – and these six were in addition to the seven Allied divisions withdrawn from Alexander's command for *Overlord*, the Normandy landing itself. What Alexander might have done with these extra divisions after the Cassino battle was won must constitute another great If of the Italian campaign. Even Montgomery, himself responsible for the Normandy landings, had recommended to Eisenhower that *Anvil* (later renamed *Dragoon*) should be cancelled, as

this will enable the commanders in the Mediterranean theatre to devote their whole attention to fighting the Germans in Italy . . . If agreed, then all the craft now being kept for *Anvil* can be released at once for *Overlord*. The effect of this on *Overlord* will be tremendous . . . Let us have two really good major campaigns – one in Italy and one in *Overlord*.[3]

Churchill too was strongly of this opinion and urged Roosevelt to think again, pointing out that 'By undertaking two operations in the Mediterranean theatre, both would be doomed to failure. General Alexander would be forced on to the defensive, while the *Anvil* force struggled slowly forward up the Rhône valley.'[4] The real difference

between the Allies was that whereas the Americans wanted to preserve *Overlord*'s priority and prevent the British from widening the
Italian campaign into a major thrust, Churchill longed for a great
victory there which might be exploited by driving through Yugoslavia
to Austria and so forestalling the Red Army. The irony of it all was
that when *Anvil* was launched in August 1944, it did nothing to help
what was happening in Normandy. Its whole purpose had been
forfeited. American insistence on it sprang not from sound strategic
reasoning, but from obstinacy. What could Alexander not have done
with those extra divisions – especially the French mountain troops –
when it came to the great battles for the Gothic Line which raged in
the Apennines during the autumn and winter of 1944. But first he had
to break the Gustav Line, and he did so in style.

Operation *Diadem* was designed to give the greatest possible
assistance to *Overlord* by destroying or containing as many German
divisions as possible. Its object was not, it must be emphasized, to
capture Rome. The taking of Rome was incidental to the idea.
Diadem was Alexander's *chef d'œuvre*. That it succeeded in its aim
was not in doubt as it contained twenty-one German divisions. That
it did not do far more and gravely damage von Vietinghoff's 10th
Army was the result of the Germans' customary skill in recovery and
withdrawal combined with the vanity of General Mark Clark, who
wanted his 5th Army to be the first to enter Rome and in order to
achieve this disobeyed Alexander's orders. Here was another opportunity missed, another chance thrown away.

Alexander's plan, like all great plans, was simple. Moreover, he
was able to achieve what all commanders strive to do when confronted with a stubborn and skilful foe – deceive and surprise.
Kesselring was persuaded to believe that the offensive was likely to be
in June, accompanied by yet another amphibious landing, this time
at Civitavecchia, north-west of Rome. In fact the attack began on 11
May at a time when some senior German commanders were away –
von Vietinghoff himself, von Senger und Etterlin, 14th Panzer Corps,
and the brave, flamboyant Baade, 90th Panzer Grenadier Division.
8th Army attacked on the right to break into the Liri valley, take
Cassino and drive along Route 6 towards Rome; 5th Army drove

through the Aurunci Mountains and advanced along Route 7 to the left of the Liri valley; then at the chosen time the six divisions at Anzio would storm forward to cut off the German forces which would be withdrawing from the two principal attacks by 5th and 8th Armies. Two weeks after the opening of the offensive, it looked as if everything was going according to plan. 5th and 8th Armies had broken through the Gustav and Hitler lines from the south; von Vietinghoff's 10th Army was retreating; the Anzio force under General Truscott had broken out and was racing forward to trap the retiring 10th Army. Thus on 25 May it looked as if Alexander was on the verge of an outstanding victory, which would enable him to drive Kesselring's armies north of Rome and pursue them to what was then known as the Pisa–Rimini position (the Gothic Line) before they had had time fully to prepare what later turned out to be its formidable defences.

In his other great book about Cassino Fred Majdalany shows how completely Kesselring had been out-generalled: his reserves committed and mauled about, 10th Army retreating in poor shape, 14th Army suffering from Truscott's advancing troops, it seemed as if the end were at hand, and the question had become: how many of the retreating Germans would be able to escape the trap's closing jaws?[25] On that same day, 25 May, Truscott's leading regiments were nearing Valmontone, and the following day would have closed the trap on Kesselring's retreating forces. Yet at this very moment General Clark ordered Truscott to alter course. He was required to switch his axis to the north-west and head for Rome. On receipt of this order, which dumbfounded him, Truscott at once challenged it: 'This was no time to drive to the north-west where the enemy was still strong; we should pour our maximum power into the Valmontone Gap to ensure the destruction of the retreating German Army,' he later recorded. His demand to speak personally to Clark by radio was refused, and he was obliged to conform with 'the order that turned the main effort of the beach-head forces from the Valmontone Gap and prevented the destruction of the German Tenth Army'. Mark Clark's obsession that *his* army should be the first in Rome is even harder to understand when it is clear that it was always Alexander's intention that 5th

Army should capture the city. Clark's fears that the British had some devious plan by which they would be first into Rome were groundless, since 8th Army's mission was to bypass the city in order to engage and damage the German 10th Army. The consequences of Clark's excessive fondness for glory were dire indeed. They seriously diminished the extent of defeat which Alexander was able to inflict on the enemy. Ronald Lewin in his book *Ultra Goes to War* made the point that Clark abandoned his mission not because of its risk or 'fear of the unknown' but 'for personal reasons which have scarcely been disguised'. With unusual restraint, Churchill called the decision 'unfortunate'.[6]

What then if Clark had not given any such order and Truscott had forged on and taken serious toll of 10th Army, much of which in the event got away to fight more battles? Napoleon's great concept of war was that, whereas the battle itself should be regarded as the breaking of the crest of a wave, it was the flood which swept irresistibly after it that constituted the actual victory. You had to get the enemy on the run. In May 1944 Alexander *had* got the enemy on the run, and if Truscott had been allowed to continue to the Valmontone Gap, cut off and account for the bulk of the German 10th Army, and then with all the advantage of overwhelming air power pursue and harass the whole of Kesselring's Army Group with his own powerful and highly mobile forces, possibly reinforced by the six divisions for *Anvil/Dragoon*, which would not then have been necessary, over country with no naturally strong defensive line until the Pisa–Rimini position, and moreover had done all this in June 1944 with three or four months of good campaigning weather ahead of him, what might not have been achieved? It might even have been possible to bounce the Gothic Line, which in the event was not reached and attacked until late August and early September. The idea of winning the Italian campaign in the autumn of 1944 instead of the spring of 1945, as it turned out, is something to make the most cynical armchair strategist sit up. Yet any exuberant ideas of this nature need to be balanced against the views of that practised observer and chronicler of war, Alan Moorehead, who wrote:

Many of us who followed the Italian campaign still think it was wasteful, and the insensate battering of the Gothic Line in the north appears to have been especially futile . . . It was a campaign which never had a definite and reasonable military object in view. It could end only in the Alps, the worst possible place.[7]

We may perhaps take issue with Moorehead in two respects. First, whatever Churchill's grand vision of major strategic gains by a largely British-run Army Group as a culmination of the Mediterranean strategy might have been, the fact was that the Italian campaign did provide a major distraction of German effort at a time when real decision was being reached on the Eastern and Western Fronts. In this way it *did* have a military object. Second, an early and successful conclusion of the fighting for Italy did not have to end in the Alps. Victorious Allied armies could have branched off through Piedmont into France or through Slovenia towards Austria, and thus provide a further distraction for Hitler's hard-pressed Wehrmacht.

The Italian campaign is full of Ifs and Buts. Yet two things are clear. Churchill's soft underbelly turned out to be uncomfortably hard, and whereas during the campaign the Germans seized every opportunity going and never forewent an advantage, the Allies made a habit of forgoing advantage and letting opportunity slip. The Germans' skilful defence of Italy, however, availed Hitler nothing in the end. The summer of 1944 brought him crisis in the east and the west. Although his subordinates told him that the war was lost, he would not listen to them. Knowing that the Führer was the only obstacle to making peace, some of these subordinates, not for the first time, decided to get rid of him.

TEN

Conditional Surrender

I have just had the greatest piece of luck in my life.

It may have been a piece of luck for the Führer. It was not for those who caused him to say it. The attempt to assassinate Hitler at Wolfsschanze, his headquarters near Rastenburg in East Prussia, had failed, and his retribution was terrible. During his military conference there, little comfort was to be found in reviewing the situation. The strategic position of the Third Reich was, if not hopeless, critical in the extreme. The Wehrmacht was having a rough time of it on all fronts in the summer of 1944. As we have just recorded, although the skilful and relentless generalship of Kesselring in Italy had enabled him to hold the Winter Line until May, Alexander's offensive had obliged the Germans to withdraw and allow the Allies to enter Rome on 4 June.[1] There was nothing for it now but to establish a further – and as it turned out formidable – defensive zone on the Gothic Line. In Normandy Montgomery not only had won a firm foothold, but was also winning the battle of the build-up, for by 18 June he had twenty divisions ashore and opposing him were eighteen, some so under strength that their fighting capacity was but three-quarters of that number. Hitler, as was customary with him, refused to acknowledge the realities of the situation when on the previous day he conferred with Rommel and von Rundstedt at Margival,[2] in the command post which had been specially constructed for the Führer to supervise the invasion of England four years earlier.

Rommel's Chief of Staff, Speidel, was present at this meeting and reported that Hitler appeared 'worn and sleepless, playing nervously with his spectacles and an array of coloured pencils which he held between his fingers'. While Hitler sat on a stool, the two Field-Marshals stood and were treated to a condemnation of their conduct of the defence. The Supreme Commander of the Wehrmacht could not yet see there was no question of throwing the invaders back into the sea so that he could turn back once more to deal with the Red Army. It was annihilation he wanted, and meanwhile every foot of territory was to be contested while the V weapons brought England to its senses. When Rommel urged Hitler to end the war, he was sharply told to look to his own front and leave the war's future to the Supreme Commander. Later that month both Rommel and von Rundstedt renewed their efforts to persuade Hitler to end the war. But facts and reason had no interest for Hitler and certainly could not prevail upon him to the extent of making him change his mind. When the battle of the Odon removed any chance the Germans might have had to split the Allied invasion force by striking at Bayeux, von Rundstedt warned OKW that the battle for Normandy was lost. Keitel[3] was in despair. 'What shall we do?' he wailed. 'Make peace, you fools,' was von Rundstedt's uncompromising reply. He was replaced by von Kluge. Hitler could not admit that he was in the wrong: in his view just one more of the 'gentlemen who write *von* in front of their names' had let him down. But neither von Kluge nor any other soldier could alter the realities of the situation, and von Kluge himself was obliged to concede a few weeks later that 'in the face of the enemy's complete command of the air, there is no possibility of our finding a strategy which will counterbalance its truly annihilating effect, unless we give up the field of battle'. He added that in spite of his determination to stand fast, as the Führer had ordered, the price to be paid was the destruction of his armies and the dissolution of the front. Events were to prove his prediction all too accurate.

With things going so badly in the south and the west, was there any comfort to be derived from those operations being conducted by the bulk of the Wehrmacht – on the Eastern Front? None whatsoever! June 1944 heralded the Red Army's summer offensive. The German army's attempt to hold lines which were far too extended to defend properly and which Hitler would not agree to shorten led to an inevitable result. In July Minsk, Vilna, Pinsk and Grodno were all taken. Even East Prussia was threatened. The Eastern Front had disintegrated. No wonder there were those in the Wehrmacht and outside it who once more plucked up the courage to get rid of the man as a result of whose disastrous military policies Germany was heading for total defeat.

Ever since 1938 there had been conspiracies hostile to the Nazi régime. Among the conspirators were General Ludwig Beck, former Chief of Staff, Dr Karl Goerdeler, who had been Oberbürgermeister of Leipzig, Ulrich von Hassel, ex-Ambassador to Rome, and Colonel, later General, Hans Oster of the Abwehr, the counter-intelligence branch of OKW. One use of this last organization was to try to discover what sort of peace the Western Allies would be willing to make after Hitler's overthrow, but attempts to do so met with no response. It has to be remembered that at the Casablanca meeting in January 1943 Roosevelt had called for 'Unconditional Surrender' and thus if the conspirators were to act, it would be without any reassurances from outside. Beck and Goerdeler had hoped to recruit the support of senior commanders in the field, among them Field-Marshal von Kluge, who in the early part of 1943 was in command of Army Group Centre on the Eastern Front, but Kluge, like others, was only willing to co-operate after Hitler's death or arrest. Any attempt to proceed therefore had to be made without support from the Army High Command. Proceed it did with the assistance of General Olbricht, who was Deputy Commander of the Home Army, and two more converts to the plot – General von Tresckow, a senior staff officer at von Kluge's headquarters, and one of his subordinates, Lieutenant Schlabrendorff. On 13 March 1943 these two men secreted a time-bomb on the aeroplane which flew Hitler from von Kluge's headquarters at Smolensk back to East Prussia. Hitler's luck was in that day, for the bomb failed to explode. The attempt was not discovered, however, as Schlabrendorff flew to Hitler's headquarters and calmly removed the bomb before it was found. Hitler's luck was to continue, for although further plots were hatched, they came to nothing until in July 1944 Count von Stauffenberg stepped on to centre-stage.

Von Stauffenberg had been in the wings for some time. He was a gallant front-line soldier, who had been gravely wounded in the Tunisian campaign. Before that, while serving on the staff in the Russian campaign, he had been made privy to the conspiracy by Tresckow and Schlabrendorff, and in June 1944, having recovered from his wounds – which had cost him his left eye, his right hand and two fingers of his left hand – he was appointed Chief of Staff to General Fritz Fromm, Commander-in-Chief, Home Army, whose deputy was a leading conspirator, General Olbricht. Von Stauffenberg became a key player in the plot, and in his new appointment was well placed to act as he would be required to attend Hitler's staff conferences at times when Home Army matters were on the agenda. Together with Olbricht, von Stauffenberg prepared plans – under the pretext of emergency measures to be taken should there be a revolt by the millions of foreign workers in Germany or landings by enemy airborne troops – by which the army would take control of the country both at home and on the various battlefronts, once Hitler had been removed from the scene. There would then be no question of interference by any 'private' forces loyal to Göring or Himmler, and with the German armies still intact in the field, there would be some grounds for hoping to negotiate a compromise peace. All the necessary orders and signals were drawn up and distributed. The code word *Walkyrie* would be transmitted to field commanders and headquarters at home that the Führer was dead and that the army was forming a new Government with Beck at his head, Goerdeler as Chancellor and von Witzleben as Commander-in-Chief of the Wehrmacht.

The conspirators had agreed that von Stauffenberg, because of his key position in being able to attend Führer conferences and having drawn up the *Walkyrie* plans, should play a dual role, both assassinating Hitler and returning to Berlin to supervise the plot's execution. He would therefore have to escape from the conference room, having planted the bomb and set it to go off, then return at once to Berlin. There was still the question of when all this was to be done, and on this vital point there was some hesitation. It was the success of the Allied invasion of Normandy that decided the issue, coinciding as it did with the Red Army's summer offensive and Alexander's offensive in Italy. Had the Normandy invasion been defeated and the Allies thrown back into the sea, so some of the conspirators believed, Germany's negotiating position with the West would have been much stronger. But by the end of June, it was clear that the Western powers were firmly established and growing ever more powerful. So paradoxically the case for acting now was strengthened by the very progress of the Allies, since it made the support of senior commanders in the field, like Rommel, more likely.

On the day of von Stauffenberg's attempt to do the deed, Chance played a leading part. 'The *putsch* would almost certainly have succeeded,' wrote Chester Wilmot,

if Hitler had not been saved by what can only be regarded as a miracle. It was mere chance that on July 20th the midday conference should have been held in a flimsy wooden hut and not in the usual concrete bunker, where the explosion would have been deadly. It was equally fortuitous that the table in the hut should have been so constructed that the main force of the blast was taken up by the solid understructure. Even as it was, three of the officers standing on Hitler's side of the table and only a yard nearer the explosion lost their lives. Yet Hitler himself survived.[4]

Hitler's escape showed him at his most remarkable and most vile. Nothing seemed able to shake his conviction that he had been chosen to shape the world's destiny. That in military failure, in defeat, when utterly doomed, he still exercised the ability – and not through fear or tyranny alone – to control events and people speaks much for his unbreakable will-power, however diabolical. Such iron resolution is rare indeed. Yet how vindictive and how appallingly comprehensive was his revenge. In his incomparable study of *The Last Days of Hitler* Hugh Trevor-Roper describes the blood-purge which followed the assassination attempt as even more drastic than that of 1934 when Hitler rid himself of Röhm, the SA leader, von Schleicher and others.[5] In this later purge there were at least 160 victims, either executed or committing suicide. Among them were von Hassell, von Witzleben, Rommel, Beck, von Stauffenberg, even Fromm. Two Field-Marshals, seventeen Generals and more than fifty other officers died. Those members of the Offizierkorps who did not know it already – and there could not have been many of them – thus had it brought home to them once and for all that the Führer was mad, bad and dangerous to know. Churchill, when exasperated by what he regarded as the caution or pusillanimity of his generals, might talk of shooting a few of them. Hitler did it. 'I'm beginning to doubt,' he declared on the afternoon of 20 July, 'whether the German people are worthy of my great ideals. No one appreciates what I have done for them.'

What had he done? He had brought Germany to the brink of total defeat in the field and there was worse to come. But what if the 20 July plot had succeeded and Hitler had been killed in the blast of von Stauffenberg's bomb? Further, what if the *Walkyrie* plans had been successfully carried out with Beck as head of state, Goerdeler as Chancellor, von Witzleben as Commander-in-Chief of the Wehrmacht and von Kluge, who had agreed to cooperate after Hitler's death, still in command of the German armies in the West? What if the German armed forces as a whole had rallied to the conspirators, and the forces likely to be hostile and adhere rather to such leading Nazis as Himmler and Göring had been neutralized? And what if Goebbels, that master of propaganda and manipulator of opinion, who in both 1943 and 1944, seeing clearly enough the disaster Germany faced, had tried to persuade Hitler to make a compromise peace, had also come down on the side of the by then successful *putsch*-makers and used all his skills to win over the German people? Finally, what if Albert Speer had added his not inconsiderable weight to the new rulers of the Third Reich and wholeheartedly supported the notion of approaching the Western Allies with offers of an armistice? Then we may be sure that von Kluge and others would have made such offers, either through diplomatic channels or directly to Montgomery's head-quarters in the field. What then would have been the Allied response? Beck, Goerdeler, von Witzleben, von Kluge, von Stauffenberg and the others all knew well enough about 'Unconditional Surrender' but they were of the opinion that an offer to withdraw the German armies in the West, thus allowing the Allies an unopposed advance to Berlin, would be too alluring to be refused.

It was in January 1943 at Casablanca that the Allied leaders, Roosevelt and Churchill, had called for 'Unconditional Surrender'.

This announcement had not been the result of previous inter-Allied consultation. The phrase itself had been used in a State Department paper to brief Roosevelt before he attended the conference, and it was on the third day of the meeting that the President first brought it out in discussions over lunch with the Prime Minister, who endorsed the idea of making an announcement to the press. Churchill then obtained the agreement of the War Cabinet, and at the end of the conference on 24 January the so-called Unconditional Surrender Declaration was given to journalists. It included what it called a 'simple formula of placing the objective of this war in terms of an unconditional surrender by Germany, Italy and Japan'. In commenting on how this declaration affected German attitudes, Trevor-Roper dismisses the idea that it frightened Germans into further compliance with Hitler's regime, for he argues that few of those Germans who would rather tolerate the tyranny of the Third Reich than endure Unconditional Surrender would have been persuaded to rebel by promises of moderate treatment by the Allies. Indeed, given Hitler's absolute grip on power, enhanced still further by the measures he took after the failed assassination attempt to complete the subservience of the army to National Socialism, it may confidently be said that Unconditional Surrender did not prolong the war. It did, however, provide Stalin with some assurance that the Western powers would not make a compromise peace with Germany, and even as late as February 1945, when Churchill, Roosevelt and Stalin conferred at Yalta, they reiterated their determination to pursue a policy of Unconditional Surrender and maximum pressure to finish the war quickly. Yet it was clear even then that as long as Hitler was alive there would be no surrender of any sort. Only two months earlier he had lectured his Generals: 'Wars are finally decided by one side or the other recognizing that they cannot be won. We must allow no moment to pass without showing the enemy that, whatever he does, he can never reckon on a capitulation. Never! Never!'

But the chance we are dealing with here is a successful *putsch*, a Third Reich freed from the iron grip of Adolf Hitler, a Germany headed by soldiers and statesmen who recognized only too well that the war could not be won, and who could show the enemy a willingness to capitulate, but it would be a *conditional* surrender – withdrawal by the Western group of armies and continued defence on the Eastern Front. However tempting such an offer might have been – and we must bear in mind that in November 1944 Eisenhower was asking the Combined Chiefs of Staff for a modification of Unconditional Surrender as he could detect no sign of an early collapse of German morale in the West – it may be supposed that the Western powers would have rejected it and stuck to their resolution of unconditional surrender. But suppose that von Kluge and his armies in the West had then simply conducted a general withdrawal – first to the Rhine, then to the Elbe, then even to the Oder – while still holding off the Red Army in Poland. What then? Montgomery's Army Group, rapidly reinforced no doubt by all the divisions still waiting in the United Kingdom and the United States, would have had little option but to follow up, so occupying Germany, Austria and Czechoslovakia, and certainly causing Kesselring in Italy to throw his hand in with von Kluge and the others. Such events would have put paid to Churchill's ever-growing fear about Russian designs on Central Europe. At this time – late summer and early autumn of 1944 – the Yalta meeting which decided how the Third Reich was to be partitioned had not even taken place. A wholly new and unexpected strategic situation would have emerged, with the Western powers in a very much more powerful bargaining position than was the case in the spring of 1945 when the Anglo-American and Red Armies agreed a junction on the Elbe–Mulde rivers. It is hardly to be thought that Stalin would lightly accept such a division of Germany as now confronted him. At the same time the Western powers, while supporting wholeheartedly a general capitulation of the Wehrmacht on the Eastern Front as well, would have wished to ensure that Churchill's great belief – 'In Victory, Magnanimity' – was the watchword. We must remember too Isaiah Berlin's contention that Churchill never hated Germany as such.

Germany is a great, historically hallowed state; the Germans are a great historic race and as such occupy a proportionate amount of space in Mr Churchill's world picture. He denounced the Prussians in the First World War and the Nazis in the Second; the Germans scarcely at all.[6]

Whether the Prime Minister would have prevailed against the combined wills of Roosevelt and Stalin is, like this hypothesis itself, a matter of conjecture. Conjecture may be entertained endlessly, but we must come back to earth and face the fact that Hitler survived the July 1944 plot.

It is ironic that less than a month after the failed attempt on Hitler's life von Kluge, the very man about whom some of this conjecture has been, who was aware of the plot but not actively part of it, caused the Führer to call 15 August 'the worst day of my life'. He was referring not to the military disasters which were overtaking his armies in the West as a result of his own direction, but to his fear that von Kluge had been planning to surrender these armies to the Allies. After Montgomery's offensive *Goodwood* had pinned down the bulk of German panzer forces in the eastern part of the Normandy bridgehead at the end of July, the Americans under Bradley and Patton broke through in the western part. Patton's armoured columns swept eastwards and the German armies were threatened with encirclement at Falaise. Now was the moment to temper valour with discretion and withdraw these armies east of the Seine and fight again another day. Just the contrary was what the Führer decided to do. He ordered von Kluge to counter-attack the American corridor through Avranches and Mortain. What is more, he laid down exactly what was to be done – all this from Rastenburg, the plan made from large-scale French maps, detailing formations, routes, objectives. The attack failed as a matter of course. It was stopped and overwhelmed by Allied air power. No explanation of the difficulties satisfied Hitler, who pronounced that 'the attack failed because Field-Marshal von Kluge wanted it to fail'. Nothing could have been more petulant, perverse or self-delusive.

A week later on 15 August, not only did the Allied landings take place in the south of France – far too late to influence the battle for Normandy – but von Kluge, visiting the front, was out of touch with his headquarters for twelve hours. It was this that led Hitler to believe that von Kluge was trying to make contact with the enemy in order to negotiate a surrender. Having made up his mind that von Kluge was bent on treachery, he was not slow to find reasons to fit in with all the related events. It was only by chance, by accident, he argued, that von Kluge's plan of surrender had not come off. 'It's the only way you can explain everything the Army Group did; otherwise it would all be incomprehensible.' Hitler was continuing to make pictures to fit his own distorted vision. So von Kluge was dismissed, Model took his place, and on his way back to Germany von Kluge committed suicide, sending one last plea to the Führer to put an end to the hopeless struggle.

Far from doing so, on the very day of the Falaise battle, 19 August, Hitler was sowing the seeds for one last throw of the dice. Jodl, Chief of Operations, OKW, noted in his diary:

The Führer discussed the equipment and manpower position in the West with Chief of OKW, Chief Army Staff and Speer. Prepare to *take the offensive in November* when the enemy's air forces can't operate. Main point: some *25 divisions must* be moved in the next one to two months.

Hitler was about to throw away his last reserves. In 1940 he had won a startling victory by smashing through the Ardennes. What he could do once, he could do again.

ELEVEN

The Gambler Keeps His Stake

If it does not succeed, I no longer see any possibility for ending the war well . . . But we will come through. A single breakthrough on the Western Front! You'll see! It will lead to collapse and panic among the Americans. We'll drive straight through their middle and take Antwerp. Then they'll have lost their supply port. And a tremendous pocket will encircle the entire English army, with hundreds of thousands of prisoners. As we used to do in Russia.

HITLER TO SPEER, NOVEMBER 1944

By September 1944 the war was being fought on the soil of Germany. The Red Army was approaching East Prussia; the British and Americans were nearing the Rhineland. Yet Hitler did not despair. For the time being the Wehrmacht held its various enemies at bay. There was no question, Hitler decided, of seeking a political solution. This could be done only in the wake of military successes, not defeats. Besides, the Allies were bound to fall out sooner or later. All coalitions disintegrated in the end. 'Since 1941 it has been my task not to lose my nerve,' he claimed, and he would not lose it now. He lived only for the purpose of leading the fight, for the battle could not be won without an iron will behind it. Therefore they would go on fighting until – and here Hitler resorted to a phrase employed by his great hero, Frederick II of Prussia – 'one of our damned enemies gets too tired to fight any more'. They would fight for a peace which would secure the German nation for the next century and which 'above all, does not besmirch our honour a second time, as happened in 1918'.

There was still a good deal to fight with. On paper the Wehrmacht totalled 10 million men, and in October Hitler proclaimed a *levée en masse* to form a Volkssturm, a Home Guard, for the Reich's protection. Moreover, the remarkable energy and organization of Albert Speer kept armament production going, even though there were shortages of petrol and oil. The German army in the West had made an astonishing recovery under the bustling leadership of Model, who had replaced von Kluge. This recovery had been assisted by Allied disagreement as to what strategy should now be pursued. Eisenhower, who had taken over command of the land battle from Montgomery on 1 September, was in favour of advancing on a broad front. Montgomery, on the other hand, was persistent in recommending a concentrated thrust on a narrow front, as he argued that a broad-front policy could not be logistically supported, would be decisive nowhere, would simply peter out and allow the Germans to complete their recovery.

With a wholly uncharacteristic fling to keep the Germans off balance and to open the way for a bold armoured thrust, Montgomery launched the airborne assault on the Rhine bridges, but discovered when the gallant attempt to turn the northern flank at Arnhem had failed, that they had in General Browning's words gone 'a bridge too far'. It seemed that the Wehrmacht had not only imposed a kind of stalemate west of the Rhine, but had done the same in the south where Kesselring was holding a new winter line north of Rimini–Florence–Pisa. For the time being East Prussia was holding firm. Indeed, Hitler had insisted on staying at Rastenburg, telling Keitel that if he left East Prussia it would fall. Not until November did he return to Berlin. By then the Balkan front was in ruins. Romania had capitulated; Bulgaria had been occupied by the Red Army; the British were in Athens; Belgrade was occupied by Tito; and the Wehrmacht was doing what it could to stem the enemy's advance on the line of the Danube in Hungary. Even Vienna was vulnerable.

Yet the Führer, having in his own mind stabilized the fronts sufficiently and ignoring the growing dangers in the East, was planning to mount one more offensive, one more gigantic illustration of Blitzkrieg which would capture Antwerp, drive a wedge into Eisenhower's armies and trap the British army, in short, be a repetition of 1940. In only one respect, however, did the idea resemble

Sichelschnitt. The chosen point for the *Schwerpunkt* would once again be the Ardennes. In making up his mind as to where this offensive should be launched, Hitler had rejected all ideas of the East. What quick or dramatic decision could be gained there? Distances were too great, logistic resources were too slender, objectives were indeterminate, the Red Army seemed to be inexhaustible. How different might be prizes in the West! To split the Allied armies, deny them a main port of entry, dismay them with the seemingly unbreakable power of the Wehrmacht, fasten upon the contradictions of an uneasy alliance, recapture the initiative at last, gain a little time and then turn on the full fury of his new secret weapons – might not a gamble of this sort pay infinite odds? In thinking along such lines Hitler was being true to his nature. He was prepared to risk all his stake money on one single turn of pitch-and-toss. But if he lost, there would be no starting again at the beginning. It was all or nothing – *Weltmacht oder Niedergang*.

The Allies might have been divided as to the proper strategy to be adopted after the battle of Normandy had been so triumphantly concluded, but on one thing they were agreed. The Germans would not, could not, attempt any large-scale counter-offensive. On 7 December Eisenhower discussed the situation with his two senior commanders, Bradley and Montgomery, at Maastricht. They were worried about the Germans' evident recovery and high morale, von Rundstedt's clear ability to conduct a stubborn and skilful defence, particularly at a time when poor weather inhibited the Allied air forces from operating freely. There was especial concern about the whereabouts and likely activities of von Rundstedt's main reserve in the West, the 6th SS Panzer Army. Yet allied Intelligence experts consoled themselves with the belief that von Rundstedt would not chance his luck by throwing away one of the most effective means of checking further Allied advances.

What must strike us as strange today, now that Hitler's supreme grip on military affairs and his absolute refusal to face facts are well known and understood, is that any senior commander on the Allied side, least of all Intelligence staffs, should have expected the Wehrmacht to conform to sensible rules of conducting war. Yet they had repeatedly been shown by the Wehrmacht's supreme commander that his strategy was not based on shrewd weighing of the military options. It was founded on intuition, will-power, total over-estimation of the Wehrmacht's ability to overcome the Allies' determination and staying power. By his impulsive and rash conduct of affairs, which had led to the disasters of Stalingrad, Tunisia, Kursk and Avranches, Hitler had demonstrated his readiness to contravene the military rules. Yet the Allied commanders in the West seemed to have been lulled into a condition of optimism by the relative stalemate of the autumn of 1944. Bradley's intelligence staff had noted on 12 December that at any moment the Wehrmacht's breaking-point might be reached. Even Montgomery, master of circumspection, observed on 15 December that the enemy could not stage major offensive operations. The following day Operation *Herbstnebel* (Autumn Mist), code-name for the Ardennes counter-offensive, began.

When we add to this unreadiness of the Allies the fact that Bradley had deployed only four divisions in the Ardennes on a front of seventy-five miles, while Hitler had assembled no fewer than twenty-eight divisions, eight of which were Panzer Divisions, we may readily comprehend that the German offensive took the Allies by surprise and enjoyed initial success. The broad plan was that three armies would attack between Montschau and Echternech. 6th SS Panzer Army under the celebrated Sepp Dietrich was to deliver the main blow in the north, crossing the Meuse at Huy and Andenne and then striking towards Antwerp; Manteuffel's 5th Panzer Army would advance in the centre through Namur and Dinant to Brussels; while 7th Army under Brandenberger would protect the southern flank. When von Rundstedt received this plan, endorsed in Hitler's hand: '*Nicht abändern!*' ('Not to be altered'), he was dumbfounded. It was so obvious to him that the forces at his disposal were quite inadequate for so ambitious an undertaking.

Aware of his own inability to move the Führer from a chosen course, von Rundstedt despatched Model instead, in the hope that his bustling, brisk style and fearless temperament might prevail. But all Model's efforts to modify the plan so that it might have some chance of being carried out duly failed. Hitler had written '*Nicht abändern*' and he had meant it. He was determined to have Antwerp.

Four days before the offensive was launched, Hitler harangued all the senior commanders who were to execute it. Lack of confidence in the plan itself could only have been deepened by the Führer's appearance as well as his words. Bayerlein, commanding the Panzer Lehr division, saw only an old, broken man reading a long prepared speech with a shaking hand. Manteuffel recalled 'a stooped figure with a pale and puffy face, hunched in his chair, his hands trembling, his left arm subject to a violent twitching'. And this was the Supreme Commander of the Wehrmacht. After rambling on about the incongruities of the Grand Alliance fighting against them, Bolsheviks hand in hand with Capitalists, imperialists in league with anti-imperialists, Russia and Britain, who for so long had been rivals in the Near and Middle East, now again at loggerheads over the Balkans and the Persian Gulf, Hitler declared that the whole thing was ripe for disintegration: 'If we can now deliver a few more heavy blows, then at any moment this artificially bolstered common front may collapse with a mighty clap of thunder.' How prophetic he was. It did collapse before long, but not until after the Wehrmacht's utter defeat and its Commander-in-Chief's self-slaughter.

This defeat was assisted and accelerated by the Ardennes offensive which began on 16 December. In spite of the initial weakness of the American forces opposing the German attacks and of the consequent advance by panzer spearheads, the attempt to reach Antwerp and Brussels was blocked and defeated. Indeed, von Rundstedt subsequently commented that had they even got as far as the Meuse they would have gone down on their knees and thanked God. As it was, the heroic defence of Bastogne, the grip established by Montgomery on the northern shoulders of the German penetration, intervention by Patton's 3rd Army and the weather's clearing on Christmas Eve, so enabling 5,000 Allied aircraft to fill the sky and swoop on the German columns, all added up to the fact, unpalatable for Hitler, that the momentum of the offensive had been broken. By 27 December it was no longer a question of being able to continue the advance. It was a matter of whether or not the surviving forces could be extricated before it was too late. Characteristically, Hitler rejected all ideas of withdrawal, although there were compelling reasons for doing so. Not only was there the danger of his armies in the Ardennes being destroyed, but there was gathering peril on the Eastern Front. Guderian, now Chief of General Staff, came to tell Hitler, now with his headquarters at Adlershorst (Eagle's Nest), Bad Nauheim, that if troops were not transferred to the East soon, the imminent Russian winter attacks could not be held. Dismissing all such threats from the Red Army as 'the greatest imposture since Genghis Khan' and demanding to know who was responsible 'for all this rubbish', Hitler ordered a resumption of the offensive in a further attempt to reach the Meuse. The result of it all was that by mid-January 1945, just one month since the offensive was launched, what remained of the attacking forces were back behind their starting lines, with nothing in the balance-sheet to compensate for dreadful losses of 120,000 men, 600 tanks and guns, 1,600 aircraft and 6,000 vehicles. Hitler's reserves had gone, and after the battle, as Montgomery later observed, 'the Germans gave no serious resistance'.

Yet ironically enough there had been a chance during the early stages of the offensive when, if Hitler had been moved by purely military reasoning, not by political leanings, he might have prolonged his possession of the initiative and even reached the river Meuse. As early as the first evening of the attack, 16 December, it was clear that Manteuffel's 5th Panzer Army was making much better progress than Dietrich's 6th SS Panzer Army. Despite the caution urged by von Rundstedt, it was at this point that Hitler, with all the authority he wielded as Supreme Commander, should have switched all available reserves, including the powerful 2nd SS Panzer Corps, to reinforce Manteuffel, in other words to stick to that invariably reliable maxim of exploiting success, not propping up failure. Such a move, while still not achieving the aim of reaching Antwerp – always too distant and unattainable an objective – would have conformed to those indispensable principles of concentration and adaptability, and by speed of movement maintained an element of surprise.

But the Supreme Commander could not see it. 6th SS Panzer Army was to be the spearhead and that was that. For political reasons Hitler wished to keep his SS Panzer Divisions under SS, that is Dietrich's, command. So the great opportunist chucked aside opportunity at the very moment it beckoned to him. Even on the night of 18/19 December when von Rundstedt was again advising Hitler to call off the operation and consolidate the gains that had been made, Model disagreed and recommended that even now, if the main weight off the attack were switched to Manteuffel, there would still be the chance of a breakthrough. Hitler would still not listen, but two days later, on 20 December, with a final ironical touch, authorized the switch. By this time it was too late.

We have noted von Clausewitz's contention that of all human activities none is so much linked to chance as that of making war. And one of the most curious features of the Ardennes battle as it developed was that the three most important parts of it – the German attempts to capture Malmedy, St-Vith and Bastogne – had been brought about by Allied reactions which owed their origins not to calculation but to chance. The US 7th Armoured Division had not been directed to St-Vith in accordance with some grand design which foresaw that its defence would be critical to the whole operation. It went there by order of a local commander because of the need at that time to meet a local threat. 101st Airborne Division and the Combat Command of 10th Armoured Division went to Bastogne merely, as Eisenhower himself admitted, 'because Bastogne was such an excellent road centre. Troops directed there could later be despatched by the commander on the spot to any region he found desirable.' By such chances are campaigns determined. Had all this not happened and had the Germans reached and crossed the Meuse and advanced towards Brussels and Antwerp, what would have been the outcome? We must remember that Montgomery's Army Group, although he was later put in charge of the northern flank and took a firm grip of it, was hardly engaged at all. As he himself said: 'The battle of the Ardennes was won primarily by the staunch fighting qualities of the American soldier.' We may recall also Patton's characteristically blunt comment on 19 December during the Allied High Command conference at Verdun: 'Let the —— —— go all the way to Paris'; then they would 'cut 'em off and chew 'em up'.[1] Indeed German losses might have mounted in proportion to how far they advanced. In any case the gambler's final throw had failed. The roulette ball had found its niche in zero!

But say that by chance Hitler had changed his mind at the last moment and having assembled those twenty-eight divisions with their powerful panzer content, had determined not to gamble them away on an offensive which his senior field commanders deplored, but instead had kept them in reserve to argue the toss with the Anglo-American armies advancing towards the Rhine and at the same time have something in hand to avert a collapse of the Eastern Front: what then? It was a time of year when Allied air supremacy was least able to influence the land battle. Even as things were, there was still much hard fighting to be done by the Allies before they restored the Western Front to what it had been before the Ardennes counter-offensive. During the first week of January two major battles were in progress. One was Patton's 3rd Army fighting to the west of Bastogne in order to widen the salient he had driven through to the town from the south and so bring ever-increasing pressure on the southern flank of the Bulge; the other was Montgomery's drive with the US VII Corps and British XXX Corps towards the key communications centre of Houffalize. There were many conditions favourable to the Germans. The intense cold – and no army on the Western Front was better equipped and better trained for winter warfare than the Wehrmacht – multiplied the inherent advantage of the defender in such weather. For skilful use of mines, booby traps and entrenched positions concealed by the ever-present snow is one thing; advancing over icy roads and impassable, boggy or mined country and so presenting yourself as a target is another. The appalling weather, having robbed the attackers of their trump card – air power – meant that every inch of ground had to be fought and sometimes refought for – some villages changed hands several times in as many days – as the Germans, more effective in withdrawal than any soldiers of the Second World War, wrested every benefit from the natural delaying strength of the Ardennes.

As Montgomery's January counter-attacks got under way, blizzards, biting winds, frozen ground, tracks too icy and slippery for even tracked vehicles to get a grip, snow and fog so thick that British and German troops kept finding themselves mixed up together, sleep and hot food out of the question – made them no joke. 'The blizzard howled and raged,' wrote one veteran of the battle, 'with ever increasing intensity and not even the massive Christmas tree regalia which the fighting soldier dons in battle could in any way relieve the numbing effect of the Arctic wind.' Another soldier recalled that tanks were required to advance up icy tracks and attempt to shoot and manoeuvre when the men were blinded by fog and soaked, with no possibility of supply vehicles reaching them with their indispensable ammunition, food and petrol, so that all these things had to be man-handled up freezing, slippery slopes.

After nearly a week's exposure to murderous enemy fire and viciously cold weather, short of sleep, food, warmth and everything that made a soldier's life tolerable, one British battalion had lost more than half its strength in killed and wounded, but was nevertheless ready to fight on. In this way the spirit of the ordinary soldier and that of his immediate leaders – battalion, company and platoon commanders – together with the staunch, resilient courage and example of the non-commissioned officers, shone triumphant. Not quite so triumphant was Allied leadership at the top, which was uneven, capricious, discordant, characterized by the drive for national or personal glorification, and at times even contradictory. On 10 January 1945 the Combined Chiefs of Staff had asked the Supreme Allied Commander, Eisenhower, what his plans were. His reply ten days later made it clear that his strategy was dominated by the Rhine: getting to it, getting over it, advancing into Germany and destroying all German forces encountered in the process. While holding to the view that the main attack should be made north of the Ruhr if possible, the Supreme Commander reserved the right to switch his main effort from north to south, that is, the Frankfurt–Kassel axis. Yet when the plan was actually spelled out, it was obvious that Eisenhower intended to continue with attacks on two main axes, that is, to persist in what always had been and was to continue to be his concept of the entire campaign – a broad-front advance. The British Chiefs of Staff did not agree with this idea at all. They wanted all resources to be concentrated in one thrust to maintain momentum. Thus on the eve of the Yalta conference when the Big Three,

Roosevelt, Churchill and Stalin, would meet to discuss how to finish Germany off militarily and then divide and administer their defeated enemy, there was a major clash of opinion between the British and their American Allies.

In commenting on Hitler's strategy – if it deserves such a name – at this stage in the war, Chester Wilmot pointed out that the Supreme Commander was prepared to court defeat on the Vistula in the hope of gaining victory on the Meuse and recovery on the Danube,[2] in other words, despite all Guderian's pleading that the Eastern Front must be reinforced from the West unless the whole thing were allowed to collapse like a house of cards, Hitler paid no attention to him. It was hardly surprising therefore that when the Red Army's great offensive started on 12 January, it swept all before it, and although it came to a halt at the beginning of February, by this time the Russians had reached the Baltic, overrun East Prussia, threatened Danzig and got as far as the river Oder at Küstrin and Frankfurt (Frankfurt an der Oder, not to be confused with Frankfurt-am-Main in the west), both less than fifty miles from Berlin. Prospects on the Western Front at the same time were very different. It was true that Hitler's Ardennes offensive had been defeated. But its defeat had not been accompanied by any giant and sweeping advances such as the Red Army had enjoyed. The American, British and French armies were still slogging their way slowly forward against skilful and determined defences. They had not even closed up to the Rhine and the Siegfried Line along its full length.

When we consider therefore how the situation might have been transformed if Hitler, instead of chucking away his carefully mustered reserve of twenty-eight divisions on the fruitless chance of capturing Antwerp, had carefully nurtured them and, while continuing to deploy sufficient strength in the west to dispute the Allied advance, had hung on to the newly formed, powerful panzer reserves in order to counter any enemy penetration of the line, he could have delayed the Anglo-American armies far longer than he did. Even so, Montgomery and Bradley did not cross the Rhine until March 1945.

Von Rundstedt, Hitler's Commander-in-Chief, West, whose name was given to the Ardennes offensive, even though, leaving aside his opposition to it and his attempts to call it off almost as soon as it had started, he had little influence over its course, pointed out after the war that every step forward simply prolonged the flanks more dangerously, making them more and more vulnerable to Allied counter-strokes. He therefore tried to stop it early on when it was clear that there was no chance of achieving its aim, but Hitler furiously insisted that it must go on. Had the offensive been called off early and the gains made been used for strengthening and deepening the German defences, further delays would have been imposed on the Allies. But this was nothing to what might have been achieved if the entire force of twenty-eight divisions had been employed in the way that Cassius had put it to Brutus before Philippi:

> 'Tis better that the enemy seek us:
> So shall he waste his means, weary his soldiers,
> Doing himself offence; whilst we lying still,
> Are full of rest, defence and nimbleness.

But, of course, Hitler would have no truck with such defensive notions. He wanted the initiative and by taking it, threw away all chance of ever recovering it. When we contemplate the maximum number of divisions that Eisenhower was planning to commit to the northern thrust – some thirty-five – we may judge how effective against them would have been the 5th Panzer Army, with eight divisions including three Panzer Divisions, and the 6th SS Panzer Army, with nine divisions including 1st and 2nd SS Panzer Corps, plus all the advantages of prepared positions, rehearsed counter-penetration plans, concealment, mines and the sheer fanatical bravery and field craft of veteran soldiers. The total force which Hitler committed to the Ardennes gamble amounted to nearly 250,000 German troops, and some 700 tanks, supported by 2,000 guns. The battles for the Rhineland were to prove slow, punishing and bloody enough for the Allies even without such powerful resistance as might have been put up by making use of this last substantial reserve. Yet had it been so employed, while Hitler might have gained some time and space in the West, the Eastern Front's house of cards would still have collapsed, perhaps with even more dire results, not just for the

Third Reich, but also for the Western Allies. Although Eisenhower had agreed to halt his Army Groups on the line of the Elbe–Mulde and join up with the Red Army there, given the circumstances that the Western Allies were still held up on the Rhine in April 1945 – because of Hitler's not having squandered the Ardennes armies in his reckless gamble there – what would there have been to stop the Red Army surging over the Elbe and racing to the Rhine itself? We may be sure that Stalin would have had no qualms about breaking his word, no matter what had been agreed or not agreed at Yalta. Pursuit of the defeated enemy, occupation of territory in order to ensure security, further support of the Western Allied armies, breakdown of communications – any excuse would have served. If by chance something like this had come about, what sort of political and military plight would Churchill and Roosevelt,[3] Eisenhower and Montgomery have found themselves in? It beggars conjecture.

On the other hand, of course, assuming still that the bulk of Hitler's twenty-eight divisions earmarked for capturing Antwerp and Brussels had not been so employed, and had Hitler, who on 15 January decided to quit Adlershorst and reached Berlin the following day, never to leave the city again, pursued more vigorously his change of strategy to the effect that the Western Front must go over to the defensive in order to allow strengthening of the East – had this been done to the extent of despatching powerful forces to the central part of the Eastern Front, it is conceivable that the Red Army would have endured a further check. Under such conditions, we look at the reverse side of the coin – the Russians held up, Montgomery's and Bradley's armoured columns, having crossed the Rhine and encircled the Ruhr, rushing on not just to the Elbe–Mulde line, but still further. For it could well have transpired that the German High Command, sensing Hitler's inability to influence matters further by virtue of being isolated in his Bunker, would have positively welcomed a more comprehensive occupation of the Fatherland by British and American troops, and so withdrawn in the path of the advancing Allies. Exactly the same sort of justification for such action, as the Russians might have pleaded, given the reverse case, would no doubt have been readily forthcoming.

Under these circumstances, given this latter sort of chance, the British and American armies might well have got to Berlin first. Could they have done so anyway under the conditions as they actually were, as opposed to these hypotheses? It is this chance – and make no mistake, the chance was there all right – that we will now examine.

TWELVE

Who Is to Have Berlin?

I say quite frankly that Berlin remains of high strategic importance . . . should [it] be in our grasp we should certainly take it.

CHURCHILL to ROOSEVELT, 1 APRIL 1945

You will see that in none of this do I mention Berlin. So far as I am concerned, that place has become nothing but a geographical location.

EISENHOWER to MONTGOMERY, 27 MARCH 1945

One of the attributes most valued in a military commander is calm. It was not one in which Hitler excelled. Rather the contrary, as was illustrated by a Führer Conference in the Berlin Chancellory on 13 February 1945. Before we see what happened there, it should be understood that by January, one month earlier, the Supreme Commander of the Wehrmacht had so disposed his armies that the most vulnerable front of all, both militarily and politically, the front in Poland and East Prussia, was in comparative terms the most weakly held, the one least likely to be capable of withstanding the knock it was about to receive. In the west were 76 divisions, in Italy 24, 10 were in Yugoslavia, 17 in Scandinavia – in short, 127 divisions were deployed elsewhere than on the Eastern Front; only a few more, 133, were in the east. In the same month of January 300 divisions and twenty-five tank armies of the Red Army were getting ready to end the war; in the north two groups of armies under Chernyakhovsky and Rokossovsky were to converge on East Prussia; Zhukov's and Konev's groups in the centre would aim at Berlin and Upper

Silesia; further south two more groups would clear Slovakia, take Budapest and Vienna; finally, Petrov was to reoccupy the Northern Carpathians.

Whereas the Russians with their seemingly limitless resources of men and material could afford to operate over such broad fronts, the number of German divisions facing them was quite inadequate to constitute an effective defence. The vital central area of East Prussia and Poland was some 600 miles wide and here only seventy-five German divisions were deployed. Against them Stalin launched 180 divisions, including four tank armies each of which contained 1,200 tanks, so that it was hardly surprising when Konev's Army Group rapidly broke out of its bridgehead on the Upper Vistula and heralded a series of disasters which engulfed the Eastern Front. Guderian had warned the Führer that this front was like a house of cards and that if it were broken anywhere it would collapse everywhere. Even so, Guderian, never one to despair, set to work in forming a new Army Group Vistula to stem the Russian advance. Its front would stretch from Poznan to Graudenz, and Guderian intended to give this Army Group all the reserves he was mustering from the west, including Sepp Dietrich's 6th SS Panzer Army. Intending to direct its operations himself – and it would have been difficult to find any general more qualified or more able to make telling used of it – Guderian proposed von Weichs as a nominal Army Group Commander. But Hitler was so disillusioned by the professional soldiers' handling of affairs, a disillusionment brought about by virtue of his own unrealistic mishandling of them, that he appointed Himmler, who had never commanded armies in the field and was already contemplating treachery against his master.

Guderian was so appalled by this appointment that on 26 January he suggested to von Ribbentrop[1] that the two of them should speak to the Führer and seek his agreement to securing an armistice on one front or the other. Von Ribbentrop lacked either the character or the courage to stand up to Hitler and refused, but was himself aghast when Guderian asked how he would feel when he found that the Russians had reached Berlin in a few weeks' time. Von Ribbentrop then asked Guderian if he really believed such a thing was possible, and was hardly comforted by the reply that because of Hitler's leadership it was not just possible, but certain. The conversation was duly reported to Hitler, who in Guderian's presence referred to it as treason, but the great Panzer Leader never lacked the courage of his convictions and tried to argue the strategic issues there and then. Hitler refused to discuss the matter.

As the first two weeks of February went by, the disagreements between Guderian, still Chief of the Army General Staff, and the Supreme Commander of the Wehrmacht concerning the conduct of the war in general and the campaign on the Eastern Front in particular grew ever more bitter and violent. At one point when Guderian counselled withdrawal and Hitler refused to give up an inch of territory, the Führer's rage and vituperation reached an absolute crescendo. Guderian's assertion that he was not being obstinate but simply thinking of Germany precipitated a furious bellow from Hitler that his whole life had been a struggle for Germany. It was all he had been fighting for. Guderian's adjutant was so alarmed by Hitler's shaking fists that he took hold of his General's tunic and pulled him back out of range. The whole sorry scene was re-enacted at the 13 February Führer Conference. This time the principal issue concerned the conduct of a counter-attack by Army Group Vistula against Zhukov's extended and vulnerable right flank. Those present included Hitler himself, Keitel, Jodl, Himmler, still in command of the Army Group, Sepp Dietrich and Wenck, whom Guderian had brought with him. Guderian was insisting that the counter-attack should be launched at once, before the Russians had time to bring up their reserves, and moreover that command should be entrusted to Wenck, not to Himmler. Hitler contested every point made by Guderian, who just as steadily contradicted him and who later recorded what occurred:

And so it went on for two hours. His fists raised, his cheeks flushed with rage, his whole body trembling, the man stood there in front of me, beside himself with fury and having lost all self-control. After each outburst of rage Hitler would stride up and down the carpet edge, then suddenly stop immediately before me and hurl his next accusation in my face. He was almost screaming, his eyes seemed about to pop out of his head and the veins stood out on his temples.[2]

Military decisions are best taken after calmly reviewing the circumstances, weighing the odds, determining the likely enemy action, keeping an eye firmly on the immediate objective and the consequences of attaining it, and then ensuring that the second great strategic rule – that of so disposing resources as to maximize the chances of success – is adhered to. Shrieking, shouting matches between senior commanders, decisions flawed by intrigue, lack of men and material, in short thoroughly bad leadership, were improbable preliminaries to taking the path of glory. They were much more likely to lead to the grave. Despite Hitler's ravings on 13 February Guderian gained his point. With his most charming smile, the Führer announced that the General Staff had won a battle that day. Guderian's subsequent comment was that it was the last battle he was to win and that in any case it came too late. The counter-attack, last of all offensives waged by the German army, petered out in failure after a few days. But was Guderian right in predicting to von Ribbentrop that the Russians would reach Berlin in a few weeks' time? Could the British and American armies have got there first? The answer is almost certainly yes, but for the procrastination of one man – Eisenhower. For it was he who followed the example of so many military commanders before him. He changed his mind.

On 15 September 1944, after the great victory in Normandy, he had sent a letter to his two Army Group commanders, Bradley and Montgomery, in which he outlined his views as to future operations and asked for theirs. At this time it was clear from his letter that he regarded Berlin as a primary objective. Having assumed that the Ruhr, the Saar and Frankfurt would before long be in Allied hands, he then designated Berlin as the main prize. 'There is no doubt whatsoever, in my mind, that we should concentrate on a rapid thrust to Berlin.' There would, of course, have to be some coordination with the Russians, but precise objectives could not be selected until later.

At this point, therefore, it was clear that Berlin was the goal. In his reply to Eisenhower Montgomery urged the Supreme Commander to decide there and then what forces were necessary to go to Berlin, and so reach agreement as to both the plan and the objectives. Moreover, these matters had to be agreed at once, not decided on later.

Montgomery also stressed that all other considerations must be secondary to the main aim and objective. The trouble was that there was no absolutely clear and clearly understood policy as to what Eisenhower was required to do after crossing the Rhine. Indeed, in spite of his reference to Berlin, Eisenhower's strategy had consistently been to advance on a broad front with primary and secondary thrusts, and then, having linked up the two advancing forces in the general area of Kassel, make one great thrust to the eastward. But where to? Lack of decision here meant that on crossing the Rhine and moving eastward, the aim of the Allied armies was far from clear.

One of the ironies of the situation was that whatever objectives the Western Allies might care to choose, they were almost certainly attainable, for the German forces in the west – now under Field-Marshal Kesselring – could no longer fight a coordinated defensive battle, however determined individual pockets of resistance might be. Although on paper there were still sixty-five German divisions on the Western Front, for practicable purposes they were only small battle groups and a few headquarter staffs, dispersed and without either proper communications or logistic support. Such penny packets would not be able to resist a firm Allied drive. Eisenhower's plan, such as it was, laid down that the Ruhr would be encircled by Montgomery's 21st Army Group plus US 9th Army to the north, while Bradley's 12th Army Group would break out from the Remagen bridgehead and link up with Montgomery. The whole area east of the Rhine would be occupied and a further advance into Germany would proceed. Montgomery's orders were for his forces to advance with all speed to the Elbe from Hamburg to Magdeburg, with great emphasis on 'getting the whips out' so that fast-moving armoured spearheads could capture airfields to ensure continuous close air support. These orders were given on 27 March, but the following day everything was changed. Eisenhower did an absolute volte-face, abandoned the idea of going for Berlin, and communicated directly with Stalin in order to coordinate his operations with those of the Red Army. Having informed Stalin of his intention to encircle the Ruhr and mop up the enemy there, Eisenhower went on to define his next task as 'joining hands with your forces' and suggesting that the junction should be

Erfurt–Leipzig–Dresden. Nothing could have been more acceptable to Stalin or unacceptable to Churchill and Montgomery. Indeed, Eisenhower had signalled to Montgomery that the US 9th Army would be removed from him after his joining hands with Bradley in the Kassel–Paderborn area, and that the main Allied thrust would be not to Berlin, but to Leipzig and Dresden. Montgomery's appeal not to change either the plan or the command arrangements was not heeded. Eisenhower reiterated his intention to divide and destroy the enemy forces and to join hands with the Russian army. He added significantly:

You will see that in none of this do I mention Berlin. So far as I am concerned, that place has become nothing but a geographical location; I have never been interested in those. My purpose is to destroy the enemy forces and his power to resist.

Why did Eisenhower change his mind? Previously he had emphasized that Berlin was the main prize, and that the Allies should concentrate everything on a rapid thrust there no matter how this was to be done. He had repeated that all his plans ultimately boiled down to exactly this – 'to move on Berlin by the most direct and expeditious route'. Now he was dismissing the city as a mere geographical location. Why? Was it that he regarded its capture as no longer feasible in that whereas 21st Army Group was still 300 miles from Berlin, the Russians on the Oder were a mere forty miles away? Was it that he was fearful that Model's Army Group in the Ruhr might even now form some formidable defensive front or that the stories about Hitler's retiring to a National Redoubt in the Bavarian and Austrian mountains, there to conduct some desperate last stand, might have some foundation and involve some further great effort? Doubts of this sort may be comprehended. What is not easy to understand in view of Eisenhower's insistence on the whole purpose of military operations being in pursuit of political aims, and the undisputed importance of Berlin as a political objective, is that he should suddenly have turned fully 180 degrees about and pronounced it to be of no significance. And the supreme irony of it all in view of Eisenhower's reiteration that what he was after was the destruction of the enemy's will to resist is that up to the very last Berlin, leaving aside its weight in the political game, contained the one military objective without whose seizure or demise the enemy's will to resist would never be broken and the war itself would never end – the person of Adolf Hitler himself. Nor is it easy to understand why Eisenhower should have chucked away the possibility of taking Berlin with his own armies before it had become plain that he could not do it. Subsequent events were to show that he could.

The reaction in Moscow to Eisenhower's change of plan could hardly have differed more from that in London. Stalin agreed with what Eisenhower had proposed and in his reply made four points: first, he confirmed the Erfurt–Leipzig–Dresden juncture for the two converging armies; second, he maintained that only secondary Soviet forces would be directed on Berlin, which had lost its former strategic importance (Churchill's comment on this point was that it was not borne out by events); third, that the main Soviet attack would begin in the second half of May (it actually began a month earlier, on 16 April, which had a strong bearing on whether or not the Western Allies could have got to Berlin first); fourth, that the Germans were further reinforcing the Eastern Front. As a result of Stalin's positive response, Eisenhower issued orders to execute his plan.

In London, Churchill took a very different view of things. As was customary with him, when it came to the big issues, his strategic instinct did not forsake him. In this case it concerned not only the final stages of one great struggle, but the seeds of another. The Russians' behaviour at Yalta had given him pause when weighing up the likely course of Soviet policy. He was anxious that the Allied armies should do all they could to put the West in the best possible position for subsequent confrontation with the Russians if such circumstances should come about. Churchill signalled to Roosevelt that he was in no doubt that the rapid advance by their armies had both surprised and displeased the Russian leaders, that their joint armies should meet the Russian armies as far east as possible, and that they should enter Berlin. But Roosevelt was a dying man and the American military hierarchy fully supported Eisenhower. There was then a further exchange of messages, Eisenhower attempting to justify his action to Churchill, and Churchill summarizing his misgivings to Roosevelt.

Churchill deplored the switch of axis from that which aimed at Berlin to one further south, and also the decision to rob 21st Army Group of the 9th US Army, thus restricting its ability to push beyond the Elbe. Berlin was still of high strategic importance. 'Nothing will exert a psychological effect of despair upon all German forces or resistance equal to that of the fall of Berlin.' The Russians would get Vienna in any case. Were they to be allowed to have Berlin too? If Berlin were within the Western armies' grasp, Churchill concluded, they should take it.

Was it within their grasp in April 1945? Before answering the question we may perhaps take a look at the one obstacle to making peace there and then, a peace which so many of the senior Wehrmacht commanders and even the Führer's henchmen, like Albert Speer, who repeatedly told his master that the war was lost, ardently desired. In other words, we should look at the Supreme War Lord of the Third Reich, which he had both created and destroyed, at genius in the Bunker. On 6 April 1945, a few weeks before the end, Hitler sent for General Wenck and appointed him to command the 12th Army. The various tasks that Wenck was given underlined the absolute absurdity to which Hitler's conduct of war had deteriorated. First of all Wenck, with just one army, and little more than a phantom army at that, was required to restore the Wehrmacht's fortunes on the Western Front, which was being overwhelmed by three Allied Army Groups. Then later he was to reverse the inevitable on the Eastern Front and relieve Berlin.

It was clear from the very outset that the first task alone was totally beyond him. His forces were inadequate in every way – in numbers, preparation, cohesion, training, concentration. The divisions theoretically under his command simply did not exist. He had no tanks, no self-propelled assault guns, no anti-aircraft artillery. And with this skeleton of an army Wenck was supposed to do what von Rundstedt and Model had already failed to do with far larger forces – stop the Western Allies from advancing. The whole thing was a non-starter. None the less, Wenck did made a start and tried to slow down the advancing American forces. Except for one small pocket in the Halle–Leipzig area, his army never got west of the Mulde–Elbe line, but by mid-April something became plain to Wenck, something so significant that it made him think again about how to employ his troops. This was that the Americans seemed to be consolidating their positions on the Elbe, without any clear intention of pushing further east. This discovery, together with the Red Army's attack across the Oder, made up his mind. He would use the 12th Army to assist on the Eastern Front. His decision to do so was powerfully supported by a visit from Field-Marshal Keitel, during one of his extremely rare absences from Hitler's side, who gave Wenck some dramatic instructions: 'Free Berlin. Turn and advance with all available strength. Link up with the 9th Army. Rescue the Führer. His fate is Germany's fate. You, Wenck, have it in your power to save Germany.' Good stirring stuff, which was almost at once confirmed and reinforced by a message from the Führer himself, calling upon the soldiers of Wenck's army to turn east and defeat the Bolsheviks in their battle for the German capital, whose defenders had taken heart from the news of Wenck's fast approach and were fighting doggedly in the belief that the thunder of his guns would soon be heard. 'The Führer has called you. You have, as in old times, started on the road to victory. Berlin waits for you. Berlin yearns for you here, with warm hearts.'

There were not many warm hearts in the Bunker on 20 April when Hitler celebrated his fifty-sixth birthday. To those who attended he presented a picture of a man in the last stages of bodily and mental decay. While the will-power which had exercised so great and enduring an influence on those about him could still be summoned up, while the dull grey-blue eyes, which often now were glazed over with a film of sheer exhaustion, still seemed able to hypnotize, fascinate and compel, the actual physical state of the man was more an object of pity than of fear. The Führer's shuffling steps, weak handshake, wobbling head, trembling hands and slack left arm were the movements and appearance of a man prematurely senile. Yet his hesitancy and indecisiveness while confirming the completeness of his disintegration were still at odds with the 'indescribable, flickering glow in his eyes, creating a fearsome and wholly unnatural effect'.

On the following day, 21 April, Hitler was giving orders for making a last stand in Berlin. There was not much time left for, by then, Marshal Zhukov's armies had got as far as Berlin's eastern suburbs, while his fellow Marshal, Konev, was nearing Dresden. Nevertheless the Supreme Commander was detailing to Göring's Chief of Staff, General Koller, an elderly, scrupulous fusspot, exactly which troops would be withdrawn from the north of the city to counter-attack the Russians in the southern suburbs. Every tank, every aircraft that could be mustered, everything and everybody would make an all-out, final, desperate effort to throw back the enemy. Obergruppenführer Steiner of the SS would command the attack. Any commanding officer who did not thrust home would answer for it with his head. It was all in vain. The attack never came off, did not even get under way; withdrawal of units from the north simply allowed the Russians to surge through there and sweep on to the city's centre. It hardly seemed possible that the military situation could worsen, yet it was just such cold comfort that Hitler was obliged to stomach.

He did not do so lightly. At the military conference the following day, when the facts were presented to him, he completely lost control of himself. One more shrieking, shouting match – a wholly one-sided affair – was duly played out. The Generals and the Staff were then treated to three hours of denunciation. Hitler had been betrayed and deserted. The army had failed him. There was nothing but lies, deceit, cowardly incompetence. It was the end. His great mission, the Third Reich itself, had come to nothing, and indeed nothing was left but for him to stay in Berlin and die. This conference, if conference it could be called, may have left his listeners bewildered and exhausted, yet its effect on Hitler himself was quite different. Decision calmed him. He seemed able to face the future, however limited it might be, serenely. Yet at the very moment of resigning himself to failure and death, he took the unwarranted, unforgivable step of resigning too from that great position which he had so long coveted and relished – command of the German army. He refused to delegate. He gave no orders to his principal military assistants, Field-Marshal Keitel and General Jodl. He simply abdicated all responsibility. From the former position of directing the entire war machine, personally, continuously and arbitrarily, he swung fully about and would have nothing more to do with it. He declared that he would stay in Berlin, lead its defence and then at the last moment shoot himself. His physical state did not allow him to take part in the fight personally and in any case he could not risk falling into enemy hands. It was not until 30 April that Hitler actually shot himself, and by then the Russians were only a few streets away from the Berlin Chancellory and the Bunker. What would have happened if the Western armies had got there first?

On 1 April 1945 Stalin was conferring in Moscow with some of his most senior commanders – Zhukov and Konev, respectively commanding the 1st Belorussian and 1st Ukraine fronts, and Antonov and Shtemenko, both of the General Staff. A telegram was read out with the unexpected information that the Anglo-American command was preparing to launch a drive to capture Berlin, the principal spearhead under Montgomery's direction. The axis would be north of the Ruhr, the shortest route, and the telegram ended by saying that Allied plans were such that they would certainly reach Berlin before the Red Army. It must be assumed that Stalin had fabricated this telegram or that it was a thoroughly bad piece of intelligence. When the Soviet leader then asked his commanders, 'Who is going to take Berlin, we or the Allies?' there was unanimous agreement that it would be themselves. The only question was whether Zhukov's or Konev's front would be charged with the task. Stalin then instructed the two commanders to prepare their ideas and two days later gave orders that whichever of the two reached a certain line between the river Neisse and the river Spree first would go on to take Berlin.

During the first week of April 1945, therefore, we have the spectacle of two Russian Army Group commanders planning how they would take Berlin, while on the Allied side Eisenhower is being pressed by the British to do so and resisting this pressure with the aid of his own countrymen. Bradley, for example, always hostile to and a rival of Montgomery, made the extraordinary estimate, quite unsupported by military considerations, that an advance from the Elbe to Berlin would cost them 100,000 men, which he regarded as too high a price to pay for a 'prestige objective'. He could not have been unaware that any such drive would be conducted by Montgomery's Army Group rather than his own, purely because of their respective deployment. He echoed Eisenhower by declaiming that postwar political alignments were less important than destroying what remained of the German army. He eschewed the idea of complicating matters with political foresight and what he called non-military objectives. Yet what are military operations for but to determine political circumstances? And it has always to be borne in mind that the German army and indeed the German people as a whole, given the option, would have infinitely preferred occupation of their country by the Anglo-American armies than the Russians.

Yet Eisenhower received further support from the US Chiefs of Staff. Speaking on their behalf, General Marshall reiterated Bradley's contention that any political or psychological advantages resulting from the capture of Berlin ahead of the Russians should not over-ride the imperative military consideration of the dismemberment of Germany's armed forces. In reply Eisenhower, while adhering to the orders he had already given, and insisting that there would be no drive on Berlin until he had joined forces with the Russians, as already agreed, none the less commented:

I am the first to admit that a war is waged in pursuance of political aims, and if the Combined Chiefs of Staff should decide that the Allied effort to take Berlin outweighs military considerations in this theatre, I would cheerfully readjust my plans.

This signal to Marshall was dated 7 April. If the Combined Chiefs of Staff had decided to order Eisenhower to go full steam ahead for Berlin there and then, could he have got there first? On the very next day, 8 April, we find Eisenhower telling Montgomery: 'If I get an opportunity to capture Berlin cheaply, I will take it.' He was hardly as good as his word. Even Bradley, finding three days later that his armies had secured a bridgehead over the Elbe at Magdeburg and were only fifty miles from Berlin, admitted: 'At that time we could probably have pushed on to Berlin had we been willing to take the casualties Berlin would have cost us. Zhukov had not yet crossed the Oder and Berlin now lay about midway between our forces.'

Chester Wilmot was in no doubt. He pointed out that there were no prepared defences to prevent Eisenhower reaching Berlin first, no serious obstacles, 'nor any resistance that could not be brusquely swept aside by the 60 divisions available for his next offensive'.[3] What is more, there were no logistic objections.

Politically, too, the way was clear for, though the German capital lay in the centre of that area which was to be occupied by the Soviet Union after the war, it had never been suggested that the military forces of one power should not enter the occupation zone of another in pursuit of the common enemy.[4]

Indeed, there had been no discussion between the Soviet Union and the Western Allies, still less an agreement, as to who was to take Berlin. At Yalta the question did not arise. Certainly there was no understanding that the city was to be reserved for the Red Army. Since Yalta the relative freedom of movement by the two converging armies had changed dramatically. Formerly the Allies had been bogged down, the Russians advancing everywhere. Now, in April 1945, the position was reversed: the Red Army halted, Eisenhower's armies free to advance. Leaving aside for a moment whether these latter armies could have reached Berlin first, if they had attempted to do so from mid-April onwards, would the German commanders in the field – notwithstanding anything the Führer or OKW might have had to say, for their orders were negligible – have allowed the Western armies to have made their way to the capital virtually unopposed? There might have been fanatical and scattered resistance from ill-organized groups, but if a decision of this sort had been left to such men as Guderian, Wenck, Busse, Kesselring, Manteuffel, Speer, Dönitz – even Himmler – the answer would in all likelihood have been yes.

Bearing in mind now that the Russian offensive across the Oder did not start until 16 April and that five days later the armies of Zhukov's front reached the outskirts of the city, any Allied attempt to take Berlin would have had to succeed before this. Given that Montgomery's Army Group, having reached the Elbe during the first weeks of April was then charged with so many tasks – to clear Schleswig-Holstein, take Wismar, Lübeck, Emden, Wilhelmshaven, Cuxhaven and Bremen – that it had to be reinforced by a US Airborne Corps,[5] it would have been impossible for Montgomery's forces to have got to

Berlin before the Russians. On Bradley's front, however, it was a different story. His elimination of Model's group of armies in the Ruhr encirclement had been so successful that by 10 April the German soldiers were surrendering *en masse*. A total of 320,000 were captured with all their weapons and equipment, a significant pointer to what might have happened on the road to Berlin. Bradley had been instructed to seize bridgeheads over the Elbe and be prepared to continue the advance. On 11 April Simpson's 9th US Army reached the Elbe astride Magdeburg and was across it the following day. On the same day, 12 April, it reached Tangemünde, just over fifty miles from Berlin. Everywhere the US armies were advancing rapidly, and by 15 April Hodges' 1st Army reached the Mulde and Patton's 3rd Army had got to Plauen, Hof and Bayreuth. On that very day Simpson proposed to Bradley that his army should expand its Elbe bridgehead and push on in force and with all speed to Berlin: this, it must be noted, on the day before the Red Army's attack began.

Eisenhower vetoed the suggestion. We may hazard a guess that had Patton been there instead of Simpson he would have pushed on anyway and asked for permission later. That Simpson could have got on seems more or less certain for in the whole of his advance up to the Elbe, his army had suffered very few casualties. Indeed, all that had opposed him – ill-equipped and unpractised divisions of Wenck's 12th Army, which had no air support at all – had been scattered. Wenck's own comment on it all was: 'If the Americans launch a major attack they'll crack our positions with ease. After all what's to stop them? There's nothing between here and Berlin.' If we assume therefore that on 15 April Simpson had despatched powerful armoured columns down the Autobahn to Berlin, with motorized infantry, artillery and engineers in support, and the Allies' unchallenged air supremacy to deal with any pockets of resistance, we may suppose that the American armies could have reached and occupied Berlin on 15 and 16 April, so anticipating the arrival of the Russians by several days. Of one thing we may be sure. They would have been welcomed by the Berliners with the most profound relief.

What about Hitler himself? Would he still have committed suicide when the information was brought to him that the American forces were in Berlin? There could presumably be no surrender, conditional or unconditional, while he still lived. Would he still have married Eva Braun, who arrived in the Bunker on 15 April? There would just have been time. Whom would the Führer have nominated as his successor? Would it still have been Dönitz? There are innumerable questions of this sort. But having assumed that Simpson's 9th Army, rapidly reinforced by elements from the US 1st, 3rd and 15th Armies, did reach, occupy and even extend eastwards beyond Berlin, we may allow ourselves further speculation. Once it was known that Hitler was dead, his nominated successor, provided it were someone like Dönitz, and not Göring, Himmler, Goebbels or Keitel, would have initiated some approach to the Western Allies to negotiate a cessation of hostilities. In view of the proximity of the Red Army, the Western negotiators would have insisted that the Soviet Union be involved in the surrender conditions. There would have to be a newly agreed junction between the two converging armies, possibly the arterial roads to the east of Berlin or the broadly defined eastern outskirts of the city. It must be assumed here too that the Red Army has been ordered not to contest occupation of Berlin.

Who would have been the principal negotiator on behalf of the Western Allies? Eisenhower, as Supreme Allied Commander, might have been a candidate, provided he were furnished with the necessary political guidance from Truman and Churchill. But such delegated authority would have been limited to surrender terms, and would not have changed what had been agreed at Yalta in February. We may be sure that at least three men would have wanted to make their presence known when it came to detailed discussions with Stalin: Truman, Churchill and de Gaulle. One other man would somehow or other have contrived not only to be involved himself, but to ensure a substantial role for the soldiers he commanded: Field-Marshal Sir Bernard Montgomery. How he would have longed to organize some sort of victory parade or celebration in Berlin's Olympic Stadium! If Churchill had been given the chance, he would no doubt have arranged for his quarters to have been at Frederick the Great's Potsdam palace, Sans Souci, and indeed had there been a Potsdam conference in April 1945, instead of July, with the Western Allies in a far more powerful bargaining position than was in reality the case, Churchill might never have experienced his subsequent disappointment and dismay as to what actually emerged in July, when he was out of power:

The line of the Oder and the Eastern Neisse had already been recognized as the Polish compensation for retiring to the Curzon Line, but the overrunning by the Russian armies of the territory up to and even beyond the Western Neisse was never and never would have been agreed to by any Government of which I was the head . . .

The real time to deal with these issues was . . . when the fronts of the mighty Allies faced each other in the field, and before the Americans, and to a lesser extent, the British, made their vast retirement on a 400-mile front to a depth in some places of 120 miles, thus giving the heart and a great mass of Germany over to the Russians . . .[6]

The heart: what if Churchill had had his way earlier and the Western armies had met the Russians not on the line of the Elbe–Mulde rivers, but on the Oder–Neisse line, with Berlin in their own hands? What then? How different a Potsdam conference might have been. Churchill's fundamental antipathy towards allowing the Russians to occupy great chunks of Central Europe was that he could see no future for these areas unless it was acceptable to – that is, controlled by – the Soviet Government. And that to him was no future at all. Yet all this apart, the American view, at a time when American counsels carried great weight, was that the Western Allies were committed to a definite line of occupation and that this commitment must be honoured. Churchill, too, was in favour of honouring commitments provided all of them were equally honoured, in other words, provided the Western Allies could be satisfied that the entire European future was being properly settled. At Potsdam in July 1945 American support for such a notion was not to hand. Would the situation have differed if Potsdam had instead taken place in April, with Berlin occupied by American and British forces and the Red Army still some way off to the east? We may be sure that Churchill, still at that point wielding much influence and power, would have moved mountains to reach a satisfactory solution.

As for Berlin itself, there would still have been quadripartite control of the city, but how different might have been its initial occupation. We have to recall that in April 1945 Berlin was *kaputt*, a bombed ruin of a city, as described by a correspondent of the Red Army, Lieutenant-Colonel Troyanovsky, who saw for himself what happened between 21 and 25 April as the battle raged:

From one end of the horizon to the other stretched houses, gardens, factory buildings, and many churches. Volumes of smoke arose from all quarters and hung like a pall over the city. The German capital was burning. The thunder of the artillery bombardment shook the air, the houses and the ground. And Berlin replied with thousands of shells and bombs. It seemed as though we were confronted not by a town, but by a nightmare of fire and steel. Every house appeared to have been converted into a fortress. There were no squares, but only gun positions for artillery and mine throwers. From house to house and street to street, from one district to another, mowing their way through gun fire and hot steel, went our infantrymen, artillery, sappers and tanks. On 25 April the German capital was completely encircled and cut off from the rest of the country. At the height of the street fighting Berlin was without water, without light, without landing fields, without radio stations. The city ceased to resemble Berlin.

'How pitiful is their Berlin!' observed Zhukov.

How pitiful too was the plight of the Berliners, particularly the women. The Red Army ran riot. Rape, looting, burning and murder were rife. Hitler's very last War Directive of 15 April had made it clear what fate threatened a defeated Germany: 'While the old men and children will be murdered, the women and girls will be reduced to barrack-room whores.' Antony Beevor, while doing his research into the fall of Berlin, was shocked by what he discovered about the depravity of the Russian soldiers. This research, says a newspaper report, 'revealed that the Russians raped hundreds of thousands, possibly millions, of Germans; the troops even raped the Russian and Polish women prisoners they freed from German camps. In some towns every female, young and old, was violated.'

The British and Americans would have behaved better. There might have been seduction, even barter, for cigarettes were treasured currency then, but rape would have been rare. When the British did enter Berlin later, they were greeted as liberators rather than conquerors. What must have been the consequence if Berlin had initially been wholly occupied by the Western armies, before its division into the four sectors, British, American, French and Russian? Is it not possible that as soon as the boundaries were made known and before the barriers and barbed wire went up, every Berliner able to do so would have quitted the Russian zone to find refuge in one of the other three? Even as things were, Germans who found themselves in the Soviet-controlled part of the former Third Reich and in East Berlin flocked to the west in their thousands until the Berlin Wall and the boundary minefields deterred such abundant emigration and denied those seeking refuge from the oppressor's wrong, the whips and scorns of uniformed bullies, the spurns of the unworthy, the insolence of jack-booted officials, the chance to do so.

It had all been brought about by one man, whom Speer called 'a demonic figure', whose 'person determined the fate of a nation. He alone placed it, and kept it, upon the path which has led to this dreadful ending. The nation was spellbound by him as a people has rarely been in the whole of history.' Was it all by chance?

THIRTEEN

Chance Governs All

What is character but the determination of incident?
What is incident but the illustration of character?

HENRY JAMES

Fate, show thy force: ourselves we do not owe.
What is decreed, must be; and be this so!

TWELFTH NIGHT

There are, so they say, two views of history. First, the determinist view that history is subject to external forces influencing human action, that everything is predetermined, appointed by fate, or chance, if you like. For those who share this view, we might say chance does govern all. This was certainly the theory embraced by Tolstoy, who would talk about Charles IX only thinking that he had decreed the Night of St Bartholomew or Napoleon only fancying he had brought about the war of 1812. Then, on the other hand, we have Thomas Carlyle maintaining that no great man lived in vain, that the history of the world is but the biography of great men. Which of them was right? Both, one or neither? Was the Second World War inevitable, preordained, or was it brought about by the activities and ambitions of Adolf Hitler? Or, indeed, had those Western political leaders, whom Hitler later described as 'little worms' shown some backbone in 1936, when German troops reoccupied the Rhineland, and been prepared to go to war there and then, would the whole sinister process of Europe's murder have been brought to a halt before it got properly under way? Or again are there simply too many factors and influences abroad in international affairs for us to count or comprehend?

Whatever we may think, we must concede that Tolstoy waxed eloquent in support of his own ideas. He wrote that however convinced Napoleon had been in 1812 that the question of whether or not to shed the blood of his peoples depended entirely on his own will, he had in reality 'never been more in the grip of those inevitable laws which compelled him to perform for the world in general – for history – what was destined to be accomplished'.[1] There is much to be said for some of Tolstoy's assertions. We may readily endorse his suggestion that the will of an historical hero is subject to events. Yet when he goes on to say that this same hero cannot rule the actions of a multitude, we part company with him. For whatever Tolstoy's attempts to convince us that the Grande Armée marched east because this great event had to occur, we may prefer to believe that it did so because Napoleon gave the necessary order. In this instance, therefore, we may argue that character determined incident. Moreover, those on the spot at the time would confirm this view of things.

One of the Emperor Napoleon's most devoted followers was the Marquis de Caulaincourt, Duke of Vicenza, who accompanied him on the Russian campaign. Few men were better qualified to offer an opinion about the whole affair. Caulaincourt had been the French Ambassador at St Petersburg from 1807 to 1811, and when he returned to Paris he had a conversation with the Emperor, which lasted for five hours, about Czar Alexander's attitude to war and peace. He told Napoleon that the Czar did not want war, but was concerned about what appeared to be hostile troop concentrations in Danzig and Prussia. He also referred to Napoleon's Continental System, which had been agreed at Tilsit and was designed to cripple Britain by stopping all trade with her, maintaining that Russia had not breached the agreement, although in making this assertion he was either mistaken or deliberately misleading. Indeed, he went so far as to remind his master that he himself had authorized French merchant vessels to trade with England.

Caulaincourt then urged Napoleon to preserve the Russian alliance, emphasizing that Alexander did not wish to make war on France, but adding the Czar's warning that if it should come to war, it would not be a short one. He, Alexander, would not be the first to draw his sword, but he would certainly be the last to sheathe it. No matter how great a general Napoleon was, how valiant his lieutenants, how spirited his veterans, *space* was still a barrier, and he had infinite space at his command. The Russian climate, the Russian winter would be his allies. What all this boiled down to was that it would be for Napoleon to choose between peace and war. Caulaincourt beseeched the Emperor when he decided on his course to bear in mind not only his own welfare, but that of France.

Alas, two months later, in August 1811, when Napoleon held a reception at the Tuileries to celebrate his forty-second birthday, it became all too clear that Caulaincourt had wasted his breath. The Emperor chose this of all inopportune occasions to vent his grievances about the Czar's behaviour to the Russian Ambassador. Still worse, he did so in a raised voice, using violent language. Russia, he complained, was conducting two-way trade with Britain, and had moreover imposed heavy duties on French imports. Russian troops were menacing peace, the Czar was putting an end to their alliance. He, Napoleon, did not want war, but if it came to that, if he was obliged to make war, he would win. He had 800,000 troops at his command. Besides, he always did win. How could Russia hope to match him? Where would Alexander find allies? Not Austria, from whom Galicia had been seized. Here Napoleon strayed from the truth, as he frequently did when justifying his actions or reporting his battles. In fact Napoleon had presented Alexander with part of this Austrian province in return for Russia's nominal, but insubstantial, support during France's 1809 campaign against Austria. Nor could Alexander look to Prussia for aid. Napoleon had thrashed the Prussian army in 1806 and Frederick William III was totally subservient. Sweden too could not be relied on, for Russia had stolen Finland from her and longed to avenge this humiliation. Here Napoleon overlooked or chose to ignore the point that one of his own Marshals, Bernadotte, became Crown Prince of Sweden in 1810, heir to King Charles XIII, and would not be slow to turn against his former master when the time was ripe. None the less, in his outburst to Prince Kurakin, the Russian Ambassador, Napoleon concluded that 'the entire Continent will be against you'.

Yet we must concede that the French Emperor did have some cause for anger at what he thought of as Alexander's shilly-shallying. The trouble was that the Czar wanted to have it both ways. His inclination was to remain on friendly terms with Napoleon. But such friendship would involve his acceptance of some liberal principles, which might not be compatible with his continuing to be Czar of all the Russias. His own nobles deplored the establishment of the Civil Code in the Grand Duchy of Warsaw. They regarded any ideas about political rights for all races or freedom for serfs as dangerous nonsense. Who could say what effect the proximity of such revolutionary notions might have upon their own countless serfs? The nobles intimated to Alexander that unless he changed his ways, he would, like his father, end up by being strangled to death. Such a threat was sufficient for the Czar to turn about and demand from Napoleon a large chunk of the Grand Duchy of Warsaw. It was therefore becoming plain to Napoleon that Alexander was not content to play second fiddle, but was as intent on expanding his own empire as he himself had been – and at France's expense! This was enough for Napoleon to decide at the end of 1811 that preparations for a great military venture must be put in train. The Grande Armée, he told de Cessac, Minister of War, would be required to cover long distances and advance in several directions. It would all start by crossing the river Niemen, which formed the frontier with Russia. It was in this way that the French Emperor chose war. So much then for Tolstoy.

But suppose Napoleon had listened more carefully to Caulaincourt, had weighed the military odds more fully, had appreciated by careful calculation the sheer logistic difficulties of campaigning in the wastes of Russia, had thought twice about those two unavoidable factors in war, time and space, and, knowing his own recipe for winning wars by bringing his enemy's armies to rapid and decisive action, had cogitated upon the possibility of the Russian forces simply withdrawing in the face of the advancing Grande Armée, choosing to avoid battle, imposing ever-lengthening lines of communication, without any decisive engagement, the enemy husbanding his strength while weakening his opponent's – what then? If Napoleon had heard the way in which Alexander predicted with uncanny accuracy the course of things to come – 'Space is a barrier, and if, after several defeats, I withdraw, sweeping the inhabitants along with me, if I let time, deserts and climate defend Russia for me, then perhaps I shall have the last word' – he might have changed his mind.

Then, instead of invading Russia, Napoleon might have staged another Erfurt, the medieval city in Saxony where in September 1808 he had aimed to dazzle Alexander with the spectacle of his power. On that occasion all the vassal sovereigns of Bavaria, Saxony and Würtemberg, together with the Princes and Dukes of the Confederation of the Rhine, had assembled in order to show Alexander that except for Britain, Spain and Sweden, the whole of Europe was either ruled by Napoleon or allied to him. It was all laid on in order that Napoleon might strengthen his friendship with and reliance on Alexander, but thanks largely to the treachery of Talleyrand, it failed. Talleyrand made an astonishing overture to the Czar:

Sire, it is in your power to save Europe, and you will only do so by refusing to give way to Napoleon. The French people are civilized, their sovereign is not. The sovereign of Russia is civilized and his people are not: the sovereign of Russia should therefore be the ally of the French people.

Thereafter Alexander's demands grew while his undertaking to support France diminished. It was from the time of Erfurt that relations between the two sovereigns of France and Russia deteriorated until the Grande Armée crossed the Niemen on 24 June 1812.

Now put the case that this did not happen, that instead Napoleon called for another meeting with Alexander, perhaps at Danzig. The Grande Armée would be intact and put on some huge display of might and precision. The other sovereigns would have been summoned, Talleyrand left behind in Paris to smoulder, some concessions made by Napoleon both with regard to Poland and the Continental System, in short an uneasy alliance would have been patched up. With so much power at his disposal, Napoleon would have little to fear from Metternich and Austria. Moreover, he could have despatched to Spain such a powerful army as would bring the Peninsular War to a close before it bled the French army white, then by restoring Ferdinand to the throne in Madrid cure the festering Spanish ulcer once and for all. By putting an end to the countrywide guerrilla resistance, backed up by the half-hearted efforts of the Spanish army, the French armies in Spain would have been able to do what they had never in fact been able to achieve – concentrate their forces spread about the Peninsula into one; and then even Wellington with his limited numbers would have been unable to resist them.

But Napoleon was resolved to teach Alexander a lesson and so threw away half a million men, countless thousands of guns and horses, and at the end of it all, while conceding that the Grande Armée had been destroyed, comforted the French nation with the declaration that the Emperor had never been in better health. We too may be comforted by the reflection that but for Napoleon's 1812 adventure, we would never have had Tolstoy's *War and Peace*. If we can say therefore that Napoleon repudiated the determinist view of history, so too surely did one of his predecessors, another sovereign and soldier, Frederick the Great. Like Napoleon, Frederick showed what resolution and endurance could achieve. Unlike the Emperor, Frederick never deluded himself. Towards the end of his career Napoleon tended to make pictures, to live in a world created by his own ambitions and imagination. Frederick might find the truth, the facts, unpalatable, but he did at least recognize them for what they were. Right from the start he did not pretend to believe idle tales about Prussia's claim to Silesia. Perhaps no soldier, and certainly no king, was as prolific with the pen as Frederick, and his Memoirs contribute much to our understanding of what really determined events. 'Ambition, interest, the desire of making people talk about me', he wrote, 'carried the day; and I decided for war.'

Was the battle of Mollwitz destined to be fought, subject to one of history's inevitable laws, or was it brought about by the chance of Frederick's ambition and keen desire for military glory? We may incline to the latter view, while acknowledging that this particular battle did not in the event yield much admiration for either his military skill or his personal courage. Although Silesia had been occupied easily enough in the winter of 1740–41, when spring came and Frederick rejoined his army, there was a battle to be fought against the

Austrians advancing to relieve those fortresses which still resisted. At this time Frederick knew little of how to manage a battlefield and had never commanded a large body of troops in action. It was fortunate for him that there were among his commanders those who were both experienced and competent, while the discipline of his soldiers, most notably the infantry, was unrivalled. Yet Frederick, himself in command of the cavalry, was so disconcerted when they suffered a reverse and so dismayed by the uproar and slaughter of battle that he allowed himself to be persuaded to quit the field, leaving it to others successfully to complete the business of Mollwitz. We may conclude therefore that in this particular case, whereas the character of Frederick brought about the incident of Mollwitz, his subsequent flight from the battlefield was not illustrative of his character, whereas in his two next battles, Chotusitz and Hohenfriedberg, he displayed vigour and personal bravery in the former and mastery of the military art in the latter.

Disraeli once observed of Wellington that he had left the nation a great legacy – contemplation of his character. And indeed it bears contemplation, for the Iron Duke was honest, brave, loyal, magnanimous, honourable and kindly. When we look at Frederick the Great, we get a different picture. He was regarded by many of his contemporaries as completely lacking political morality or human decency, consumed by predatory ambition and a master of intrigue. At the same time they recognized his growing competence as a general, his skill as a negotiator, his sure touch in administration – all in all, a man of substance. Yet he could neither feel nor inspire affection. Despite his encouragement of religious toleration and press freedom, despite his devotion to the arts and the enjoyment of good company, Frederick was guilty of malice, a love of humiliating others, a petty display of power, a mean close-handedness and a sly cynicism, an inability to tolerate any will but his own that modify our admiration of his achievements. But then, had it not been for this hardness, this inflexibility, this reluctance to compromise and the inexorable refusal to spare himself, Frederick would have been unlikely to have won lasting military renown in the Seven Years War.

In December 1757, with 40,000 men, Frederick won a battle

against 60,000 Austrians at Leuthen. It was a victory conspicuous for Frederick's brilliant handling of his army and for the skill and resolution of his Prussian troops. Napoleon called it a masterpiece which, apart from anything else, entitled Frederick to rank himself among the very greatest generals. 'The King's fame filled all the world,' wrote Macaulay.

He had during the last year maintained a contest, on terms of advantage, against three powers, the weakest of which had more than three times his resources . . . This victory of Leuthen is, to this day, the proudest on the roll of Prussian fame.[2]

Here again we find the resolution and skill of a great man calling the odds, laying down the stake and making off with his winnings. Yet the true greatness of Frederick was to be shown not in good fortune, but in adversity. And here it seemed that chance did govern all.

As the years 1760 and 1761 progressed, Frederick's military fortunes deteriorated. Berlin was occupied by the enemy, the country was ravaged, half Silesia was in Austrian hands, the Russians were triumphant in Pomerania, there was a dearth of men, horses, supplies: even Frederick felt something like despair. Yet two events were to transform the political and military scenes. In 1761 the enforced resignation of William Pitt, who had guided England with such brilliant success during the Seven Years War and overseen the Year of Victories in 1759, brought about the new Ministry's peace overtures to France, which despite Frederick's initial bitterness and alienation, did lead to a treaty between France and Britain which bound them both to neutrality with regard to Prussia's war. Of still more moment was the death of the Empress Elizabeth of Russia in 1762. Her successor and nephew, Peter, completely reversed her policy towards Prussia. Not only did he make peace, he withdrew all his troops from those provinces which Elizabeth had overrun, and to cap it all actually sent 15,000 Russian soldiers to reinforce Frederick's armies. The effect of all this on Austria, which had been unable to subdue Prussia even when allied to France and Russia, and now found herself threatened by a Turkish army on Hungary's frontiers, was such that even the implacable Maria Theresa, Empress of Austria, gave way and concluded peace with Prussia. In commenting on this astonishing turn of affairs, Macaulay points out that Frederick had conceded nothing. The entire Continent in arms against him had not been able to remove Silesia from his iron grip. 'He had given an example unrivalled in history of what capacity and resolution can effect against the greatest superiority of power, and the utmost spite of fortune.'[3] If ever we needed an instance of how character determined incident, here it is. But we must admit, too, that the incidents of Pitt's withdrawal and Elizabeth's death did not only illustrate how chance or fate could intervene, but showed what a profound effect on events such intervention could have.

We have said a good deal about battles and how their conduct and outcome were influenced by commanders, terrain, weather, chance and other circumstances, but have not faced the question: what is a battle like? Most soldiers ask themselves this when they know they are about to be committed to battle. Even if they have done it all before, they will still ponder on the nature, the hazards, the possible prizes and their own chances of survival in the battle to come. The answer will depend in large measure on positioning, in both time and space. That is to say, in Wellington's day it was just possible for a single man during a single day to view an entire field of battle and comprehend its development simply because it was so confined in both time and space. Yet even so we find Stendhal at the field of Waterloo observing: 'From noon until three o'clock, we had an excellent view of all that can be seen of a battle – i.e. nothing at all.' Wellington himself made a similar point when he likened the history of a battle to a ball. Everyone could recall with sharp clarity details here and there, at this time and at that, but few or none could comprehend or describe the whole. At the same time we must remember that Wellington in his central and commanding position, despite all the smoke and confusion, was able to see Jérôme's attack on Hougoumont and the British cavalry's charge; he observed with astonishment Ney's futile attempts to break the British redcoats' squares and was heartily relieved when he became conscious of the Prussians' arrival. His despatch described in essence the course of the battle. We may note too that Lord Raglan, from his command and observation post on top of the Sapouné Heights, had a perfect view of both the Heavy and Light Brigades' charges, indeed of the whole battle of Balaklava, so limited was it in space and time. We may even comprehend some of the Great War's ghastly offensives, so prodigal in lives, so beggarly in weighing the odds, so gallantly executed, so nugatory in dividend. But when it comes to some of the Second World War's battles, Stalingrad for example, they seem to be on too large a scale and of too long a duration to take in. Yet the battle of Stalingrad, it might be said, came about not by design, but by chance.

In June 1942 a further German offensive in the East began. Army Group B under von Bock was directed on Stalingrad with the 4th Panzer Army and von Paulus's 6th Army; Army Group A under List was headed south-east through the Caucasus with Baku as a final objective. Three weeks later things were going so well that Hitler made exactly the same error as he had made a year earlier during the initial invasion of Russia. He changed his mind, robbed himself of concentration of force, and fell between two stools. Instead of sticking to his plan that the whole weight of Army Group B should concentrate on establishing the 'Block' at Stalingrad before deciding what Hoth's 4th Panzer Army would do next – and had he stuck to the plan it is probable that Stalingrad would have fallen, for the Russians would have had far less time to strengthen its defences – instead, Hitler diverted Hoth before the Stalingrad battle was joined; what is more, he diverted it to help Army Group A which at that time did not need help, and then as resistance at Stalingrad stiffened, redirected Hoth there when it was already too late. This chopping and changing reminds us of d'Erlon's Reserve Corps at Waterloo, which was marched and counter-marched between Ligny and Quatre Bras, unable to influence either battle. With Hitler it was the old story – no patient concentration, either of mind or material, on one objective at a time, but wild dilettantism at its worst, dashing forward for all objectives at once, grossly exaggerating his own strength and the enemy's weakness, doubling his aim whilst halving the forces to achieve each one, and by doing so, achieving neither. By September the struggle for Stalingrad, the battle that saved the world, as Edward Sammis described it, was raging, and the thrust to the Caucasus had been halted by the Russians short of the main oilfields.[4] The Wehrmacht's tide was as high as it had been at any time. Henceforth it would ebb. It had not been the force of destiny that had brought this about. It had been the chance of Hitler's will.

For those commanders and staff officers poring over maps at corps, army or Army Group headquarters, such broad considerations of a campaign may have some meaning. For those in divisions and brigades, above all for those in the regiments which do the actual fighting, the mosaic has a far less disciplined pattern. For them, the infantryman, the tank crew, the sapper, artilleryman, signaller and truck driver, there is in battle a series of uncoordinated and haphazard periods of intense excitement, discomfort, activity, apprehension and sometimes elation. While most of them might on reflection agree with Rosenstock-Huessey's point that three-quarters of a soldier's life is spent aimlessly hanging about, it is the other quarter they remember.[5] The great secret of getting through a battle without having to undergo too many disagreeable moments of introspection is to be busy, so busy thinking of what to do, how to do it, how to making sure it is done and then actually doing it, while making sure also that those about you, both above and under your command, are 'in the picture', that there is little time for concern about yourself. Such industry and commitment are easier for those at the level of almost any headquarters from battalion or regiment upwards. For those who pull the triggers, advance into hostile country, get the bullets and shells fired at them, make the critical low-level decisions which turn operation orders from mere pieces of paper or groups of words into action, this total preoccupation with every minute of the night and day is less easy. Even in the thick of a battle there is a good deal of aimless waiting about, or so it often seems.

When those who have not been to war read that such and such an infantry division has launched an attack on some point or other or that an armoured division has broken out and is conducting pursuit operations against enemy rearguards, they are apt to harbour pictures of massed infantry sweeping across open ground, storming and taking all before them, or great phalanxes of tanks charging about with their guns belching flame and dismaying their adversaries into surrender or flight. It is not like that at all.

During the Second World War a British infantry division had three brigades. An attack would probably be made by two of them, with the third in reserve. Each brigade charged with the attack would deploy two of its three battalions forward and keep one in hand. So in turn battalions would position their companies, the companies their platoons, and the platoons their sections. Each section, if it were up to strength – and few were after being in action for a day or two – contained nine or ten men. So in terms of fighting soldiers, wielding rifles or light machine-guns, grenades or the bayonet, the numbers actually closing with the enemy were small in relation to the total on the ground. The division's attack would be made by four battalions, that is, eight companies, sixteen platoons, thirty-two sections, so that its leading echelon would consist of a mere 300 or so men, out of some 10,000 to 15,000 in the division as a whole if it were anything like up to strength. This sort of arithmetic helps us to understand what General Horrocks meant when he said that the front is a very small club. Of course, others in the division would also be involved in the fighting. The guns of the artillery would be an indispensable support and comfort to the advancing infantry. Assuming that the commander of the whole operation knew what he was doing – and this was by no means always the case – he would have arranged for an armoured brigade to be in close support of his infantry battalions and to work in the closest possible teams. Time after time the German army had demonstrated to the British how integrated groups of tanks, armoured infantry, artillery and anti-tank guns were the most effective means of getting and keeping the upper hand on the battlefield. Yet it was not until 1944 that the British army finally made use of proper tracked armoured personnel carriers. There was, of course, one more supremely important part of the all-arms team, which the Wehrmacht had so successfully exploited during their years of conquest – close support of aircraft. And as the tide turned against the Axis powers, this formidable weapon was largely the prerogative of the Allies.

If we turn for a moment to the conduct of defence, it will become clear to those who have not taken part in a European battle of the sort conducted in Normandy or Italy that however small the club of front-line soldiers may be, given a combination of determined, well-armed, skilfully concealed groups of panzer or parachute veterans and difficult country where roads and tracks were few and far between and the going off them treacherously boggy, it was possible for such small groups to delay and inflict damage on greatly superior numbers simply because those mounting an attack could not deploy sufficient strength forward. So we may comprehend why it was so that during those European battles, whether the axes of advance for Allied formations were in the Apennine hills, valleys and rivers, the *bocage* of Normandy or the Ardennes forest, there were times when a very few of the Germans' formidable Panther and Tiger tanks, supported by mortars and Panzergrenadiers, were able to prevent the advance of complete divisions.

It is perhaps fitting to offer an instance of such occurrences, one which also illustrates how chances may be missed by over-confidence and lack of preparation for seizing opportunity. Shortly before embarking in the *Queen Mary* on 5 September 1944 for his Quebec meeting with Roosevelt, Churchill reverted to his longed-for expectations of some great strategic triumph in Italy. His signal of 31 August to the President raised the point of what was to be done by the 5th and 8th Armies in that theatre 'once the German armies in Italy have been destroyed or unluckily have made their escape'. Once more he had glimpses of the Allies moving into Istria and Trieste, and so on to Vienna. He even mentioned the possibility of the war ending in a few months' time. Roosevelt's reply was equally sanguine in referring to what was to happen after the German forces in the Gothic Line had been broken, but he was more concerned with using Allied forces in Italy to help Eisenhower advance into the heart of Germany than to pursue what he and his advisers regarded as irrelevant strategic goals in Central Europe. Yet Churchill's *idée fixe* was not to be so easily dismissed, as was further illustrated by his signalling to Smuts that he still hoped 'to turn and break the Gothic Line, break into the Po valley, and ultimately advance by Trieste and the Ljubljana Gap to Vienna'. In the event, however, the Gothic Line proved to be a far harder nut to crack than he or the senior commanders in Italy had ever imagined, and as his own regiment, the 4th Hussars, was soon to discover.

There is an ironic touch to Alexander's attempts to break through the Gothic Line. His original intention had been to do so in the centre, using both 5th and 8th Armies, and his deception plan to accompany it was aimed at making the Germans believe that his main thrust would be on the Adriatic coast. He was then persuaded by General Leese, 8th Army commander, to change the plan so that Leese could exploit his superiority in armour, which should be more effective there than in the mountainous centre. The deception plan was all too successful, however, and Kesselring, commanding the German armies in Italy, although temporarily diverted by the landings in southern France, soon grasped where the main threat lay and acted accordingly.

The 8th Army was to advance and break into the Gothic Line through the so-called Rimini Gap, then on to the Romagna – the Rimini–Bologna–Lake Comacchio triangle – and the Lombardy Plains. This part of the country was believed by some of 8th Army's planning staff to be good going for tanks. They were to be swiftly disillusioned. 8th Army's attack began on 25 August, while further west 5th Army would break through the Futa and Il Giogo Passes and seize Bologna. Both armies fought gallantly and doggedly against the odds of rivers and ridges and rain, but the skilled defensive tactics and imaginative improvisations at which the Germans excelled and so often displayed, were too much for them. The Allies came close to success, but not close enough.

After a week's fighting on the Rimini front, the infantry divisions of 8th Army believed that they had made a hole in the German defences, and 5 Corps was ordered to break out and push on northwards. So it came about that the 1st Armoured Division was launched. It was 3 September 1944, five years to the day from the war's beginning, and as a troop leader of the 4th Hussars, the Division's armoured reconnaissance regiment – we were at the time in leaguer a few miles behind the front line – I received the order from my squadron leader to advance with all speed to the north to reconnoitre and seize crossings over the river Conco. Although far too busy at that moment with passing on the orders to my other tank commanders and looking at the map to decide on the route, it occurred to me later that none of the normal procedures had been followed.

I received no information about where our own troops were, whose positions we would be passing through before taking the lead, nothing whatever about the enemy; there was no mention of being joined by a Forward Observation Officer from our supporting artillery regiment; no question of joining up with the so-called motor battalion of the 60th Rifles, who would be ideal for holding any crossings we might secure; no indication of an objective beyond the Conco; the order was simply – Advance! I did, however, learn from my squadron leader that other squadrons of the Regiment, unwisely attempting passages cross-country, had run into soft, boggy ground and been brought to an ignominious standstill. We agreed that my troop would stick to the narrow road which led towards what from the map appeared to be a bridge across the river.

This somewhat inauspicious beginning to what ultimately turned out to be a long, costly struggle for the Gothic Line, with no clear orders, no relevant information, no sign whatever of forming a proper tank–infantry–artillery team, and apparently no preparation at all to anticipate either success in getting on or failure by being held up, had all the ingredients of chaos as far as we in the 4th Hussars were concerned. Continuing to advance during that night, with at last an objective – the village of Coriano and its tactically important ridge, the key to that part of the battlefield – I still had the honour to be the leading tank (my map reading was somewhat superior to that of my NCOs) not only of the Regiment, but of the entire 1st Armoured Division, when suddenly about a mile or so from another ridge over-looking Coriano from the south, we received the order to halt. The reason for doing so was never given, but it subsequently became clear that at that time Coriano was very lightly held by the Germans, yet during the next days was heavily reinforced, together with the neigh-bouring ideally defensive ground. This action enabled the Germans to conduct a stubborn step-by-step defence and gradual withdrawal, extremely costly to the advancing Allied troops, which ensured that the Gothic Line was not broken during the autumn and winter of 1944.

But what a chance was missed! What actually happened the follow-ing morning was that we deployed at first light on to the ridge overlooking Coriano and even attempted to penetrate the village itself, but a squadron of Sherman and Stuart tanks, totally unsupported by artillery or infantry, was quite unable to make progress against the rapidly improvised anti-tank defences deployed by the enemy. The troop which advanced to Coriano itself was shot to pieces by anti-tank guns, while those of us deployed on the ridge were subjected to the most disagreeable artillery, mortar and anti-tank fire for most of the day, while the Germans steadily reinforced the Coriano position. Yet the opportunity to win a great advantage there and then before the weather deteriorated and the whole advance became bogged down had been there. Available for action and uncommitted was the division's infantry brigade, consisting of three battalions of those intrepid and skilful warriors, the Gurkhas, who were moreover equipped with lorries to bring them rapidly to the scene of action. Also to hand was the entire divisional artillery and at that point in the affair an armoured brigade of three battle-hardened cavalry regiments, The Queen's Bays, 9th Lancers and 10th Hussars. If only on that first night even a proportion of the division's strength, say two Gurkha battalions, an artillery regiment and an armoured regiment in addition to ourselves, had been rushed forward with orders to take Coriano and be prepared after further reinforcement to exploit into the adjoining hills and ridges, we might have obtained such a foothold into the Gothic Line that the Germans would have been obliged to withdraw from it altogether. As it was, we in the 4th Hussars lost five officers, thirty-five men, nine tanks, and gained – a battle honour. And so, all along the line, the initial battles for the German defensive positions astride the Apennines – Coriano, Rimini, the Romagna, and further west the Il Giogo Pass – got under way to the accompaniment of rain, blood, mud and cold. By the end of October, some eight weeks later, it had become clear that the Allied armies would be required to spend one more winter in the mountains. Yet ironically enough, less than three weeks after 1st Armoured Division's hesitant approach to the Gothic Line, when real boldness and risk-taking could have yielded great dividends, at a time when it was far too late for such reckless action, a further attempt to break out was made on the orders of the divisional commander and against the advice and instincts of those on the spot. It was a tragic repetition of the initial Coriano battles. An armoured regiment, The Queen's Bays, was invited to advance without infantry support and without clearing a tactically vital feature on their flank, which concealed deadly 88-mm guns. The result was hardly to be wondered at. Of their fifty-two tanks half were destroyed and over sixty of their crews killed or wounded – a black day indeed for The Bays, and one not to be forgotten or forgiven by those who survived. Thus was brought home once more the point that for tanks to drive forward without infantry support in the defensive country of the Apennines was not merely taking a chance, it was defying the odds. For those taking part in this fiasco, the sheer chaos of battle was brought home with a vengeance: 1st Armoured Division had been cautious when it should have been bold, and rash when it should have been circumspect.

The curious thing is that even when operations went more or less according to plan, there was still the feeling that chaos and chance had more to do with what was going on than any ordered, controlled conduct of affairs. In the spring that followed the Gothic Line battles, when I found myself in command of a half-squadron of the 4th Hussars – by this time we were equipped with so-called Kangeroos, sawn-off Sherman tanks for carrying infantry into battle – we were required to take the lead in crossing the river Senio with a battalion of New Zealanders, those magnificent soldiers who had fought their way from Egypt to northern Italy. This time things were being done properly and we were a real team of tanks, infantry and artillery observers. The river crossing went smoothly and we succeeded in pushing on with a few skirmishes over another river. There was relatively little opposition from the Germans, and so confident did the New Zealand battalion commander become – he was with me in my armoured vehicle – that he turned and said, 'This must be the break-through.' No sooner were the words out of his mouth than we were subjected to the most vicious shelling and mortaring imaginable, and it was clear that stiff opposition was being encountered at the next river ahead.

A prolonged artillery duel was followed by a night attack which succeeded in dislodging the German opposition. At dawn we resumed the advance and I found myself proceeding down a country road with the troops I was responsible for deployed on either side. Suddenly that fearsome tearing noise, like an express train going past, occurred, and it was clear that someone was firing armour-piercing shot at us. I moved off the road to a large, strong-looking farmhouse where I found the New Zealand battalion commander. I asked him what the situation was, and have always admired his answer, which was a splendid euphemism for admitting that he had no idea. He looked at me steadily and replied, 'Fluid!'

It may perhaps be imagined that if, as was the case here, a battalion commander and his immediate armoured supporter have little or no notion of what is happening to themselves and their own front line, how much smaller still will be their understanding of what is going on to their flanks. My own grasp of the situation was not aided by a radio message from my own 4th Hussar squadron leader that a number of German self-propelled guns were heading towards me. Being in a vehicle without any armament other than a machine-gun, I demanded by radio that these unwelcome intruders should be engaged by artillery fire. I received no reply, but happily the German SP guns did not appear. After a few more scrappy actions and struggles to get over rivers whose bridges had been blown up and whose banks were mined, we found ourselves advancing faster and faster towards the Po. It was maps we needed now rather than ammunition. It was the breakthrough at last and a wonderful feeling of freedom swept over us. The situation was fluid indeed.

One of the most enduring of impressions from being involved in battles of this sort is that of uncertainty as to what is going on, an uncertainty not assisted by the constant revision of orders and a persistent dearth of reliable information. Those in command of divisions, even brigades, seem to have an insatiable appetite for chopping and changing. This in turn nearly always resulted in delay – delay in making decisions, delay in transmitting orders, delay in preparing to obey them, delay in actually carrying them out, by which time, more often than not, the situation has again changed, for as we have seen and as von Moltke emphasized, no plan survives contact with the enemy, and however much you may hope to oblige the enemy to dance to your tune, nine times out of ten he is disinclined to do so. Such is the nature of a battle. Chance, mischance, chaos, confusion set the scene and dominate the stage.

If this could be the case in the tiny actions I have described, think how it must have been with the numbers involved and the strategic stakes multiplied thousands of times over. Think for example of Mons or Gallipoli! The battle of Mons in August 1914 was an extraordinarily chancy affair. In the first place, when the Prime Minister, Asquith, presided over a council of war on 5 August, one day after the declaration of war, it had not been decided how much of the British Expeditionary Force (BEF) should go abroad, where it should go or what it should do. On the first two questions there was much disagreement, on the last no agreement at all. It was not helped by the fact that Wilson, Director of Operations, regarded the other fifteen members of the council as almost entirely ignorant of what was being discussed. This was a severe judgement on those present, who included the Secretary of War, Kitchener, the BEF's Commander-in-Chief, French, his Chief of Staff, Murray, the two corps commanders, Haig and Grierson, and Field-Marshal Roberts; also present, apart from Asquith himself, were the three ministers most concerned: Haldane, Grey and Churchill;[6] the First Sea Lord, Battenberg, and Sir Ian Hamilton, Home Defence, completed the council. Wilson made it plain that the plans he had agreed with the French, that the BEF should deploy on the French left at Maubeuge, were complete in detail and could not be altered. For a moment the matter rested there.

But the following day Kitchener raised serious objections. He pointed out that if the Germans' Schlieffen Plan were executed it would mean that an all-powerful German right wing would advance through Belgium in a bid to encircle and roll up the French army. In this event the BEF would be exposed to an overwhelming attack. He therefore urged the Cabinet to change the BEF's destination to Amiens. This was agreed, but not for long. Wilson returned to the charge and brought the influence of his French military associates to bear on Kitchener, arguing that the BEF had to act with its Allies and show total commitment to have any effect at all. The French, of course, were only too anxious that the British should be involved in the fighting from the outset. Kitchener gave way and the BEF did concentrate at Maubeuge. During the various Cabinet discussions Kitchener made the remarkable prediction that the war would last for at least three years[7] and that Britain would have to deploy an army of millions to fight a series of bloody campaigns on the Continent. He therefore set about raising such an army. How he arrived at this all too accurate a conclusion was never clear. He seemed to be possessed of flashes of brilliant strategic instinct.

As things turned out, the deployment of the BEF on the French left, done for political reasons rather than strategic ones, although worked out in precise administrative detail, had a profound effect in thwarting von Moltke's version of the Schlieffen Plan. The whole essence of the original plan was that of a powerful right wing which would move with great speed and maintain momentum and advance to the west of Paris, avoiding distractions elsewhere. Fortunately for the Allies the Germans failed to adhere to these conditions. In the first place, expecting to walk through Belgium without meeting any resistance, von Kluck's 1st Army was delayed by four days when it encountered fierce defence of the Liège fortress. A further unwelcome surprise awaited the Germans when, having calculated that the British army's support for the French would be too late and too insignificant, they encountered the five divisions of the BEF at Mons – an unlucky chance indeed for von Moltke. This blocking of their advance caused the German High Command to abandon the essential feature of the Schlieffen Plan – a further enveloping movement by the right wing – and turn their thrust to the east, instead of the west, of Paris, thus exposing flank and rear to a counter-attack by the French. Worse was to follow from the German point of view when von Moltke, breaching a fundamental principle of war, failed to concentrate in the area where decision was possible, the right wing, and so regain the momentum, and instead mounted a strategically irrelevant attack on Nancy. Everything had gone wrong and resulted in von Moltke's replacement by von Falkenhayn.

But the almost chance encounter between von Kluck's 1st Army and the BEF on the morning of 23 August 1914, when four German corps and three cavalry divisions mounted their main attack against a mere two British divisions of Smith-Dorrien's 2nd Corps, an encounter which became known as the Battle of Mons, figures still as a legend in this country's military history. In her book *August 1914*, Barbara Tuchman wrote that it

was given a place in the British pantheon equal to the battle of Hastings or Agincourt. Legends like that of the Angel of Mons settled upon it. All its men were valorous and its dead all heroes. The deeds of every named regiment were chronicled down to the last hour and bullet of the fight until Mons came to shine mistily through a haze of such gallantry and glory as to make it seem a victory.[8]

In fact it was a retreat, for the BEF was obliged to conform to the movements of the French army. Next came a counter-move by the French and British which forced the Germans to conduct a general withdrawal to the river Aisne. Then all manoeuvre and mobility virtually ended.

Now came the greatest spite of fortune that could have befallen any armies of this generation. The Germans, as A. J. P. Taylor put it, had unwittingly 'stumbled on the discovery which shaped the first world war: men in trenches, with machine-guns, could beat off all but the most formidable attacks. The Allied advance ground to a halt.'[9] Trench warfare had begun. It was never part of some grand strategic vision, but a mere chance, and one which baffled Kitchener, who in spite of his prediction about the length of the war and its millions of participants commented: 'I don't know what is to be done. This isn't war.' Had Kitchener had his way earlier and deployed the BEF at Amiens instead of Maubeuge, it might never have happened at all. If in fact there had been no resistance at Mons, no blocking of von Kluck's 1st Army, the Schlieffen Plan might have worked, the French army have been rolled up, Paris taken and a repetition of the 1870/71 disaster have overtaken the French nation, with Wilhelm II and von Moltke strutting about in the Palace of Versailles forty-three years after the first German Emperor, William, and his architect of victory, Bismarck, had done so.

But trench warfare had come to stay. It was a chance which was to cost the armies taking part hundreds of thousands of young lives.

Even though Kitchener professed that he did not know what was to be done, there were plenty of other British generals who thought they did. Yet in fact the real trouble facing the British as 1914 ended and 1915 began was that no one had any clear idea as to what was to be done to defeat the Germans. Kitchener believed the German defensive lines to be impregnable to frontal assault. Despite this the generals in the field, French and Haig, were planning to indulge in a series of frontal assaults, which resulted in no strategic gains and ever-mounting casualties. The fiasco of the attack at Neuve Chapelle in March 1915 cost the British army 600 officers and 12,000 men. For what? A useless salient about two miles wide and a little more than half a mile deep. No lessons were learned from this failure. The whole thing was repeated at the Aubers Ridge in May where it failed with heavy losses. No matter! They would plan another attack. The battle of Loos in September 1915 began with a wholly inadequate artillery programme. Then thousands of British infantrymen, massed together, advanced across open country towards the intact defences of the German lines. Never before, one German regimental diary recorded, had there been such a target. Never before had the machine-guns done their work so effectively. The whole affair lasted three and a half hours until at length, despite incredible courage and perseverance,[10] having endured terrible losses – of the roughly 10,000 soldiers in the attack, 385 officers and 7,861 men were lost – the pitiful survivors made their way back to their own trenches. The Germans called the battlefield *Leichenfeld von Loos*, field of corpses, and as the remnants stumbled back 'no shot was fired at them from the German trenches for the rest of the day, so great was the feeling of compassion and mercy for the enemy after such a victory'.

Surely, the strategists asked themselves, there must be a way of using British sea power in an indirect approach which might obtain a foothold somewhere and threaten the German homeland from a flank. There was. When Turkey entered the war on the German side in October 1914, these strategy-makers sought a theatre of war where the Germans would be unable rapidly to interfere. A possible theatre was not difficult to identify when it became clear that Turkish forces were advancing south through Palestine and would before long pose a threat to the Suez Canal. No one embraced the idea of employing the Royal Navy in a bold strategic enterprise more ardently than the First Lord of the Admiralty, Winston Churchill; at a meeting of the War Council on 25 November 1914 he suggested that the way to defend Egypt would be to mount an attack on the Gallipoli Peninsula. Once successful, the British would have control of the Dardanelles and would be in a position to dictate terms at Constantinople. Exactly what effect all this would have on the Western Front was not made clear, but it could conceivably aid the Russians, who three months earlier had suffered a severe defeat at Tannenberg.

Grand strategic ideas are all very well when acted upon expeditiously, but there then ensued a long period of dithering, argument and uncertainty. In particular, the War Council could not make up its mind whether it would be possible to force the Dardanelles by ships alone or whether it would be necessary to mount a joint operation. The extent of the controversy may be gauged by recording that at one point Kitchener maintained that 'We have no troops to land anywhere' and at another offered the entirely intuitive opinion that the Gallipoli Peninsula could be captured with 150,000 troops, then, having finally agreed that a military force would include the Royal Naval Division, the 29th Division, Australians and New Zealanders, Indian Army units and French troops, acceded to the idea that after all the Royal Navy would first have a go with ships alone. No good could come from such shilly-shallying.

And no good did come of it. When on 18 March 1915 a combined fleet of Royal Navy and French battleships attempted to force the Straits, the Turkish defenders enjoyed a day of absolute triumph. Despite a furious bombardment of the Turkish forts, only four guns were destroyed out of 180 positioned to defend the Dardanelles. There were 400 mines in the waters. Not one was cleared. Three Allied battleships were sunk, a further three disabled. Hamilton, who had been appointed by Kitchener to command the operation, now signalled him to say that the Straits could not be forced by battleships, but that the army would have to be deployed in strength to make a passage for the navy. But what if the initial attempt by the navy had been successful and battleships had made their way to Constantinople?

What would they have done then? No doubt they could have bombarded the city, even sent landing parties ashore, but little else. Unless the ships had then returned to the open seas, they would have been vulnerable to hastily mobilized shore batteries or enemy submarines. In any event, once Kitchener had concurred with his recommendation, Hamilton took his army away to Alexandria to reorganize before setting about the business of taking the Gallipoli Peninsula. This delay robbed the Allies of all hope of surprise and allowed the Turks to reinforce Gallipoli three-fold, bringing its garrison up to some six divisions. The whole idea of the venture was to seek an alternative to a war of attrition on the Western Front. Now the British were about to indulge in an amphibious assault on unreconnoitred country which was defended by more soldiers than Hamilton had under his command. It was not exactly a recipe for success.

Even at the outset there was disagreement as to how the assault should be made. Hamilton favoured the Gallipoli Peninsula itself as the main objective, that is, the European part of the Dardanelles, while Birdwood, in command of the ANZACs, wanted to go for the Asian shores. In the end Hamilton had his way, and apart from diversionary landings on the Asiatic shores, the main efforts were at Cape Helles and south of Suvla. The plan was full of holes. There was no secrecy. Everyone seemed to know the expedition's destination. Although both the ANZACs and the 29th Division got ashore, the Turks' reaction under the dynamic leadership of Mustapha Kemal was swift, resolute and effective. The great strategic *coup*, designed to turn the flank of the Central Powers as an alternative to the dreadful carnage of France and Flanders, became another scene of futile slaughter. The British then indulged in their seemingly favourite activity of reinforcing failure. Another great effort was made at Suvla Bay in August: result – furious counter-attacks by the Turks and stalemate. In October Hamilton was recalled and replaced by Monro, who at once recommended evacuation.

The British army, with the indispensable aid of the Royal Navy, was good at evacuations. They had had much practice during the French Revolutionary and Napoleonic Wars, and were to have more in the war still to come. In mid-December 1915 the Suvla and

ANZAC beaches were evacuated, and the Helles beaches three weeks later. This was the most successful part of the whole enterprise, for it was all done without loss. But the overall losses had been grievous – 25,000 killed, three times as many wounded, 10,000 missing, thousands more sick. It had simply shown that the German army on the Western Front could not be outflanked by Mediterranean adventures, a lesson largely ignored during the Second World War, when the indirect approach was once more favoured by British strategists. In this latter case it did at least prove a significant distraction to the Wehrmacht's endeavours on the Western and Eastern Fronts. In the case of Gallipoli, it failed to provide a distraction. And suppose it had succeeded, and half a million Allied soldiers had occupied the Gallipoli Peninsula, taken Constantinople and routed Mustapha Kemal, what then? Where would the army have gone? How would it have been supplied? How could such a force have succeeded in building up its strength and capability more quickly than the Central Powers with their rapid and secure lines of communication? And what would have been the effect on the battles in France and Flanders, the only theatre of war where in the end decision could be attained? These were questions that never required an answer. There was, of course, one other casualty of the whole affair, the man regarded, not justly, as its architect and greatest advocate – Winston Churchill. He was the chosen scapegoat, and in his own heroic way sought redemption by commanding an infantry battalion in the trenches and no-man's-land of the Western Front. The tragedy of Gallipoli is in great measure explained by the character of its commander, Hamilton, described by Robert Rhodes James as an attractive, intelligent and sensitive man who, however, 'lacked that element in a commander which is so difficult to define with exactitude, that inner confidence, that basic common sense, that understanding of reality . . . that mental and moral toughness . . .'[11]

Thus it was that character determined incident and incident illustrated character. Decision and indecision, chance and chaos: the history of war and the chronicle of battles are laced with them. Let us look at a few more.

Charles Gordon was one of the great Victorian soldier heroes, a man of infinite truth and integrity, the ever-victorious general, a legend who seemed to bear a charmed life and had led his Chinese troops into battle during the suppression of the Taiping rebellion calmly holding a swagger cane. William Butler said of him that he was 'the noblest knight among us all' and Richard Burton called him 'a phenomenon in the nineteenth century'. In 1884 Gordon had been sent to Khartoum to evacuate the Egyptian garrisons there in view of the dangers posed by the Mahdi's successful uprising. This move was strongly opposed by the British Consul-General in Cairo, Sir Evelyn Baring, who knowing Gordon's character and courage feared that he might not stick strictly to his instructions but would take the sort of action which would get everyone, especially the British Government, into trouble. His fears were justified. When Gordon arrived in Khartoum in February 1884, he decided not to evacuate the garrisons but to defy the Mahdi and hold both Khartoum and the Nile valley. Three months later the Mahdist armies had completely cut off Gordon by taking Berber, nearly 200 miles to the north. Anticipating such difficulties, both Baring and the British army's Commander-in-Chief, Field-Marshal Lord Wolseley, had urged the Government to prepare for just such an eventuality by mounting a military expedition to relieve Gordon. Wolseley even went so far as to produce a detailed plan, described by him as the biggest operation the English army had ever undertaken. Wolseley was a general who enjoyed war for its own sake. He had distinguished himself in countless engagements – Burma, the Crimea, the Indian Mutiny, China – and had commanded with marked success in suppressing a rebellion in Canada's Red River, destroying Ashanti power in the Gold Coast, crushing Arabi Pasha at Tel-el-Kebir. He had given the phrase 'All Sir Garnet' to the nation as an unfailing recipe for getting things right. Disraeli called him 'an egotist and a braggart' but took some of the sting away by adding, 'So was Nelson.'

Had Wolseley been allowed to get on with his plan when he first proposed it in April 1884, he might well have relieved Gordon. But even Wolseley could not induce the Prime Minister, Gladstone, to act there and then. Gladstone was far too preoccupied with his Reform Bill and was in any case most reluctant to indulge in military adventures. It was not until August that Wolseley was appointed, and still no preparations had been made. What this all amounted to was that one man, Gordon, by refusing to obey his orders, by showing that he was determined to remain in Khartoum, had forced the British Government's hand to mount an expedition to relieve him, destroy the Mahdi and reoccupy the Sudan. So much for the forces of destiny! Yet it was already too late. Wolseley arrived in September and his army set off from Wadi Halfa the following month, reached Korti in November, won a battle against the Mahdi's forces at Abu Klea on 17 January and eleven days later came within sight of Khartoum, to see the Mahdi's banners fluttering above the city. Gordon had been killed two days earlier.

> Too late! Too late to save him,
> In vain, in vain they tried.
> His life was England's glory.
> His death was England's pride.

What had Gordon been up to all this time? When Wolseley landed in Egypt Gordon was almost the sole remaining European in Khartoum. Ever since March the Mahdi's forces had been drawing closer to the city. Gordon's attempts to disrupt their advance and to establish an escape route had failed. The despatch of his trusted assistant, Colonel Stewart, and the British and French consuls along with a dozen others downstream in the steamer *Abbas* ended at Abu Hamed, north of Berber, when it went aground and all aboard except a stoker were killed. But in Khartoum itself Gordon did not despair. All his talents for organizing and inspiring others were employed to keep the enemy at arm's length and the morale of 'his people' in good order. Every sort of device was put to use – fortifications, mines, patrols, messages smuggled out so that they would be intercepted with their claims to be able to hold out indefinitely, bogus communications from Wolseley's relief force. Factories turned out ammunition, medals were minted for the Siege of Khartoum, bands thumped out martial music. Gordon's energy, commitment and defiance were absolute. When God was distributing fear to all those in the world, he would tell a Khartoum merchant, his own turn was last of all and by then there was no fear left. He might, like Coriolanus, have cried, 'Alone I did it,' recalling Caius Marcius's fluttering of the Volscians, like an eagle in a dovecote, at Corioli, but it would have been quite uncharacteristic of him. He would have been more likely to call for another b and s. (Gordon's favoured tipple was brandy and soda.) He rejected the Mahdi's call for surrender with the retort that he was in Khartoum like iron, awaiting the imminent arrival of the English. Yet, as James (later Jan) Morris has reminded us:

He admired his Mahdist enemies, he enjoyed war and responsibility, and if he despised his Egyptian soldiers, he was indubitably attracted by the stalwart Sudanese . . . He was terribly alone. He had no intimate friend in the city – he spoke little Arabic, nobody else spoke English. Yet he never sounds unhappy. He had, like so many of the Victorian imperial heroes, like Napier, like Hodson, like Colley, a vivid sense of theatre: and there in the throttling heat of his palace roof he was playing the most splendid of all tragic roles, to the best of audiences. He made sure it was all recorded for posterity, and he did not fail to stage manage the last curtain to legendary effect.[12]

It was not fate which staged this tragedy. It was the leading actor. Let us glance briefly at the other three heroes that James Morris selects. They too defied the odds, took chance after chance and made their own particular mark on history. Lieutenant-General Sir Charles Napier, of Peninsular fame, conquered Sind ('Peccavi') in the early 1840s and governed it. He suppressed *suttee*, widow-burning, in a simple, effective way – 'When men burn women alive, we hang them.' He was in every way a remarkable man. Fearless in action, full of common sense, in no doubt about the benefits of British rule, totally honest about the real purpose of taking Sind – that is, to the East India Company's advantage – but genuinely believing that his rule would be infinitely better than that of the Amirs, he defined the Imperial mission of conquest as a process of administering a good thrashing, followed by kindness – in short, cruel only to be kind. James Morris instantly excites our sympathy and admiration for Napier when he explains that 'he felt only a vehement contempt for most politicians, most civil servants, most bigwigs of the East India Company and all the Amirs of Sind'. A man with feelings like that, we may tell ourselves, must have been a good fellow.

The Indian Mutiny was better named by the Victorians the Sepoy War, for it was not a national uprising against the British, but a revolt by only a portion of the Bengal army. The Bombay and Madras armies did not mutiny, while many of the native regiments remained loyal and fought with the British to restore their rule. Also, a number of irregular regiments were newly raised at the time, among them Hodson's Horse. James Morris describes William Hodson as 'Hotspur brought to life' and with his relish for combat and his splendid swagger, he proved a brilliant commander of irregular troops. In his regiment's first action against the mutineers with some 400 cavalrymen he took on five times his number, deceived them into thinking he was withdrawing, then turned about, charged into the thick of the enemy horsemen, slashing and shooting, utterly routing them. 'In three days,' runs his account of the action, 'we have frightened away and demoralized a force of artillery, cavalry and infantry some 2,000 strong, beat those who stood or returned to fight us twice, in spite of numbers, and got fed and furnished by the rascally town itself.' On another occasion, when ordered to arrest the last of the Moghul Emperors, Bahadur Shah Zafar, who had taken refuge at the tomb of Humayan, Hodson with fifty of his troopers galloped wildly through the refugees from Delhi frantically trying to shield themselves from this terrifying squadron of horsemen, and on arrival outside the gate of the tomb demanded the submission of Bahadur Shah, 'half an Englishman, half a Sikh, dusty, lithe, ardent, dressed in the haphazard flamboyance dear to irregular cavalrymen down the centuries'. Hodson was killed at the retaking of Lucknow, but his regiment lived on.

One of the less edifying and less successful incidents in British Imperial history concerns our dealings with the Boers. When Gladstone became Prime Minister in 1880, he refused to reverse the annexation of the Transvaal which had been effected while Disraeli was still in office. Negotiations came to nothing. Kruger and Joubert, champions of Transvaal independence, took up arms against the British, and in December 1880 the first Boer War began. Major-General Sir George Colley, one of Wolseley's favourites, had taken over from his former chief as High Commissioner, and like so many others still to come fatally underestimated both the Boers' determination and their formidable skill as mounted infantry. Moreover Colley, a chivalrous, introspective man wholly lacked the iron will, tactical know-how and sheer competence to take on the Boers. Time after time his attempts to invade the Transvaal from Natal went horribly wrong. First the Connaught Rangers were ambushed on 20 December 1880 and suffered appalling casualties. Then, when Colley with 1,500 young soldiers made a second sortie, they were completely outmanoeuvred and outfought by the Boers' mounted Commandos and their guerrilla tactics of rapid fire and movement. Despite this further reverse Colley decided to capture Majuba Hill on the border between Natal and Transvaal. Majuba, which was 6,000 feet high, dominated the border country as if it were some sort of sentinel, but it had no tactical significance. Colley did not even plan to take artillery with him, nor to establish a strong defensive position there. He simply seemed to believe that possession of Majuba would in some way have an influence in his favour to settle his contest with the Boers. His assault on it certainly influenced the outcome of the affair, but not as he hoped. It led to his own disgrace and death.

During the night of 26 February 1881 a mere 359 soldiers climbed up the steep southern slope of Majuba Hill. With Colley were men of the Gordon Highlanders, 58th Foot, 60th Rifles and even some sailors, all dressed in their colourful red tunics, kilts, white helmets and other accoutrements. When the soldiers reached the small plateau at the summit they took no proper measures of defence, there was no cover, no listening posts or look-outs were established. The tiny force simply took it easy. Colley had told them that they must hold the position for three days. There was no reasoning behind this curious instruction. In the event they held it for less than half a day. On the morning of 27 February the Boers on their ponies made their way up to the northern crest of the hill, unseen and unheard, and then, totally surprising Colley's force, poured volley after volley into them at close range. About three-quarters of the British soldiers were killed, wounded or captured, the remainder fleeing ignominiously down the hill. Colley himself was among those killed, and there were rumours that it had been a matter of self-slaughter, for what could have been a more fitting end to so tragically empty a gesture as the attempt on Majuba Hill, than an Othello-like exit?

And if these Victorian Imperial heroes had never lived or done the things they did, what then? If Gordon had not disobeyed orders, and evacuated the Egyptian garrisons in the Sudan, as he might have done had he acted at once, such an Imperial retreat would hardly have restrained the Mahdi and his Dervishes from their fanatical *jihad*. Egypt would have been invaded and even the reluctant Gladstone would have been obliged to respond. No doubt Herbert Kitchener, the most pushing, opinionated and unscrupulous soldier in the British army until the advent of Henry Wilson in the First World War and Montgomery in the Second, would have been there to defeat any such incursion into Egypt, as indeed he did in 1889. But there would have been no need for the Omdurman campaign of 1898, when Kitchener was Sirdar of the Egyptian Army and set about preparing what he had long desired – reconquest of the Sudan. It had been the desperate chances taken by Gordon that had led to his death in 1885 and a long wait before this death could be avenged at Omdurman. Taking chances was an essential part of the Imperial pattern, otherwise Napier would never have seized Sind, Hodson would not have founded his famous Indian cavalry regiment, Colley would never have indulged in the enormous folly of Majuba Hill. The fabric of Empire would have lacked some notably colourful threads.

Men like these left a great deal to chance. Sometimes fortune favoured their risking all on one turn of pitch-and-toss, sometimes not. Yet we are reminded of Halifax's point about not leaving anything to chance and thus not doing ill. During the War of the Spanish Succession, while Marlborough was enjoying an unbroken run of success at Blenheim, Ramillies, Oudenarde and Malplaquet, in Spain itself Galway was not doing so well. He could not be faulted for breaking all the rules of war. He was universally acknowledged to be an experienced commander. He was familiar with campaigning conditions in Spain. He was also strongly of the opinion that war was an exact science from which all unconventional ideas should be excluded. In short, he took no chances. The result was that having embarked on the battle of Almanza in 1707, employing methods with which the textbooks could have found no fault, it took him only a few hours to lose the best part of 20,000 men, all his guns and baggage, over 100 colours, the campaign itself and almost the whole of Spain. Such are the fortunes of war.

Does chance govern all, as Milton suggests? Was von Clausewitz justified in claiming that no human activity is so bound up with chance as that of war? Here again we must distinguish between the various types of chance. For sheer good luck the chance presented to the 9th US Armoured Division on 7 March 1945 as it led the 1st Army along the northern part of the Eifel and approached the Rhine town of Remagen must take some beating. Up until then bridge after bridge over the Rhine between Koblenz and Duisburg had gone crashing into the river. But as Chester Wilmot tells us,

It was early afternoon when the leading Americans reached the last ridge above Remagen and saw to their astonishment that the Ludendorff railway bridge was still intact. A motorized platoon raced down the hill and into a town crowded with stragglers. At a quarter past three a prisoner reported that the bridge was to be blown at four. At ten minutes to four the Americans reached the waterfront and dashed for the western end. While engineers cut every demolition cable they could see, the infantry raced on across the standing span. One small charge went off and then a second. The bridge shuddered, but the detonator of the main charge failed to fire and, before another could be set, the defenders had been overpowered. Reinforcements poured across, cleared a shallow bridgehead and scaled the heights beyond to silence the flak defences. Before dark the line of the Rhine was inviolate no longer. The Americans had breached the last barrier in the West.[13]

There was little risk in exploiting this wonderful opportunity. But risk was at the heart of other great victories. The battle of Assaye, counted by Wellington as the greatest of his victories, was fought in September 1803 and was, like Waterloo, a near-run thing. Wellesley, as he then was, decided to bring the joint armies of Scindia and Rajah Bonslah to battle by harrying them to the north and east until an opportunity came to strike at them effectively. On 23 September, with 7,000 men and some twenty guns – he had only three British regiments, two of

Foot, one of Light Dragoons – Wellesley found himself confronting the entire Mahratta armies of some 50,000 infantry, countless cavalry and 100 guns. Wellesley, like Nelson, believing the boldest measures are usually the safest, realized that only by attacking so formidable an army from the flank could he hope to prevail, and he staked everything on being able to cross the river Kaitna. Despite his native guides' assurance that there was no crossing, Wellesley caught sight of two villages divided only by the river, and in his own words,

I immediately said to myself that men could not have built two villages so close to one another on opposite sides of a stream without some habitual means of communication either by boat or a ford – most probably the latter. On that conjecture, or rather reasoning, in defiance of all my guides and information, I took the desperate resolution, as it seemed, of marching for the river, and I was right; I found a passage, crossed my army over, had no more to fear from the enemy's cloud of cavalry, and my army, small as it was, was just enough to fill the space between the two streams, so that both my flanks were secure.[14]

Diseases desperate grown, By desperate appliances are reliev'd, Or not at all.

Wellesley's position was still charged with danger. Although his flanks were secure, his small army was still facing one vastly superior in infantry and artillery. Moreover, Mahratta cavalry swarmed on the far banks of the river. If the taking of calculated risks, backed by extreme boldness and inspiring leadership, is the key to winning battles, Wellesley certainly showed at Assaye that he held this key firmly in his grasp. The battle was a bloody affair, a frontal assault against far greater numbers and fire-power. Wellesley's own personal command of the left flank was decisive when he came to the rescue of his right-hand battalion, first by despatching British and native cavalry and then leading the 78th Highlanders to sweep down on Mahratta artillerymen and cut them to pieces, leaving their infantry with little stomach for the fight. He was always in the thick of the action, cool and collected, and overseeing the Highlanders' final advance which took Assaye and ninety-eight of the enemy's guns. His victory was complete, but at the cost of half his British troops and nearly 1,000 sepoys. After his defeat of Mahratta power, Wellesley displayed another great trait of character, one which Churchill advocated and embraced throughout his military and political career – magnanimity. Animosity, urged Wellesley, should be forgotten. If it were not, war would be never-ending. The doings of a great Empire must not be marred by mean acts of retribution. He was anticipating Charles Napier's prescription of a good thrashing followed by kindness.

Although the two men could hardly have been further apart in upbringing and character, Wellington and Nelson shared a capacity for extreme daring in battle and agreeable benevolence in the wake of victory. We have seen that although before closing with the French fleet at Aboukir in 1798, Nelson had conceded that in a sea-fight, something must be left to chance, there was no If as to whether he would win or not. He was wholly confident of success. Yet nothing could have been bolder than his tactic at Aboukir. It was a master-piece of quick thinking, indomitable courage, brilliant seamanship and devastating gunnery. We have noted that among the aces of leadership which embellished Nelson's hand were imagination and the offensive spirit. At the battle of the Nile he played them with over-whelming effect. By concentrating against Admiral Bruey's battleships on either side of them, that is, by means of sailing some of his own ships between the French line and the shore, at the end of the action ten of Bruey's thirteen sail of the line had been taken, one was blown up, and two escaped. As Nelson observed, victory was hardly a strong enough term for such a result. Thus were Napoleon's dreams of con-quering the East thwarted. Nor would it be the last time that Nelson would stand in Napoleon's path. Yet ironically enough, the Royal Navy's prevention of any grand ideas that the Corsican ogre would descend on the shores of Sussex and Kent led to the Emperor's most spectacular victory when he too showed that when chances presented themselves, they had to be seized no matter how high the stakes or how awe-inspiring the risk.

In 1805 both Nelson and Napoleon were at the peak of their form. Nelson's crushing defeat of the French and Spanish fleets at Trafalgar put paid once and for all to ideas of the Grande Armée's lounging about in Hyde Park or clanking through the corridors of St James's

Palace. Even before that famous day Napoleon had abandoned any such adventure and turned his attention instead to the growing threat from Austria and Russia. The movement of his army from the camps at Boulogne to concentrate against Mack's Austrian army at Ulm was a classic example of how to combine deception of intention and rapidity of marching. In just over six weeks the Emperor succeeded in positioning some 150,000 soldiers, coming from as far apart as Hanover, Utrecht, the Rhineland and the Pas-de-Calais, to the north of Mack's 30,000 men, clouding this great movement by deploying a huge screen of the Reserve Cavalry under Murat to conceal his intentions. Before Mack had any idea of what was going on, his entire army was surrounded and captured. So far, so good, but Napoleon's greater triumph was still to come. Having entered Vienna and crossed the Danube, despite appalling weather, exhaustion and a severe shortage of food, forage and other supplies, the Grande Armée finally confronted the combined Austro-Russian forces at the Moravian village of Austerlitz on 2 December 1805. It was greatly to Napoleon's advantage that Alexander I of Russia and Francis II of Austria were nominally in command of their armies, and even though Kutusov was present to do their thinking for them – he would no doubt have advised a waiting game until powerful reinforcements had reached them, while the French were at the limit of their supply lines – the two Allied Emperors had their prestige to protect and insisted on fighting the pretentious little Corsican usurper there and then. With the sun of Austerlitz looking down on them, Napoleon ordered Marshal Soult's corps forward, together with those of Bernadotte and Oudinot, Bessières' Imperial Guard being in reserve. The vital piece of ground was in the centre of the Allied position, and when Napoleon asked Soult how long it would take him to get there, Soult replied: 'Twenty minutes, Sire.' Twenty minutes after Napoleon's order to advance had been given, the vital ground was in Soult's hands. The Austro-Russian centre was destroyed, their left wing rolled up, and the whole thing was over. Austria made peace, the Russian armies faded away, the Third Coalition was finished and, as Sir Charles Petrie put it, 'Napoleon's domination of the Continent was more firmly established than ever.'[15]

Austerlitz was a great triumph for Napoleon and he would often recall it. Even during the ill-fated expedition to Moscow when the Emperor mounted his horse on the morning of 7 September 1812 and the sun rose just before 6 a.m. on the field of Borodino, he declared: 'The sun of Austerlitz.' But Borodino was a bloody slogging match, and although the combined furious efforts of Ney, Davout and Murat succeeded in forcing the Russians from their strong defences, the absolutely crucial climax to a Napoleonic battle – the pursuit – when a beaten, retiring enemy would be cut up and destroyed, never came. For once Napoleon was too far back from the scene of decision, and when the three assaulting Marshals pleaded for the Guard to be sent up to finish off the business, the Emperor listened instead to Bessières, commanding the Old Guard, who reminded him that they were 800 miles from Paris. The Russian army withdrew in good order. Had Napoleon destroyed it there and then, Czar Alexander might after all have come to terms, and Napoleon would not have been obliged to brood in Moscow from mid-September until 19 October, waiting for a message from Alexander which never came.

In one way it was the very success of Austerlitz which in the end led to Napoleon's downfall, for it gave him still more appetite for conquest and territorial gain. It must be remembered that the Austerlitz campaign, like that of Marengo and indeed the first and most startlingly novel success of the then General Bonaparte, the Italian affair of 1796-7 – was defensive warfare. The invasion of Russia in 1812, and that of Spain in 1808, were wars of aggression, in the former case when the French Emperor was supreme in Europe. What then if Napoleon had not won the battle of Austerlitz? What if he and the Grande Armée had been forced to retire, with the Third Coalition still in being, and William Pitt, already cheered by Nelson's victory at Trafalgar, further encouraged by the justification of his policy, no longer calling for the map of Europe to be rolled up: 'It will not be wanted these ten years.' Would such a reverse have threatened Napoleon's throne? He would still have been at war with the three Coalition powers. Yet with the Grande Armée still powerful and its Marshals still loyal, there would have been little inducement for them to attempt a *coup* against the Emperor. There would have been little, if any, enthusiasm for inviting the gouty, obese Anglophile émigré, the Bourbon, Louis XVIII, to return to France some eight years earlier than he did. Among the eighteen Marshals appointed by Napoleon when he became Emperor of the French in May 1804 were Berthier, Murat, Masséna, Augereau, Bernadotte, Soult, Lannes, Ney and Davout – about as glittering an array of military talent as any nation has boasted at any time. Having only recently discovered that '*Tout soldat français porte dans sa giberne le baton de Maréchal de France*,' they might have been somewhat reluctant to risk having their batons removed in favour of princes of the blood or members of a Bourbon royal household. And although Napoleon himself observed that 'Men are never attached to you by favours,' he went on to shower favours on his subordinates. Like Antony, crowns and coronets walked in his livery, he dropped realms and islands from his pocket as plates. The Bonaparte family did uncommonly well in terms of crowns and coronets. The Marshals had little to complain of with their batons, their dukedoms and their principalities. In 1806, having humbled the prestige of the Habsburgs and Romanovs at Austerlitz, Napoleon started ennobling the Marshals in order to bind their loyalty more closely to his own Imperial dynasty. And as A. G. Macdonnell enquired, 'What duke in his senses could contemplate a return to Bourbonism if it entailed the instant loss of his dukedom?'[16] So Murat became Grand Duke of Berg and Cleves, Berthier was given the Princedom of Neufchâtel, Bernadotte was promoted to be His Highness and Marshal, Prince and Duke of Ponte-Corvo. Even the professional turncoat, Talleyrand, no soldier but a powerful pawn on the political chessboard, became Prince of Benevento. There was no shortage of favours under Bonaparte. And as long as his star went on shining, men were attached to him. But when the game went wrong, the men went too.

If Napoleon risked much at Austerlitz, how infinitely much more Henry V risked at Agincourt. In his *History of the English-Speaking Peoples* Churchill calls Agincourt 'the most heroic of all the land battles England has ever fought'. It was not a defensive battle, but one in which a mere 1,000 knights and men-at-arms with some 4,000 archers advanced to attack a French army of about 20,000. The confidence of King Henry was infectious. 'We few, we happy few, we band of brothers', he called his army, and with these few 'the Lord can overthrow the pride of the French'. For their part the French were equally confident as they awaited the attack of less than a third of their own numbers. Yet when at 11 a.m. on 25 October 1415 the English advanced to within a few hundred yards of their massed enemy, the French found that their own deployment in three lines, closely packed together, prevented their cannon and cross-bowmen from bringing effective fire on the dismounted English soldiers and archers who had planted their stakes before them. The French, both horse and foot, confident that their overwhelming numbers would carry the day, trudged down towards the English line, only to be met by a hail of arrows from the long-bows. Down went horse and foot alike in the field which had turned into a treacherous bog. Undaunted French reinforcements endeavoured to struggle on over this dreadful carpet of dead and wounded, but robbed of momentum, they were an easy prey to the English archers, who had now slung their bows and rushed forward with swords to fall upon their helpless foes. Then ensued a hand-to-hand contest between the French second line and English knights and yeomen; King Henry was himself in the thick of things, coming to the rescue of his brother, Humphrey of Gloucester, who had been felled by the Duke of Alençon. Alençon was killed. Henry and Gloucester survived. The third French line left the field without a further attempt against the everywhere triumphant English. There had been one tragic mistake, for when King Henry, hearing of enemy camp-followers pillaging his camp to the rear, took this to herald an attack from behind at a time when he was still confronted by an unbeaten force ahead, he ordered the killing of prisoners. Thus perished many of the French nobility. Henry had risked all. It had been a matter of winning or dying. Yet, as Churchill put it, 'he had decisively broken in open battle at odds of more than three to one the armed chivalry of France. In two or at most three hours he had trodden underfoot at once the corpses of the slain and the will-power of the French monarchy.'[17]

But what if, by chance, Henry had been killed in the battle at the very moment when victory was complete? What would have happened then? His subsequent campaign from 1417 to 1419 during which he subdued every French stronghold in Normandy and captured Caen would never have taken place. There would have been no Treaty of Troye in May 1420, by which the French King Charles VI acknowledged Henry as his heir to the French throne and Regent until his death. There would have been no marriage to Charles's daughter, Princess Catherine, and thus no son, no Henry VI, whose long reign, if reign it can be called, brought about a period in English history bound in shallows and in miseries. Who would have become king in Henry's place? Presumably his brother John, Duke of Bedford. The former King John had not exactly endeared himself to his subjects, but this second John was of a very different calibre, and likely, had he been put upon, to have proved most royal. Even as things were, on Henry V's death in 1422, Bedford became both one of the Protectors, together with Henry's other brother, Humphrey of Gloucester, and Regent of France. He was, as Churchill recorded, a Commander-in-Chief and successor to Henry of the highest military quality. Of course, France would have been lost to England anyway in the end, but the Wars of the Roses might never have pursued their blood-stained course through most of what remained of the fifteenth century.

If we wished to choose two instances of Henry James's contention that character is predominant in determining incident, we might well take Henry V as the first. The great historian William Stubbs had this to say about him:

No sovereign who ever reigned has won from contemporary writers such a singular unison of praise. He was religious, pure in life, temperate, liberal, careful, and yet splendid, merciful, truthful, and honourable; 'discreet in word, provident in counsel, prudent in judgment, modest in look, magnanimous in act'; a brilliant soldier, a sound diplomatist, an able organiser and consolidator of all forces at his command; the restorer of the English Navy, the founder of our military, international, and maritime law. A true Englishman, with all the greatness and none of the glaring faults of his Plantagenet ancestors.[18]

A paragon indeed, and one who never resorted to treason, stratagems or spoils, but was open, generous and considerate. Nor – and what a virtue this was – would he ever seek refuge in evasion, circumlocution or intrigue, but would deal with matters of state with a concise and definite yes or no. How remarkable, how refreshing and how improbable it would be to find such a man in power today! Yet it must be conceded that he set England on its path to dispute the throne of France, which led to such tragic events. 'Agincourt was a glittering victory,' wrote Churchill, 'but the wasteful and useless campaigns that followed more than outweighed its military and moral value, and the miserable, destroying century that ensued casts its black shadow upon Henry's heroic triumph.'[19] Thus did character determine incident.

When it comes to talking of power and conquest, it is but a step from the heroic to the demoniac. For if we were to seek an example of ruthless, tyrannical use of power and unbridled lust for conquest, we would not need to look further than the career of Adolf Hitler. One of the Führer's Army Commanders-in-Chief was Field-Marshal Walter von Brauchitsch, who when contemplating his master's evil genius, observed that 'Hitler was the fate of Germany and this fate could not be stayed.' Had he and some of his fellow generals made up their minds during the series of bloodless victories which Hitler brought off in the Rhineland, Austria and Czechoslovakia that he was leading them inexorably down a path to world war, they might even then have stayed his hand. But for those who embrace the determinist view of history, perhaps the advent of Hitler was an instance of fate doing its worst. We must, however, be thankful that the decision to take on both Russia and the United States, two immensely powerful states which longed to be left alone, appeared to be his and his alone. Yet on the very day of his declaring war on America, 11 December 1941, we find the Man of Destiny suggesting otherwise:

I can only be grateful to Providence that it entrusted me with the leadership in this historic struggle which, for the next five hundred or a thousand years, will be described as decisive, not only for the history of Germany, but for the whole of Europe and indeed the whole world . . . A historical revision on a unique scale has been imposed on us by the Creator.[20]

It is strange and somehow ridiculous to find Hitler putting forward this Tolstoyan theory, when no better examples of events being subordinated to human will exists than his own.

Some of his subordinates believed in the Führer even when the game had begun to go wrong. Jodl, Chief of Operations at OKW, told an audience of Gauleiter towards the end of 1943 that Hitler 'is the soul not only of the political but also of the military conduct of the war, and that the force of his will-power and the creative riches of his thought animate and hold together the whole of the Wehrmacht'. Commanders in the field were not so sure. Rommel, whose loyalty had not been in question, thought otherwise when he heard the Führer announce that if the German people were incapable of winning the war, they could rot. Rommel had no illusions about Hitler's short-comings as a strategist. He might have been dazzled by the initial successes in Poland and France, but he had been overruled too often in Africa and Normandy, had seen too many opportune chances missed, too many mistakes made, to be in doubt. Guderian, too, one of the architects of Blitzkrieg and a superb field commander, acknowledged Hitler's extraordinary will-power with which he compelled men to follow him, but found that the boldness of Hitler's strategic vision was not matched by comparable boldness in its execution. Guderian was an advocate of von Moltke's recipe for winning wars: weigh the considerations first, then take the risks. Hitler's concept was to take risks, backed by huge force, and let the considerations take care of themselves. It worked in France because France's spirit collapsed. Britain remained defiant, demanding a very different strategy, involv-ing careful preparation. So Hitler turned on Russia and here his strategy, 'lacking in consistency and subject to continual vacillation in its execution', crashed in ruins. Hitler, Guderian maintained, was

a man lacking wisdom and moderation . . . going in solitary haste from success to success and then pressing on from failure to failure, his head full of stupendous plans, clinging ever more frantically to the last vanishing prospects of victory . . . with a fanatic's intensity he grasped at every straw which he imagined might save himself and his work from destruction. His entire and very great will-power was devoted to this one idea which was now all that preoccupied him – never to give in, never to surrender.[21]

Of one thing we can be sure. It was Hitler's war!

Missed opportunities – the history of war abounds with them. 'Next to knowing when to seize an opportunity,' observed Disraeli, 'the most important thing in life is to know when to forgo an advantage.' No doubt he was speaking as a politician, as a statesman, as a connoisseur of society, not as someone in charge of military matters. The instances of forgoing an advantage advantageously might be more difficult to identify when it comes to matters of strategy or some immediate tactical circumstance involving armed forces in conflict with one another. Yet we have seen that at the battle of Loos in September 1915, the German machine-gunners refrained from firing at the stunned, stumbling British soldiers as they made their way back to their own trenches. There was a touch of noblemindedness in this restraint. It might be said too that when 8th Army succeeded in breaking out at El Alamein, Montgomery chose to forgo his advantage, dismissed the opportunity of a grand outflanking manoeuvre to trap and destroy Rommel's Panzerarmee – which he had been specifically instructed to do by Churchill – and chose instead to conduct a deliberate following-up of Rommel's forces in what one participant described as a dull and measured affair. Yet given the strategic circumstances of the time, it is difficult to find fault with Montgomery's decision. He simply could not risk coming off second best in a pell-mell armoured encounter with the Desert Fox. His own comment, 'No more manoeuvre; fight a battle' admirably summed up his military doctrine. Victory, no matter how methodical, unglamorous or costly, was all important, and after Alamein, as Churchill not altogether accurately claimed, we never had a defeat.

There is, of course, a world of difference between strategic and tactical opportunity. As already recorded, Hitler may be said to have missed a unique opportunity in 1941, before his invasion of Russia, in not listening to Raeder, invading North Africa in strength, taking Egypt and the whole Middle East, and so rendering Britain strategically impotent. Furthermore, the self-styled greatest strategic genius of all time, Commander-in-Chief of the all-powerful Wehrmacht, could not see that however advantageous he might have believed Japan's attack on the United States had been to the Axis powers, to have forgone a declaration of war on America until an undertaking had been obtained from Japan to mount an instant assault on the Soviet Union would have been of paramount importance. Whether such an undertaking would have been forthcoming is not relevant. Nor is the likelihood of America's declaring war on Germany germane. Hitler's blunder lay in his inability to weigh the considerations, to be circumspect, to shed for a time his Man of Destiny role, and instead resort to his former uncannily accurate *Vorhersehung* – foresight – which had led to the bloodless victories and his lightning conquest of France. Fortunately he did not do so.

If we look at the other side of the coin, that is to say, Allied strategic opportunity, we see a very different picture – one of patience, perseverance and, albeit gradual, the presentation of a great prize. This is not to say that the Allies did not forgo advantage. But they did at least seize opportunity with prudence. It was just as well for Allied counsels that the wisdom, experience and eloquence of Winston Churchill and General Sir Alan Brooke prevailed over the impetuous, bull-at-a-gate preferences of the Americans. Any attempt to invade France in 1942 would simply have been to invite a bloody repulse, as indeed was the outcome of the Dieppe raid, and although the idea of seizing the whole of North Africa and developing further operations from there had little appeal to the US Chiefs of Staff, it became clear that this was the only practicable option for 1942. Thus the so-called Mediterranean strategy emerged with its inevitable sequel of invading Sicily and Italy. Slow but sure, sometimes too much so, for as has been argued, an immediate assault on Tunis might have finished off the North African campaign much earlier, while the possible dividends to be gained by Italy's desire to be rid of her Axis chains were marred by indecision and caution. Yet it must always be borne in mind that the longer German divisions of exceptional calibre could be kept fighting in North Africa – and forced to capitulate there – or occupied in defending with determination and skill the natural defensive country of Italy, the longer too these same divisions would be prevented from contributing to the battles of real decision on the Eastern and Western Fronts. Michael Howard's conclusion that it still needs to be shown that there was a better Allied Grand Strategy than that actually employed stands unchallenged today.

When it comes to tactical opportunity, particularly in battles of former centuries, we are on firmer ground, for the conditions of time and space alone clarify judgement. Thus in the autumn of 1793, when French Royalists were holding Toulon against the revolutionary cause, we find General Carteaux, whose only distinction was his impressive black moustache favoured by the French light cavalry, in command of the forces besieging Toulon and with no very clear idea of what to do. Along comes Major Bonaparte who sees at once that the key to taking Toulon is to force the British fleet supporting the Royalists to withdraw, and that to do so the Jacobin army must capture the Le Caire peninsula with its two forts, thus enabling them to bring direct artillery fire on to the Royal Navy's warships. Once the British left, Bonaparte insisted, the Royalists' position would collapse. Although the first attack on Le Caire faltered through lack of troops, Bonaparte persisted, arranged for the removal of Carteaux, his replacement by Dugommier and acceptance of his, Bonaparte's, plan to seize the crucial objective, Fort l'Aiguilette, commanding the harbour entrance. 'There is Toulon,' he said, and on 17 December 1793 a successful assault against the fort, led by Bonaparte himself, who sustained a bayonet wound in the thigh, proved him wholly right. On the morning following the fort's capture, the British fleet departed. It was the end of Toulon's defiance. More than that, it was the beginning of great things for Major Bonaparte. Later that month he became a *général de brigade*. He was only twenty-four. Within just over two years he would be commanding the Army of Italy, and the whole concept of warfare would be turned upside down. No more dramatic illustration of character's determination of incident could be found. It sprang from the recognition and seizure of opportunity. But it was quite by chance that Bonaparte was at Toulon in the first place.

It was a strange chance too that another star player on the French revolutionary war's stage was also to be found at Toulon in the autumn of 1793 – Captain Horatio Nelson, commanding the *Agamemnon*. He had been despatched earlier that year to join Lord Hood's Mediterranean fleet, engaged first in the blockade of Toulon and later in assisting the Royalists to hold it. When Hood required reinforcements to man the city's defences, he sent Nelson to enlist support from the Kingdom of the Two Sicilies, ruled by Ferdinand IV, the bulbous-nosed, uxorious Bourbon monarch, passionately addicted to hunting most four-legged beasts, and husband to Marie-Antoinette's sister, Maria-Carolina. Nelson's mission was successful and reinforcements were forthcoming. Of even greater significance for Nelson – and for the application of England's sea power in the Mediterranean – was that when he went ashore with despatches for the British Ambassador at Naples, Sir William Hamilton, he encountered for the first time the beautiful and desirable Emma. Perhaps of all British naval commanders Nelson was the most outstanding in perceiving and then acting upon tactical opportunity. We have seen with what effect he did so at the battle of St Vincent, which he was to repeat at Aboukir. At Trafalgar, of course, he had made up his mind beforehand what was to be done, explained the Nelson Touch to his captains, and then, when the chance to put it into practice arrived, executed it with brilliant success.

Although Nelson's great contemporary, Wellington, was sometimes thought of as a Fabian general, for the care he took of Britain's only army in the Peninsula, when opportunity presented itself, he could act with the same speed of decision and magnitude of effect as Nelson. During the afternoon of 22 July 1812, while Napoleon was driving the doomed Grande Armée ever deeper into the inhospitable space of Russia, his great friend and comrade-in-arms, Marshal Marmont, was manoeuvring his army south-east of Salamanca and attempting to envelop Wellington's right flank. In doing so he greatly extended the gap between his left wing and his centre. This was enough for Wellington. He saw his chance and took it instantly. Flinging away the pieces of chicken he was eating, he despatched ADCs with orders and galloped three miles to where his brother-in-law, Edward Pakenham, was in reserve with the 3rd Division. Wellington's order to Pakenham was a model of clarity, brevity and informality. 'Ned, d'ye see those fellows on the hill?' pointing to the French left. 'Throw your division into column; at them! and drive them to the devil.' Pakenham did so, and by giving comparably curt but effective orders to his other divisional commanders, Wellington won a famous victory. By the end of the action, which featured a devastating charge by Le Marchant's heavy cavalry including the 4th and 5th Dragoons, Wellington, usually chary of praising the cavalry, observed that he had never seen anything so beautiful in his life – almost a third of Marmont's army had been eliminated. Marmont, who realized too late that his opponent was not after all the cautious, defensive general he had supposed, was himself wounded early on in the battle. Clausel took over, and the best part the French played was in their rearguard action which successfully covered the withdrawal of the army. Had one of Wellington's Spanish officers obeyed his orders to guard the crossing of the Tormes Alba, it may be doubted whether the French would have got away at all. Yet to the dismay of the French, who knew all about Wellington's defensive tactics, they now had to concede that he had shown himself to be a master of manoeuvre, winning a battle, as General Foy put it, 'in the style of Frederick the Great'.

Wellington gave it as his opinion that one of the marks of good generalship was to know when to retreat and dare to do so. Much to his chagrin and the disgust of his army, despite his success at Salamanca, his triumphant entry into Madrid and his advance further north, his good fortune ran out at the siege of Burgos in September 1812, and he was obliged to retreat once more via Salamanca and Ciudad Rodrigo to Portugal. His army's resentment of this setback was aggravated by bad weather, shortage of supplies, sickness and – here their Commander-in-Chief acted entirely out of character – Wellington's blaming the regimental officers for failing to maintain discipline and neglecting their duty. This harshness was quite unjustified, for the shortcomings of a supply system that normally worked well could not be laid at the door of regimental officers. Here was a case where incident did not illustrate character, but on the contrary showed that even the most just and equable character can by unfavourable circumstances be betrayed into shifting responsibility from its own shoulders on to others'. When it came to writing despatches after the winning of battles, however, Wellington's true character shone forth.

Much could be revealed about the character of a commander from the manner in which he couches his subsequent report of a battle.

Wellington's renowned Waterloo despatch was so restrained that some who read it thought that he had suffered a defeat. 'The stupendous event, the titanic endurance, the blaze of glory, the oceans of blood', wrote Elizabeth Longford, 'deflected him not an inch from his accustomed brevity and restraint.'[22] He simply referred to the army's good conduct, the example set by the division of Guards and that 'there is no officer nor description of troops that did not behave well'. There was reference to bravery – the Guards at Hougoumont, to steadiness – the infantry at Quatre Bras, and to glory – Picton's death at the head of his division. One NCO who took part in the battle praised the despatch's 'noble simplicity, perfect calmness and exemplary modesty', but many were disappointed and dismayed by its neglect of naming both regiments and individual commanders.

How different we find some other post-battle reports. After El Alamein Montgomery crows to the press about 'total victory', and in commenting on the Ardennes counter-offensive talks of his 'tidying up the battlefield', describing the operation as 'one of the most interesting and tricky I have ever handled', and referring to his employment of 'the whole available power of the group of British armies' causing immense ill-feeling and resentment among the United States generals, even though he gives proper acknowledgment to the major part played by the American soldiers. He may not have intended to imply that he, Montgomery, had saved the situation. Yet by the tactless phrasing of his statement to the press, this was the very impression he gave to men like Bradley and Patton.

Hitler relished superlatives. On 5 June 1940 he issued an Order of the Day: 'Dunkirk has fallen . . . with it has ended the greatest battle of world history. Soldiers! My confidence in you knew no bounds. You have not disappointed me.' Or after the initial triumph in Russia, when the panzer groups of Kleist and Guderian closed the pincer movement 120 miles east of Kiev with a bag of nearly 700,000 prisoners, Hitler again refers to 'the greatest battle in the history of the world'. And at the end of it all, when Hitler has given up manipulating phantom armies in the Bunker, with the Russians only a few days from reaching the Berlin Chancellory, he adds a postscript to his testament, a valediction to the Wehrmacht, in which, while admitting that 'the people and the Armed Forces have given their all in this long and hard struggle', he turns on the General Staff and disparages their achievements. Out of thy own mouth will I judge thee! For the General Staff had simply obeyed his orders.

How different were the public pronouncements of Winston Churchill. After the Battle of Britain, he speaks of how much is owed by so many to so few. When later he refers to his warning the French Government that Britain would fight on alone whatever they did, and their Generals predicted that in a few weeks' time England would have her neck wrung like a chicken, he reminds the British people of their calibre: 'Some chicken! Some neck!' When again it seems that the tide has turned, with the battle of Alamein won and the North African landing successful, Churchill indulges in no bombast, but simply tells us that it is not the end, not even the beginning of the end, 'but it is perhaps the end of the beginning'.

On Churchill's desk in his study at Chartwell reposed two busts – one of Nelson, one of Napoleon. When Nelson composed his despatch after Aboukir, he wrote: 'Almighty God has blessed His Majesty's Arms in the late Battle by a great Victory over the Fleet of the Enemy, whom I attacked at sunset on the 1st August, off the mouth of the Nile.' When Napoleon phrased his bulletins for publication in Paris, the actual circumstances of the moment would always take second place to what was politically expedient.

'Talk'st thou of me of ifs?' demanded Richard III. Well, yes, I do. This whole book has been a treatise of Ifs. One of the most enduringly interesting of these, despite Jac Weller's wincing, remains Waterloo. Lord Rosebery's *Napoleon: The Last Phase* stimulates our interest once again. Napoleon is at St Helena:

The third great subject of regret is, of course, Waterloo, over which we sometimes seem to hear him gnash his teeth. 'Ah! if it were to begin again!' he exclaims. He cannot understand how he lost it. Perhaps the rain of the 17th? Had he had Suchet at the head of Grouchy's army, had he had Andreossi in Soult's place, could Bessières or Lannes have commanded the Guard, had he given command of the Guard to Lobau, had Murat headed the cavalry, had Clausel or Lamarque been at the War Office,[23] all might have been different. Should he have waited a fortnight longer? He would then have had the 12,000 men employed in La Vendée. But who could tell that La Vendée would soon be pacified? Should he have attacked at all? Should he not have concentrated all his troops under Paris, and awaited events? Perhaps then the Allies would not have attacked him.[24]

And so on. Speculation about the chances and mischances of war and battles seems endless. There seems to be no final version of history. Every generation takes a new look. Controversy may lead to acrimony, but there is always comfort to be found in avoiding the reply churlish, the reproof valiant, the countercheck quarrelsome. You may avoid them with an If. There is much entertainment to be derived from rewriting history with reference to chance – a chance opportunity missed, a risk taken or not taken, the intervention of fate or fortune. But should discussion deteriorate into bitter quarrel, should tempers flare and combat between opposing advocates of this or that threaten, we may always resort to an If. Touchstone[25] has the last word. 'Your If is the only peace-maker; much virtue in If.'

Notes

Prologue: Chaos and Chance

1. Field Marshal Count Helmuth von Moltke (1800–91), Prussian Army Chief of Staff (1857–70).
2. Field Marshal Lord Carver, former Chief of Defence Staff, prolific historian.
3. Michael Carver, *El Alamein*, Batsford, 1962.
4. Ibid.
5. Fred Majdalany, journalist and soldier. His book about Cassino, *The Monastery*, John Lane The Bodley Head, 1945, describing his own battalion's part in the battle, is a classic.
6. Nigel Hamilton, *The Full Monty*, Penguin, 2001.
7. Majdalany, *Cassino: Portrait of a Battle*, Longmans, Green & Co., 1957, p. 261.
8. 'What is fortune? Is it fate or destiny chancing to any man by the will of God without man's providence', Thomas Becon (1512–67), *The Catechism of Thomas Becon*, J. Ayre (ed.), CUP, 1844.
9. Martin Gilbert, *Finest Hour*, Heinemann, 1983.
10. It was said that when William had paid an official visit to England in 1051, Edward had given a promise that William would be his heir.
11. George Savile, Marquis of Halifax (1633–95), the 'Trimmer', statesman who played a prominent part in the Glorious Revolution of 1688.
12. The point was underlined in the *Dictionary of National Biography*'s estimate of General Henry Rundle, Governor of Malta in 1909: 'He never took a risk, and was rewarded by never meeting a reverse.'
13. J. A. Williamson, *The Evolution of England*, Oxford, 1931, p. 68fn.
14. Ibid.
15. Originally The Tangier Troop, garrison of Tangier fortress, part of the dowry of Charles II's queen, Catherine of Braganza.
16. Macaulay, T. B., *History of England*, vol. I, Dent, 1906, p. 578.
17. At this time a dragoon was a foot soldier who used horses to move about. Later he became what Macaulay called 'a mere horse soldier'.
18. Ibid., vol. III, p. 188.

19. Who can forget Kipling's lines from 'The Irish Guards':
    'We're not so old in the Army List,
    But we're not so young at our trade,
    For we had the honour at Fontenoy
    Of meeting the Guards' Brigade.'
    Or, indeed, the Duke of Cumberland's oath of regret, as he watched the
    Irish Brigade sweep into action at Fontenoy, on the laws 'that made those
    men our enemies'.
20. Macaulay, T. B., *Critical and Historical Essays*, vol. I, Dent, 1907, p. 495.
21. After further great service to India and England, Lord Clive was threatened
    with impeachment. In a fit of depression he committed suicide in 1774.
22. Isaiah Berlin, *Mr Churchill in 1940*, John Murray, 1964, p. 39.
23. Macaulay, *Essays*, vol. I, p. 402.
24. A. Doughty and George Parmelee, *The Siege of Quebec and the Battle for
    the Plains of Abraham*, Dussalt & Proulx, Quebec, 1901.
25. J. Steven Watson, *The Reign of George III*, OUP, 1960, p. 86
26. Edmund Burke, speech on conciliation with America, 1775.
27. Sergeant Roger Lamb, *Memoirs*.

ONE St Vincent: 14 February 1797

1. Terry Coleman, *Nelson: The Man and the Legend*, Bloomsbury, 2001, and
   'Spinning Nelson', a lecture by Colin White, National Maritime Museum,
   November 2001.
2. Arthur Bryant, *The Fire and the Rose*, Collins, 1965, p. 193.
3. Elizabeth Longford, *Wellington: The Years of the Sword*, Weidenfeld and
   Nicolson, 1969, p. 110.
4. Christopher Hibbert, *Nelson*, Viking, 1994, p. 237.
5. We may recall with pleasure Miss Crawley's comment in William
   Thackeray's *Vanity Fair*: 'That was the most beautiful part of dear Lord
   Nelson's character. He went to the deuce for a woman. There *must* be good
   in a man who will do that.'
6. Arthur Bryant, *The Years of Endurance, 1793–1802*, Collins, 1942, p. 180.
7. Arthur Bryant, *The Fire and the Rose*, Collins, 1965, p. 167.
8. Ibid., p. 168.
9. Ibid., p. 160.
10. Not in this case Dr Johnson's 'last refuge of a scoundrel'.
11. Tom Pocock, *Horatio Nelson*, The Bodley Head, 1987, p. 20.
12. Ibid., pp. 317–18.

TWO Marengo: 14 June 1800

1. Sir Charles Petrie, *When Britain Saved Europe*, Eyre and Spottiswoode, 1941, p. 135.
2. A. G. Macdonnell, *Napoleon and His Marshals*, Macmillan, 1950, pp. 76–7.
3. Ibid.
4. Correlli Barnett, *Bonaparte*, George Allen & Unwin, 1978, p. 77.
5. Evangeline Bruce, *Napoleon and Josephine*, Weidenfeld and Nicolson, 1995, pp. 312–13.
6. Ibid.
7. Vincent Cronin, *Napoleon*, Collins, 1971, p. 192.
8. Macdonnell, *Napoleon and His Marshals*, p. 85.
9. The noble animal has even inspired a book – *Marengo* by Jill Hamilton – in which she points out that on many occasions the grey ridden by Napoleon could not have been Marengo.

THREE 18 June 1815

1. Andrew Roberts, *Napoleon and Wellington*, Weidenfeld and Nicolson, 2001.
2. A. G. Macdonnell, *Napoleon and His Marshals*, Macmillan, 1950, p. 318.
3. Victor Hugo, *The Battle of Waterloo*, Haldeman-Julius Company, pp. 22–3.
4. Vyvyan Ferrers, *The Brigadier*, Art and Educational Publishers, 1948, p. 2.
5. Robert Cowley (ed.), *What If?*, Macmillan, 2001, pp. 217–18.
6. For that matter, what if Wellington had been killed early on in the battle as he might well have been? Uxbridge would have taken command, but he had never held a senior command in battle and did not even know Wellington's plans. Would Hougoumont have held or would the French have taken it?
7. A. P. Herbert, *Why Waterloo?*, Methuen, 1952, pp. 383–4.
8. Lord Rosebery, *Napoleon: The Last Phase*, A. L. Humphries, 1900, p. 197.
9. Ibid., pp. 199–200.
10. Ibid.

FOUR Playing – and Losing – the Great Game

1. Philip Woodruff, *The Men Who Ruled India*, Cape, 1963, pp. 274–5.
2. Ibid.
3. James Morris, *Heaven's Command: an Imperial Progress*, Faber & Faber, 1973.
4. Ibid., p. 95.
5. Ibid.
6. Ibid., p. 91.

7. George MacDonald Fraser, *Flashman*, Herbert Jenkins, 1969, p. 98.

8. John Lawrence told the people of the Kangra that having ruled them by the pen, he would if necessary rule them by the sword. If they rebelled they would be punished. He would be in their midst with irresistible force. It was said of John Nicholson, who ruled the Punjab, that no Punjabi could hear his name spoken without shivering in his pyjamas. We have met Clive already. We shall meet Major-General Frederick Roberts, known to one and all as 'Bobs', later.

9. They are playing it again now in Afghanistan, but this time it's a different sort of Great Game and, in accordance with Rudyard Kipling's plea, the white man's burden is being shared by America and Britain, a savage war of peace to quell al-Qaeda and the Taleban, and furthermore to fill the mouth of famine and bid the sickness cease.

10. Marquess of Anglesey, *A History of the British Cavalry*, Leo Cooper, 1982, vol. III, p. 262.

FIVE Balaklava: 25 October 1854

1. Russell was war correspondent for *The Times*. His reports on the Crimean War, the Indian Mutiny, the American Civil War and the Franco–Prussian War had great influence.

2. The Regiment in which the author had the honour to serve.

3. In fact, 607 charged; 198 were at roll-call afterwards.

4. It was an odd comment. Chilianwala was a fiasco, but although the cavalry disgraced themselves, there were very few casualties among them.

5. The Holy Places were in Bethlehem, Gethsemane and Jerusalem. The dispute about their custody was between Greek and Latin Christians, or put another way, between Russia and France.

6. Arthur Bryant, *The Years of Endurance 1793–1802*, Collins, 1942

7. Cecil Woodham-Smith, *The Reason Why*, McGraw-Hill, 1954, pp. 193–4.

8. The ludicrous excuse given by the French was that the men had left their knapsacks behind during the advance and had to go back for them.

9. Ibid., p. 189,

10. Ibid., p. 219.

11. Perhaps one reason for this is that although Tennyson composed poems about both charges, his Heavy Brigade effort is dull compared with the gripping appeal of the Light.

12. Ibid., p. 223.

13. Ibid., p. 224.

14. Ibid.

15. In his masterly *History of the British Cavalry*, the Marquess of Anglesey maintains that Lucan must have know which guns were really meant. He

had been there when they were captured earlier and referred to them later in despatch. Anglesey suggests that Lucan's frustration and resentment resulted in a temporary loss of reason and judgement. He was not called Lord Look-on – a title earned by his inaction at the battle of Alma – for nothing.

16. Woodham–Smith, *The Reason Why*, pp. 240–1.

SIX May–June 1940: Disaster and Deliverance

1. Herman Rauschning, *Hitler Speaks*, 1939.
2. Heinz Guderian, *Panzer Leaders*, London, 1952.
3. Rauschning, *Hitler Speaks*.
4. Ibid.
5. Hence the operation's code name, *Sichelschnitt*.
6. Alistair Horne, *To Lose a Battle*, Macmillan, 1968.
7. Jean Bruller Vercors, *The Battle of Silence*, Faber & Faber, 1968.
8. Chester Wilmot, *The Struggle for Europe*, Wordsworth, 1997, first published 1952.
9. W. S. Churchill, *The Second World War*, Penguin, 1989, p. 264.
10. John Strawson, *The Battle for North Africa*, Batsford, 1969, p. 17.

SEVEN The Peg on Which All Else Hung

1. Kirkpatrick was a Foreign Office German expert who had served in Berlin.
2. John Strawson, *Hitler as Military Commander*, Batsford, 1971, p. 118.
3. Michael Howard, *The Mediterranean Strategy in the Second World War*, Weidenfeld and Nicolson, 1968.
4. Strawson, *Hitler*, p. 128.
5. Ibid.
6. Robert Cowley (ed.), *What If?*, Macmillan, 2001, p. 297.
7. If what follows had occurred, Rommel might, like Tamburlaine, have ridden in triumph through Persepolis too.
8. HMSO, *History of the Second World War: The Middle East and the Mediterranean*.

EIGHT Master Plan Manqué

1. Fred Majdalany, *The Battle of El Alamein*, Weidenfeld and Nicolson, 1965.
2. Nigel Nicolson, *Alex (Field Marshal Alexander of Tunis)*, Weidenfeld and Nicolson, 1973.
3. Martin Gilbert, *Road to Victory*, Heinemann, 1986, p. 215.

4. David Irving, *The Trail of the Fox*, Weidenfeld and Nicolson, 1978.
5. Ronald Lewin, *The Life and Death of the Afrika Korps*, Batsford, 1977.
6. Field Marshal The Viscount Montgomery, *Memoirs*, Collins, 1958.

NINE The Hard Underbelly of Europe

1. Round-Up was the codename for the invasion of Western Europe.
2. Fred Majdalany, *The Monastery*, John Lane The Bodley Head, 1945.
3. John Strawson, *The Italian Campaign*, Secker & Warburg, 1987, p. 159.
4. Ibid.
5. Fred Majdalany, *Cassino: Portrait of a Battle*, Longmans, Green & Co., 1957.
6. Ronald Lewin, *Ultra Goes to War*, Hutchinson.
7. Alan Moorhead, *Eclipse*, Hamish Hamilton, 1946.

TEN Conditional Surrender

1. Harold Macmillan, an Etonian, sent a telegram to Alexander, saying how thoughtful it was of him it was to have taken Rome on 4 June. Alexander replied, 'Thank you. What is the fourth of June?' He had been at Harrow.
2. Rommel commanded Army Group B; von Rundstedt was Commander-in-Chief, West.
3. The compliant, obsequious Field-Marshal Keitel was Chief of Staff, OKW.
4. Chester Wilmot, *The Struggle for Europe*, Wordsworth, 1997, first published 1952.
5. H. R. Trevor-Roper, *The Last Days of Hitler*, Book Club Associates, 1971.
6. Isaiah Berlin, *Mr Churchill in 1940*, John Murray, 1964, pp. 17–18.

ELEVEN The Gambler Keeps His Stake

1. General Horrocks rather agreed, suggesting that the Germans be allowed to cross the Meuse and then be destroyed in a final battle on the field of Waterloo!
2. Chester Wilmot, *The Struggle for Europe*, Wordsworth, 1997, first published 1952.
3. Roosevelt died on 13 April 1945, Truman then became president.

TWELVE Who Is to Have Berlin?

1. Joachim von Ribbentrop, a former champagne salesman, was German Ambassador to Britain 1936–8, and Foreign Minister 1938–45. He was pliant, subservient, vain and a blunderer. He was tried at Nuremberg in 1946 and hanged.

2. Heinz Guderian, *Panzer Leader*, London, 1952.
3. Chester Wilmot, *The Struggle for Europe*, Wordsworth, 1997, first published 1952.
4. Ibid.
5. It must be remembered that by this time the 9th US Army had been removed from Montgomery's command and had reverted to Bradley's.
6. John Strawson, *The Battle for Berlin*, Batsford, 1974, p. 160.

THIRTEEN Chance Governs All

1. Leo Tolstoy, *War and Peace*, Penguin, 1957, first published 1869.
2. T. B. Macaulay, *Critical and Historical Essays*, vol. II, Dent, 1907, p. 174.
3. Ibid., pp. 184–5.
4. Edward R. Sammis, *Last Stand at Stalingrad*, New York, 1966.
5. W. H. Auden and Louis Kronenberger (eds), *The Faber Book of Aphorisms*, Faber & Faber, 1964, p. 243.
6. Respectively Lord Chancellor, Foreign Secretary, First Lord of the Admiralty.
7. Kipling too forecast that the war would last for three years and end only when Germany had had 5 million casualties. He was one year and one million out.
8. Barbara W. Tuchman, *August 1914*, Constable, 1962, pp. 279–80. It was of this time, August 1914, that Winston Churchill wrote in *The World Crisis*, 'The terrible ifs accumulate.'
9. A. J. P. Taylor, *English History 1914–45*, OUP, 1965, p. 11.
10. Ludendorff was right when he declared that British soldiers 'fight like lions'. Colonel Hoffmann was equally right when he replied that they were 'led by donkeys'.
11. Robert Rhodes James, *Gallipoli*, 1965.
12. James Morris, *Heaven's Command: an Imperial Progress*, Faber & Faber, 1973.
13. Chester Wilmot, *The Struggle for Europe*, Wordsworth, 1997, first published 1952.
14. Arthur Bryant, *The Great Duke*, Collins, 1971, pp. 55–6.
15. Sir Charles Petrie, *When Britain Saved Europe*, Eyre and Spottiswoode, 1941.
16. A. G. Macdonnell, *Napoleon and His Marshals*, Macmillan, 1950, p. 115.
17. W. S. Churchill, *A History of the English-Speaking Peoples*, Dodd Mead, 1956, p. 406.
18. Ibid., pp. 409–10.
19. Ibid., p. 410.
20. Alan Bullock, *A Study in Tyranny*, Penguin, 1962, p. 663.

21. Heinz Guderian, *Panzer Leader*, London, 1952.
22. Elizabeth Longford, *Wellington: The Years of the Sword*, Weidenfeld and Nicolson, 1969.
23. Then the invaluable Davout would have been available to command in the field. This indeed might have turned the scales.
24. Lord Rosebery, *Napoleon: The Last Phase*, A. L. Humphreys, 1900, pp. 201–2.
25. But not forgetting Rudyard Kipling. The opening lines of what is said to be the nation's favourite poem, 'If', are singularly apt when applied to those charged with leadership in battle:

    If you can keep your head when all about you
        Are losing theirs and blaming it on you,
    If you can trust yourself when all men doubt you,
        But make allowance for their doubting too;

    What is more, despite Rosenstock-Huessey's contention that three-quarters of a soldier's life is spent aimlessly hanging about, I know of no surer way of filling the unforgiving minute with sixty seconds' worth of distance run than that of having been a soldier.

Bibliography

Anglesey, Marquess of, *A History of the British Cavalry*, Leo Cooper, 1982

Barnett, C., *Bonaparte*, George Allen & Unwin, 1978

Berlin, I., *Mr Churchill in 1940*, John Murray, 1964

Bruce, E., *Napoleon and Josephine*, Weidenfeld and Nicolson, 1995

Bryant, A., *The Years of Endurance 1793–1802*, Collins, 1942

– *The Fire and the Rose*, Collins, 1965

Carver, M., *El Alamein*, Batsford, 1962

Churchill, W. S., *The Second World War*, Penguin, 1989

Coleman, T., *Nelson: The Man and the Legend*, Bloomsbury, 2001

Cowley, R. (ed.), *What If?*, Macmillan, 2001

Cronin, V., *Napoleon*, Collins, 1971

Doughty, A. and Parmelee, G., *The Siege of Quebec and the Battle for the Plains of Abraham*, Dussalt & Proulx, Quebec, 1901

Ferrers, V., *The Brigadier*, Art and Educational Publishers, 1948

Gilbert, M., *Finest Hour*, Heinemann, 1983

– *Road to Victory*, Heinemann, 1986

Guderian, H., *Panzer Leader*, London, 1952

Hamilton, J., *Marengo: The Myth of Napoleon's Horse*, Fourth Estate, 2000

Hamilton, N., *The Full Monty*, Penguin, 2001

Herbert, A. P., *Why Waterloo?*, Methuen, 1952

Hibbert, C., *Nelson*, Viking, 1994

HMSO, *History of the Second World War: The Middle East and the Mediterranean*

Horne, A., *To Lose a Battle*, Macmillan, 1968

Howard, M., *The Mediterranean Strategy in the Second World War*, Weidenfeld and Nicolson, 1968

Hugo, V., *The Battle of Waterloo*, Haldeman-Julius Company

Irving, D., *The Trail of the Fox*, Weidenfeld and Nicolson, 1978

Lamb, Sergeant R., *Memoirs*

Lewin, R., *Ultra Goes to War*, Hutchinson

– *The Life and Death of the Afrika Korps*, Batsford, 1977

Longford, E., *Wellington: The Years of the Sword*, Weidenfeld and
Nicolson, 1969

Macaulay, T. B., *History of England*, vol. I, Dent, 1906

– *Critical and Historical Essays*, Dent, 1907

MacDonald Fraser, G., *Flashman*, Herbert Jenkins, 1969

Macdonnell, A. G., *Napoleon and His Marshals*, Macmillan, 1950

Majdalany, F., *The Monastery*, John Lane The Bodley Head, 1945

– *Cassino: Portrait of a Battle*, Longmans, Green & Co., 1957

– *The Battle of El Alamein*, Weidenfeld and Nicolson, 1965

Field-Marshal The Viscount Montgomery of Alamein, *Memoirs*,
Collins, 1958

Moorhead, A., *Eclipse*, Hamish Hamilton, 1946

Morris, J., *Heaven's Command: an Imperial Progress*, Faber & Faber,
1973

Nicolson, N., *Alex (Field Marshal Alexander of Tunis)*, Weidenfeld and
Nicolson, 1973

Petrie, C., *When Britain Saved Europe*, Eyre and Spottiswoode, 1941

Pocock, T., *Horatio Nelson*, The Bodley Head, 1987

Rauschning, H., *Hitler Speaks*, 1939

Roberts, A., *Napoleon and Wellington*, Weidenfeld and Nicolson, 2001

Lord Rosebery, *Napoleon: The Last Phase*, A. L. Humphries, 1900

Strawson, J., *The Battle for North Africa*, Batsford, 1969

– *Hitler as Military Commander*, Batsford, 1971

– *The Battle for Berlin*, Batsford, 1974

– *The Italian Campaign*, Secker & Warburg, 1987

Trevor-Roper, H. R., *The Last Days of Hitler*, Book Club Associates,
1971

Vercors, *The Battle of Silence*, Faber & Faber, 1968

Watson, J. S., *The Reign of George III*, OUP, 1960

Williamson, J. A., *The Evolution of England*, Oxford, 1931

Wilmot, C., *The Struggle for Europe*, Wordsworth, 1997, first
published 1952

Woodham-Smith, C., *The Reason Why*, McGraw-Hill, 1954

Woodruff, P., *The Men Who Ruled India*, Cape, 1963

Index

INDEX

ROBERT COWLEY (ED)

What If?

Military Historians Imagine What Might Have Been

PAN BOOKS

*'Anyone interested in military history or indeed
history in general will find it fascinating to read'*
Spectator

What If? is a collection of counterfactual essays dealing with military events. Concentrating on some of the most intriguing military-history turning points of the last 3,000 years, twenty celebrated historians, including Alistair Horne and John Keegan, have come together to produce a group of essays that enhance our current understanding of decisive events.

'Pure, almost illicit pleasure . . .
What makes these essays tremendously diverting is how
little they strain one's sense of credibility'
Andrew Roberts, *Sunday Telegraph*

'These informed, elegant essays authoritively
analyse incidents over the past 3,000 years'
The Times

'One of the delights of the book is that broad
speculative analysis is built from a mass of exciting detail.
This make for a top-class bed-side read'
Financial Times

ROBERT COWLEY (ED)

More What If?

Eminent Historian Imagine What Might Have Been

PAN BOOKS

More What If?, the sequel to the acclaimed *What If?* examines history's most fascinating what might have beens.

More of the world's leading historians, including Geoffrey Parker, Theodore K. Rabb, Cecilia Holland and Caleb Carr postulate on what might so easily have been. Concentrating on the crucial and the seemingly insignificant, *More What If?* is an entertaining and brilliantly provocative look at the way our world could easily have been.

What if William hadn't conquered? What if the enigma code remained uncracked? And would this even matter if Lord Halifax had become Prime Minister rather than Churchill? This selection of alternative history is both provocative and stimulating and gives us a valuable insight into the way things could so easily have been.

'Marvellously entertaining as well as thought-provoking
– the finest intellectual parlour-game around'
Noel Malcolm, *Sunday Telegraph*

NIALL FERGUSON (ED)

Virtual History

Alternatives and Counterfactuals

PAN BOOKS

What if Britain had stayed out of the Second World War and what if Germany had gone on to win the war?

These are just some of the questions answered in *Virtual History*, a revolutionary book in which leading historians explore what would have happened if nine momentous events had turned out differently.

'Fluent and entertaining'
The Times

'Ferguson . . . constructs an entire scenario starting with Charles I's defeat of the Covenanters, running through three revolutions, the American, the French and the Russian – that did not happen and climaxing with the collapse of the West, ruled by an Anglo-American empire, in the face of a mighty transcontinental, tsarist Russian imperium . . . A welcome, optimistic assault on an intellectual heresy that has done much, much more harm than good'
Brian Appleyard, *Sunday Times*

'Quite brilliant, inspiring for the layman and an enviable tour de force for the informed reader . . .
A wonderful book . . . lucid, exciting and easy to read'
Claus von Bulow, *Literary Review*

'Sizzling essays hot from the academic griddle'
Piers Brendon, *Mail On Sunday*

MAX HASTINGS

Going to the Wars

PAN BOOKS

Memoirs from one of the greatest war reporters of our time

Max Hastings grew up with romantic dreams of a life among warriors. But after his failure as a parachute soldier in Cyprus in 1963, he became a journalist instead.

Before he was thirty he had reported conflicts in Northern Ireland, Biafra, Vietnam, Cambodia, the Middle East, Cyprus, Rhodesia, India and a string of other trouble spots. His final effort was as a war correspondent during the Falklands War.

Going to the Wars is a story of his experiences reporting from these battlefields. It is also the story of a self-confessed coward: a writer with heroic ambitions who found himself recording the acts of heroes.

'Max Hastings is one of the greatest living war correspondents'
John Keegan

'A wonderful account of the wars of our times'
William Shawcross, *Literary Review*

'His memoirs have . . . honesty, pace and readability'
Jeremy Paxman

'The chapters on the Falklands War are . . . one of the best things written about warfare in half a century'
John Simpson

FIELD MARSHAL LORD CARVER

The National Army Museum Book of
The Boer War

PAN BOOKS

A vivid military history of what was Britain's first modern war, written with original sources chosen by one of Britain's foremost soldiers and military historians. Published in cooperation with the famous National Army Museum, it quotes extensively from the museum's unpublished archive of diaries, letters and documents. The text is complemented by unpublished photos from the museum's collections, together with seven detailed maps devised by Lord Carver.

Field Marshal Lord Carver was one of the most distinguished British soldiers of our time. His previous book, *Britain's Army in the Twentieth Century*, received superb reviews: 'particularly readable' – *Sunday Telegraph*; 'masterly' – *Spectator*; 'vivid . . . masterful' – *Military Illustrated*; 'lucid' – *Soldier*.

'Sobering reading, laced with sudden infusions of raw excitement as some violent encounter comes to life in a soldier's own words'
John Spurling, *Times Literary Supplement*